WHERE STORIES DWELL

by I.A. Watson

PULP
STUDIES

PROSE ⚖ PRESS

WHERE STORIES DWELL
By I.A. Watson

A Pulp Studies Book, Published by Pro Se Press

Edited by Nikki Nelson-Hicks, Tommy Hancock and Morgan Minor
Editor in Chief, Pro Se Productions-Tommy Hancock
Director of Corporate Operations- Morgan Minor
Publisher and Pro Se Productions, LLC-Chief Executive Officer-Fuller Bumpers

Pro Se Productions, LLC
133 1/2 Broad Street
Batesville, AR, 72501
870-834-4022

proseproductions@earthlink.net
www.prose-press.com

Cover Art by Jeff Hayes
Print Production by David J. Foster and Sean Ali
E-Book Design by Russ Anderson

New Pulp Seal created by Cari Reese

WHERE
STORIES
DWELL

***Dedicated** to the creative and long-suffering writers, artists, and editors of the Pulp Factory mailing group, who have already had to hear from the author at length on many of these topics, and whose erudition, intellect, good humour and baffled bemusement have shaped much of the content of this volume. May their keyboards never clog, their punctuation never falter, and their biographies never be as interesting as some of those contained herein.*

TABLE OF CONTENTS

PART THREE: BIOGRAPHIES
In which the author reveals illuminating incidents from others lives and his own

***

Starring:

The Duke of Marlborough,
swashbuckler, soldier, adventurer, and ladies' man
Medea of Colchis,
seductive sorceress and woman scorned
Eleanor of Aquitaine,
the most powerful woman in Europe
Brutus Giantslayer,
who overcame Gog and Magog to found a nation
William Paget, Earl of Uxbridge,
and especially his right leg
Princess Enheduanna,
High Priestess of the Moon Goddess Nanna
William the Conqueror,
a bastard by name, birth, and nature
Sir Francis Dashwood,
wicked master of the wicked Hell Fire Club
King Arthur Pendragon,
rightwise born King of All Britain
Kings Henry II, IV, V, and VIII,
who average to King Henry IV¾, plus a guest Edward
Rhodopis of the Stolen Slipper,
a damsel in distress with familiar problems
Acting Major William Martin,
a Royal Marine who died before he was ever born
Inspector-General James Barry MD,
a military surgeon who never existed at all
Spring-Heeled Jack,
fire-breathing iron-clawed terror of the night
The Lone Ranger and **Tonto**

With a full cast of gods, monarchs, smiths, Celts, Hussites, supervillains, sacrificial virgins, Londoners, knights, heretics, lighthouse-keepers, Methodists, spectral hounds, Loathly Ladies, pulp writers, revolutionaries, spies, gasogene-fillers, and souvenir-vendors to match all tastes.

PART ONE: YARNS

In which we review the nature of stories and the power of words

1.
A Slipper of the Tongue

A YOUNG GIRL loses her father. A tragedy.

Her stepmother abuses her. A crime story.

Her godmother grants her wishes. A fairy tale.

She meets the man of her dreams. A romance.

She vanishes from him at the stroke of midnight. A mystery.

He finds her despite nefarious attempts to thwart him. An adventure.

The lovers are reunited, the evil are punished, and the deserving live happily ever after to the end of their days.

Any story, even the ones we learned in our cots, can be told many different ways. When Charles Perrault first recorded *Cinderella* in 1697,[1] he was not writing for children but to entertain a sophisticated courtly audience in Paris' salons. Jacob and Wilheim Grimm's version[2] was at least in part a revenge drama; the stepsisters and their wicked mother all faced horrible punishments for their behaviour. Or else the story shows that true breeding and "the right stuff" show through despite rags and circumstance; the nobility are innately noble. Or else it teaches that a selfless act of kindness to an old woman can sometimes be wonderfully rewarded. Or it's an archaic throwback to a time when women were defined by the men who rescued them. Or in post-modern versions, it's about a spunky heroine who takes her future into her own hands and carves a destiny.

Stories are how we shape our world around us, and how we are shaped.

Cinderella wasn't the first girl to have a magic slipper, of course. Italian poet Giambattista Basile collected children's stories for his *Pentamerone*

---

1 *Histoires ou contes du temps passé or Les Contes de ma Mère l'Oye* (*Fairy Tales From Times Past With Morals, or The Tales of Mother Goose*) Charles Perrault, Paris, 1697.

2 In "Aschenputtel" *Grimm's Fairy Tales*, 1812, the sisters had "beautiful faces and fair skin, but hearts that were foul and black". They sliced off their heels and toes to try and fit into the slipper but seeping blood betrayed them They were punished at the heroine's wedding by birds Aschenputtel summoned to peck out their eyes (Disney take note), blinding and disfiguring them. Other versions see the sisters and their mother rolled in tar-barrels or simply executed.

(1634-1636), and included an account of Princess Zezolla, who was abused by her governess' daughters and turned into a kitchen slave, but who met and fled from a king and was recognised again by the footwear she had lost.

Miscellaneous Morsels from Youyang, written by Duan Chengshi around A.D. 860, tells of hardworking orphan Ye Xian, who is helped (by a fish who is a reincarnation of her mother, a recurring trope of Eastern stories[3]) to attend the king's banquet, where she leaves her slipper. The king seeks her out, frees her from her murderous stepmother and stepsister, and makes her his wife.

Go back further. Strabo's *Geographica*, Book 17, 1.33, written between 7 B.C. and A.D. 23, recounts the life of Rhodopis of Nautcratis in Greek Egypt. Beautiful fair-haired foreigner Rhodopis (her name means "Rosy-Cheeked") was despised by her fellow slave-girls, all the more so when her aged master gave her ruby-coloured slippers for her skilful dancing. When Pharaoh Ahomose II invited all to a great celebration in Memphis the other girls piled Rhodopis with chores so she could not attend. As the girl was scrubbing clothes in the river an eagle snatched her slipper. The bird flew off with it and dropped it into the pharaoh's lap. "Stirred by the shape of the sandal", the king sought, found, and wed its owner.[4]

Remarkably, Herodotus' *Histories* (450-420 B.C.) also mentions a Rhodopis as a Thracian slave of Iadmon of Samos – the man who also owned Aesop of *Fables* fame! She was taken to Egypt by her new master and freed for a huge sum by Charaxus of Myteline, brother of the poet Sappho.[5]

But there's more. The sixth dynasty of Egypt is currently dated as ending in 2181 B.C., but its possible final queen, Nitocris, has been expunged by modern archaeologists and historians as being a probable fiction. This is the

---

3 In some variants of the my-dead-mother-is-my-helpful-fish story, the heroine is forced by her oppressor to cook and eat the tutelary familiar. However, she keeps the creature's bones and it is they who guide her to her destiny.

Writing on possessed fish being eaten in some cultures, Robert Graves in *The Golden Bough* discusses Indian rituals where such a fish is eaten as a fertility rite to reincarnate the spirit in a new child. The same ancient Greek word for fish and womb is *delphos*, suggesting ancient associations between fish and fertility; some speculate that this is the symbolism of the mermaid.

4 Also possibly history's first recorded foot fetish.

5 There are no slippers in this version. Herodotus is discussing Greek hetaera, those superior female courtesan companions, educated and erudite, the only women whose presence was welcomed and well-regarded in the Greek symposia. Rhodopis is one of only two hetaera he names (the other is Archdyke).

If historical Rhodopis was indeed an hetaera then Charaxus must have paid a high purchase price indeed for it to be noted. Demosthenes records that the hetaera Neiara bought her freedom for 30 minas, perhaps $575,000 in today's currency.

Sappho later wrote a poem accusing Rhodopis of conning her brother out of his property.

young woman, who, according to Herodotus, took decisive action after the murder of her pharaoh brother by inviting all those who had conspired to a banquet to dedicate her new feasting hall then flooded it and drowned all those within. Manethon, Egyptian historian and priest from Sebennytos during the 3rd century B.C., attributes Nitocris with building the third pyramid (other historians may vary).

And Herodotus goes out of his way to tell us that all rumours of Rhodopis building the third pyramid are wrong.[6] Yes, there were popular associations between Rhodopis and Nitocris, so strong that the scholarly historian felt obliged to prove them erroneous in his text. Or, to put it another way: Cinderella built a pyramid.

Nitocris slinks into pulp fiction again in Lord Dunsany's play *The Queen's Enemies*, in H.P. Lovecraft's stories "The Outsider" and "Imprisoned with the Pharaohs", and in Tennessee Williams' "The Vengeance of Nitocris". In Lovecraft's second tale, written in the first person for Harry Houdini, the escape artist encounters the undead queen of shambling human and animal-headed mummies. Cinderella, mistress of the undead.

John Basalt's 1929 novel *Der Blau Basalt*, translated to English as *Nile Gold*, was the first modern work to resurrect the Rhodopis/Nitocris connection. It speculates that Rhodopis became Queen Nitocris by marriage to the pharaoh who found her slipper.

But, as Herodotus concludes before moving on, "This is enough about Rhodopis."

For at least two and a half millennia, oppressed girls have been losing footwear and royal suitors have come to return it. In 1893, the Folklore Society of Britain identified 345 variant versions of the story.[7] In the Philippines, misused Maria is helped by Mariang the crab. Malaysian Bawang Merah, enslaved by the stepmother who killed her parents, is guided to her prince by the bones of a fish that her mother's spirit occupied. In Vietnam, downtrodden Tâm Cám is likewise helped by a dead fish to boil her stepsister

---

6 The full quote, from *Histories* 2.134.1&2 (Loeb) is "Some Greeks say that it was built by Rhodopis, the courtesan, but they are wrong; indeed, it is clear to me that they say this without even knowing who Rhodopis was (otherwise, they would never have credited her with the building of a pyramid on which what I may call an uncountable sum of money was spent), or that Rhodopis flourished in the reign of Amasis, not of Mycerinus."

Several historians attest that Rhodopis dedicated a great deal of treasure at the Oracle of Delphi however, which was on display for centuries thereafter.

7 *Cinderella: Three Hundred and Forty-Five Variants of Cinderella, Catskin and, Cap o'Rushes, Abstracted and Tabulated with a Discussion of Medieval Analogues and Notes*, Marian Roalfe Cox, 1893.

alive and feed her to her stepmother. Kongjwi in Korea, Ashenputtel in Germany, and the youngest sister in "The Eldest Lady's Tale" from *1001 Nights* are all different takes on the same basic events.

This tells us two things; three if there's a lesson to be had about carelessness with slippers. Firstly, a good story lasts and travels. It's a tool that is put to many uses as circumstances demand. Secondly, the *way* we use the story tells us quite a bit about ourselves, our values, our culture, and our character.

This volume is about stories. It has plenty of stories in it, from ancient myth to biographies of some great eccentrics, from ghostly mysteries to neglected histories. But it's also about telling stories. How we tell them. Why we tell them. What are they for?

I don't have any great revelations to offer. Then again, understanding stories isn't a matter of revelation so much as inspiration. Once one can see our consensus reality as one defined by the words by which we name things and the stories by which we contextualise events, then one knows why the pen is mightier than the sword: swords can only kill you; words can make you immortal.

Squeezing the Pulp

PAUSE FOR A MOMENT and inspect the cover. Authors don't usually get much say about what goes on there, but Pro Se is usually pretty good at that stuff. I'm willing to bet there'll be a publisher's logo for on it somewhere though, and if you know Pro Se you'll know they're a small, hungry, growing publisher that mostly specialises in pulp fiction.[8] They must be pretty smart too – they printed my stuff![9]

The point, though, is that Pro Se is at the vanguard of the New Pulp movement, the great revival of techniques and traits, and sometimes of the characters and situations, that reached its most prominent peak back in the cheap mass-produced monthly magazines and dime-store novels of the 1930s. The stories in those old publications had to grab the reader by the throat and bring them back next time. They had to make the purchaser feel

8 Pulp is a portmanteau team for a genre of action-oriented character-rich plot-driven writing that provokes gut reactions in its readers. It is typified by the cheap 1920s and 30s mass-marketed U.S. magazines such as *Weird Tales* that popularised the term, but includes a wide range of sources and is still a popular literary medium today. Horror, romance, adventure, mystery, it's all got to get the heart pumping and keep the pages turning..

9 Readers are directed to www.prose-press.com and to the volumes *The New Adventures of Richard Knight* and *Blood-Price of the Missionary's Gold: The New Adventures of Armless O'Neil*.

his hard-earned two bits had been well spent. And to achieve that, those pulp writers had to dig deep into stories and come up with the undistilled stuff.

Pulp was visceral, demanding an emotional reaction from the reader. It was popular, in both senses of the word, being cheaply mass-produced for a large audience and being aimed at the masses rather than the elite. Rising from the 'penny dreadfuls' and monthly gentleman's magazines of the Victorian era – which gave us such pulp characters as Sherlock Holmes and Allan Quartermain – pulp literature spawned much of modern popular fiction.

Many of our most recognised media "franchises" are rooted in that era. Some are directly from it – James Bond and Tarzan, for example, along with every hard-boiled street-pounding 'tec and high-flying space adventurer. Others merely owe their existence to the tropes popularised in that period; Star Wars, Indiana Jones, Batman, take a bow.

Don't worry, we'll bring that cast back later in the book.

The conditions that led to the growth of the pulp genre back then were the development of a new mass market through cheap print publishing; bleak economic circumstances developing an audience appetite for worlds where justice prevailed, however rough, and where heroes tackled villains; and a thirst for escape from "the real world" into the entertainment and catharsis of a good story.

Strangely, those are conditions that might be said to prevail as much in the present age as in the 1920s and 30s. A new mass market has opened with the arrival of online book sales via Kindle and Amazon and their competitors. In 2011 my book royalties reached the tipping point where more income comes from e-sales than from paper copies; other authors seem to echo my experience.[10] We are currently enduring global recession, with the consequent disillusionment in our institutions and leadership that makes fictional characters seem our only refuge for integrity and heroism. And our Western society has become obsessed with stories again, from TV and movies to video games and comic books.

This is where the "new" part comes in with "new pulp".

There's a fresh growth of publishing with the internet age. The balance of power has shifted from the bookstores to the internet, from the big publishers to the self-publishers. The old paradigms have crumbled. We mourned the loss of local bookstores decades ago, but now we're seeing even the national

---

10 "Kindle ebook sales have overtaken Amazon print sales, says book seller", *The Guardian*, 6th August 2012

chains begin to vanish; and yet book sales haven't massively diminished, only shifted to other sales venues.[11] The next generation of household name authors won't be "discovered" by a literary agent and signed-up for life by a major imprint, they'll rise from the talent using CreateSpace and Amazon Kindle and all the other ways there are now for writers to sell print-on-demand or electronic copies of their work.

And somewhere in that list will be some of the luminaries of the New Pulp wave. Or it might be the Genre Fiction wave. Or the Slipstream wave. The terminology arguments can go on forever. What its harder to argue about is that pulp, noir, whatever term wins dominance in the end, is back to stay – and its all because of *the story*.

So another thing you'll notice about this book is that it keeps harking back to the pulp genre. Partly that's an artefact of this volume's origin. Much of the material included herein first circulated privately to a list of pulp fiction writers (see the dedication page) and so was slanted to their interests and experiences. The book itself is published and distributed by a pulp publisher. But I hold that pulp is itself a throwback to some of the earliest forms of storytelling, to fairy tales and myths, and that the three things naturally go together. I'll try and convince you as the stories pile up.

For now, let's just remember that pulp also describes 1. a recycled product and 2. the stuff you squeeze out when you really want some refreshment.

Stories vs. Atoms

PUT TWO PEOPLE in a room for long enough, and if they don't kill each other they'll start to tell stories. They'll probably start by saying their names – names used to tell stories themselves; ask Mr Smith, Mr Weaver, Mrs Tanner, Ms MacDonald. Then they'll say what they do for a living. Then

---

11 This is perhaps contentious. There are all kinds of conflicting statistics out there for book sales, confused and confounded by commercial confidentiality and optimistic marketing. Perhaps the most robust US stats come from the Census bureau, which records year-on-year book sales income as follows: 2002= $15.45bn, 2003=£16.24bn, 2004=$16.88bn, 2005=$16.89bn, 2006=$16.99bn, 2007=$17.18bn, 2008=$16.87bn, 2009=$16.05bn, 1010=$15.66bn; 2011=$15.53bn.

Codex Group, which describes itself as "the leader in book audience research and pre-publication book testing", released statistics through their website at http://www.codexgroup.net/ based upon a quarter of a million interviews since 2004. Their research suggests that within two years the percentage of purchasers who discovered new books in-store has dropped from 35% to 17%. In the same period, books bought because of personal recommendation rose from 14% to 22%, of which three-quarters were face-to-face recognition.

they'll share something about their family. Stories.

As far back as humans can remember, and probably further than that, we've been telling stories. Ask Cinderella.

Don't ask the semiotics. They'll talk about signs as the building blocks of meaning, then discuss semantics, then describe how signs combine in codes to transmit messages in a discourse of varying modalities and forms. No offence to well-meaning academics doing valuable work into language and psychology, but deconstructing stories to find what they're about is like performing an autopsy on a cadaver to find the soul.

Consider instead this story:

During the earliest days of Soviet rule in Communist Russia, a good deal of effort was put into stamping out the Orthodox Church's grip on the peasantry. Clever young Party men were sent out to lecture on the follies of religion and the virtues of the state, so that the masses would understand that they had been freed from the tyranny of theology.

One such meeting took place on a snowy Easter Day in some rural village, in what had been the church hall. Every member of the community was expected to attend. The distinguished visitor spoke for upwards of three hours on Marxist ideals and the benefits of atheism. When he finally finished his proofs that God did not exist he asked, nay challenged, his cowed audience if they had any comment.

The parish's former priest stood and spoke only three words: "Christ is risen."

Whereupon the entire assembly rose and replied to the traditional Easter proclamation with the traditional response: "He is risen indeed!"

Now I've heard this story told in church as testimony to the faith of religiously-oppressed people. I've seen it repeated in text as proof of the way the church brainwashes its adherents. Many people are sceptical of the tale's veracity; after all, no specific time or place is mentioned and there is no mention of the aftermath of such civil disobedience. It sounds like a parable suitable for an instructive homily.

The point is, though, that the story has resonance. Religious or not, it demands a response of us. No dissection of the relationship of form and style[12] really gets to the bottom of *why*. No listing of the tropes the story has in common with other narratives[13] helps explain why we have to listen to it.

12 This would be Russian Formalism, Viktor Borisovich Shklovsky's 1930s work on understanding narrative.

13 *Morphology of the Folktale* (1928, but not translated to English until 1958) by Vladimir Yakovlevich Propp analysed the basic plot components of Russian folk tales to identify their simplest irreducible narrative elements.

In fact we only understand the story by experiencing the story; that is to say, hearing it and thinking about what we hear.

Stories are a very sophisticated type of communication. They are excellent teaching tools because they give us associations and context for important information ("And that's why we don't cry "wolf" when there's no danger, children!"). They reinforce social behaviour and create community identity ("And so it is that we never eat the flesh of the pig"). They form our opinions ("Now Goldilocks knew that she shouldn't go into the house..."). They influence our expectations ("He saw her and fell in love at once").

Consider wallpaper. I once had to redecorate my bathroom entirely because, as I was soaking in the tub one day, I realised that there were faces in the patterns. And they were watching me. Now once you've made random blobs into a face you can't un-see it. Ask all the people who find Elvis on a burger bun or the Virgin Mary in a damp stain. So the wallpaper had to go, and my baths could again be private.

Seeing faces where there are none, seeing monsters where no monsters lurk, are both primitive survival techniques. Its better to have a hundred false alarms, where the primitive proto-human startles at nothing, then to miss one alert where the predator is real. Evolution has given us pattern recognition.

Our developing cognitive processes and memory capacities have given us non-visual pattern recognition as well. Now we can draw associations and extrapolate from them. At its simplest, the story we work out for ourselves probably started out as: "Well, the day before yesterday the tasty game animals came to this water to drink. Yesterday the tasty game animals came to this water to drink. Perhaps then the tasty game animals will come again today. Where's my spear?"

From that we go on to personal stories and family histories, to tales that explain the world and tales that simply amuse, and from there to the whole body of literature that defines mankind.

But when I see a face in the wallpaper, I'm not really seeing a face. It's not there. Neither is the wallpaper. Neither is the wall.

Zen, huh? But since physics insists that solid matter isn't solid, just a bunch of subatomic particles with vast spaces between them, coupled with strong and weak forces, bouncing photons back to specialised electrochemical cells in my eyeballs, then what we see isn't what's really there. It is, in fact, the story our brain constructs for us so we can understand and cope with what's there.

On a fundamental level, reality as we perceive it is determined by the narrative we put to it. Change the story, change the universe.

***

2.
Babbling, or History's First Author

WITHOUT LANGUAGE there are no stories. There are no lies and no truths. Without language we cannot name the world to understand it and control it.

Humanity is distinguished from the rest of life on Earth because we have a sophisticated method of communicating ideas, information, history, feelings, instructions, even objections. When things go wrong, the voice of reason says, "Let's talk this over."

The ancient sources of the Bible understood the importance of language. Whether one chooses to believe that the priests and prophets who first wrote those texts received dictation direct from God or distilled many generations of diverse folklore into a single unifying narrative, those Jewish texts reflect the importance of words in creation.

"In the beginning, God said…"14

"God also gave Adam the gift of naming the things of the universe." 15

"You shall not take the name of the LORD your God in vain, for the LORD will not hold him guiltless who takes his name in vain."16

The first story in the Bible that's really about words, about language, is found in *Genesis* 11, 1-9. But before the theology, a little geology.

The Middle East was, of old, defined by two rivers. The Tigris and the Euphrates run south through arid desert, transforming the locality through which they drain into lush fertile corridors. In ancient times, annual river floods irrigated pasture nearby, allowing a thriving early civilisation to rise up on the Akkadian delta. Archaeologists agree with historians on that one.

14 Book of Genesis, Chapter 1, verse 3.
15 Genesis 2: 19-20: And out of the ground the LORD God formed every beast of the field, and every fowl of the air; and brought them unto Adam to see what he would call them: and whatsoever Adam called every living creature, that was the name thereof. And Adam gave names to all cattle, and to the fowl of the air, and to every beast of the field…
16 Exodus 20.7, the third of the Ten Commandments; also listed in Deuteronomy 4.11

The most effective form of survival was to cultivate local resources, which meant herding and farming. Success meant the population rose, which meant that resources had to be contended for. Humans banded together for mutual defence and because it allowed specialisation. A man who knew how to make pots well could make pots all day and exchange his pots for another man's fruit or meat. Specialisation requires trade, and trade requires marketplaces, and marketplaces cause villages. And villages are targets, so they require soldiers, another specialised trade, and as those settlements get wealthier and larger they require walls. And suddenly there are cities.

That part of the world was short of some resources, though. In particular, wood was scarce and stone was hard to quarry. The natural building materials of much of the world were difficult to come by, but one thing the inhabitants by the Tigris and Euphrates had in plenty was mud.

Make a box one cubit long by half a cubit wide and deep – a cubit is the length of a man's arm from elbow to middle fingertip, around eighteen inches, and its one of the oldest measurements. Fill the box with river mud. Toss in some straw for texture if desired. Leave it to dry in the blistering sunlight for a couple of hours. Tip out the brick that solidifies in that time and you'll have a building material that's pretty durable. In fact it can withstand weight from above as well as some types of rock.

The Akkadians built their villages, then their towns, then their walled cities, out of mud brick – which is fine until you have a Flood.

I don't mean a flood, the seasonal descent of waters drained from higher land. I'm talking Flood, the sort of thing that Bible described in *Genesis* 6-9.

Another thing geology has confirmed for us is that the Tigris and Euphrates have, from time to time, modified their courses after major cataracts. This might have been natural or it could have been one of the world's first man-made eco-disasters.

As cities grew along the riverbanks, with rising populations competing for limited arable land, some unrecorded genius had the idea of digging a trench from the river out into the desert, bringing the life-giving water to turn barren waste into farmable plots. The science of irrigation was born. Canals were cut along the lengths of the great watercourses, extending the seedable and grazable lands far beyond the half-mile corridor that had previously confined civilisation.

The cost of those channels was that the natural riverbanks had to be compromised, allowing water onto the flat plainlands beyond. When the floods rose again there was no defence.

If you don't take a fundamentalist view that the Biblical Flood happened because God simply dropped a lot of water, here's a mechanism by which "all the lands" might be covered. After all, as Einstein contended, "Coincidence is God's way of remaining anonymous." In any case, it could be argued that with their increased prosperity and a science that had overcome nature and brought about an age of plenty, the Akkadians felt that they no longer needed God to send them the necessary things of life. Their hubris was their downfall.

The story of the Great Flood appears in many mythologies. The Sumerian King-List distinguishes between the massive longevities of rulers before the Flood and the mortal spans of those after. The Biblical account of Noah is similar to the story of Utnapishtim in the *Epic of Gilgamesh*. A variant account appears in the Yazidi *Mishefa Reş*. Hindu texts such as the *Satapatha Brahmana* mention a man escaping a great deluge in a boat by intervention of Vishnu. Quiché, Mayas, and Greek mythologies likewise feature survival of great floods.

So the cataracts came; and mud-bricks, while excellent for holding up buildings against wind and weight, are useless when submerged by rising waters. Mud bricks + river = mud. No wonder the Flood washed away all the cities of the Earth.

Anyway, in each of the stories the waters eventually passed. The ark's survivors emerged from their boats and began to rebuild and repopulate the land of the two rivers. But as time went on they either forgot the lesson of the past or had a very human reaction to it.

If God had caused the Flood in response to human sin and might do so again (rainbows notwithstanding) then there were two possible responses: 1. Do not sin. 2. Get rid of God.

Hence the Tower of Babel, that amazing folly described in the eleventh chapter of Genesis[17], in that first story about language.

---

17 "And the whole earth was of one language, and of one speech. And it came to pass, as they journeyed from the east, that they found a plain in the land of Shinar; and they dwelt there. And they said one to another, Go to, let us make brick, and burn them thoroughly. And they had brick for stone, and slime had they for mortar. And they said, Go to, let us build us a city and a tower, whose top may reach unto heaven; and let us make us a name, lest we be scattered abroad upon the face of the whole earth.

And the Lord came down to see the city and the tower, which the children of men builded. And the Lord said, Behold, the people is one, and they have all one language; and this they begin to do: and now nothing will be restrained from them, which they have imagined to do. Go to, let us go down, and there confound their language, that they may not understand one another's speech.

So the Lord scattered them abroad from thence upon the face of all the earth: and they left off to build the city. Therefore is the name of it called Babel; because the Lord did there confound the

The Babylonian cosmos-view, and probably that of the whole Middle East in ancient times, held that the Earth was positioned over a void, possibly the abode of the dead, in a vast and eternal sea. Above us was the canopy of the stars, a frame or series of frames upon which sun, moon and planets wheeled. A great dome of the sky was the final starry backdrop. On the other side of that was heaven, the dwelling place of God.

So, taking that as a scientifically proven given, it is perhaps not too ridiculous to plan a huge high tower that can be built all the way up to that celestial canvas. A little cutting work on the cloth of the universe and an invasion of heaven becomes very feasible. Why not organise a pre-emptive strike against God before he can send another Flood?

Or, if you prefer a more allegorical reason for the Tower, it was an expression of human dominance, an "in-your-face, God," defiance; or a temple to some pagan fire deity requiring human sacrifice; or a political statement demanding the unification of all peoples of Earth under a single authority. Commentaries vary, and have done since the Jewish *Midrash*.

In any case, the myth insists that a great tower was raised at Babel (what we would call Babylon in ancient Mesopotamia, modern day Iraq), and it was pretty damned high, and it was pretty bothersome to God.[18] In fact the Bible records his response as, "Behold, the people is one, and they have all one language; and this they begin to do: and now nothing will be restrained from them, which they have imagined to do."

It also described His response. "Go to, let us go down, and there confound their language, that they may not understand one another's speech."

Later sources describe the Tower's spectacular destruction, where the top part is consumed by fire and the bottom crumbled into the earth, but

language of all the earth: and from thence did the Lord scatter them abroad upon the face of all the earth."
Book of Genesis XI:1-9, King James Version
18 Many sources differ as to the dimensions and construction time of the Tower of Babel, but all agree that it was made from baked river mud-clay and mortared with bitumen (asphalt), the common construction technique of that part of the world at that time, and still sometimes used today. For example, the apocryphal *Book of Jubilees* 10:20-21 states, "And they began to build, and in the fourth week they made brick with fire, and the bricks served them for stone, and the clay with which they cemented them together was asphalt which comes out of the sea, and out of the fountains of water in the land of Shinar. And they built it: forty and three years were they building it; its breadth was 203 bricks, and the height [of a brick] was the third of one; its height amounted to 5433 cubits and 2 palms, and [the extent of one wall was] thirteen stades [and of the other thirty stades]" (Charles' 1913 translation). This description suggests that the Tower was over one and a half miles tall. In 2010 the world's tallest building was Burj Khalifa in Dubai, United Arab Emirates, at 2,722 feet a meagre half-mile high.
Genesis offers no dimensions but makes clear that the construction never met its intended height.

the Genesis account says nothing of that. Confounded by God giving them not one but many languages (and by implication many cultures, beliefs, and world-views), the builders could no longer co-operate and so abandoned their efforts. The Tower fell because of the birth of politics, or sectarianism, or arguments about definitions.

Language defines the world. A culture with no word for "apology" can't have any concept of it. Another might invent such a useful word, for example schadenfreude, that it has to be adapted into other languages so the concept can be properly expressed. How interesting that the world's most internationally recognised word, *okay*, was unheard of a little over a century and a half ago.[19]

Maybe we're getting to the point where we can build Babel again. Perhaps if we build it the right way this time it won't be displeasing to God.

That's our story and we're sticking to it.

The World's First Writing Credit

WHO WAS the world's first author? More properly, who was the first author who included a name on their work, "signing it"?

The first known, named author, poet, epic-writer, and the first person to attempt to codify theology was...

Princess Enheduanna, High Priestess of the Moon Goddess Nanna[20] in Ur, somewhere around 2250 B.C. And she didn't just sign her work; she left us an "about the author".

In fact Enheduanna is one of the earliest women in history whose name

---

19 J.F.D. Smythe's *A Tour of the Unites States of America* (1784) records a Negro slave saying, "Kay, massa, you just leave me, me sit here," from which some etymologists suggest a West African origin for okay in the Wolof and Bantu word waw-key or the Mandingo phrase o ke. Other scholars date the work back to the 1830s Boston comical misspellings abbreviation fad, citing O.K. as a shortening of "Oll Korrect". Democrats claim it for its use in their "Vote for OK" 1840 presidential campaign for Martin Van Buren of "Old Kinderhook", New York. This campaign also introduced the "O.K. sign" with the forefinger and thumb circled and the other fingers raised and curved – possibly the politest gesture originating in politics. It was fashionable until the 1960s to claim okay was a borrowed Chactaw word. Others believe the word a corruption of the Scots "Och aye," the Lakota "hokahey", Finnish "oikea", German "ohne korrectur", or the Greek "Ola Kala."

20 There are several variants of the name of the powerful Sumerian goddess of sexual love, fertility and warfare. The most prevalent is Inanna or Inana. Her Akkadian name was Ishtar. She shares many correlations with other love goddesses such as Aphrodite/Venus, including associations with the morning star, with doves, and with octangles.

we know.[21] She was eldest-born of Sumerian dynasty founder Sargon the Great, and was daughter, sister, and aunt of kings. She was a very smart, very powerful woman, exiled for her politicking then returned to power.

She's even got a link to the Tower of Babel. Her father, Sargon the Great, was a seminal figure in Sumerian history. He is sometimes equated with Nimrod the Hunter, or described as a descendant of Nimrod, and many early sources (but not the Bible) place Nimrod as king of Babel at the time of the tower's rise and fall. Some historians and mythographers have attempted to patch a biography in which Nimrod escapes the destruction of Babel and founds his new empire at Sumer.

In any case, Enheduanna understood words. She is the first woman in history known to have been literate (although the Babylonian goddess Nindaba was the gods' scribe, suggesting that writing things down may have been a common noble female role in that culture).

Born in 2285 B.C., Enheduanna was the eldest daughter of Queen Tashlultum, about whom stories have also been told. *Tashlultum* translates as "I carried her off as spoils". She may previously have been wife to Uruk's sole third dynasty king, Lugul-Zaggisi (other spellings are also available), before Sargon of Akkad came along and conquered everything.

Sargon appointed his daughter as High Priestess of Ur. It was a smart political move, securing the south of his empire under the control of a competent and trusted caretaker. Enheduanna took her duties very seriously and began her writing as part of them. Her surviving works include the epic and autobiographical *Exhalation of Inanna*, the mythological *Inanna and Ebih*, the fragmentary *Inanna sa-gura* and forty-two hymns and poems. It is from Enheduanna that we have a good understanding of Sumerian myth and culture and some of the earliest poetry and literature in the world.

Of course, Enheduanna is a pen name. It means "High Priestess, Adornment of the God". Another first for her. And she's the earliest named woman whose image has survived to the modern day. A Sumerian statue depicts her carrying the sacred instruments of her office and a head-dress of authority, and otherwise wearing traditional female Sumerian dress, i.e. nothing. So she may be the first identified cheesecake too. She does have

---

21 The same source that names Enheduanna also names her mother Tashlultum, who by the irreductable logic of biology was born first. Other early named women are Kubaba, a tavern keeper who rose to be the only queen to appear on the Sumerian King List (because she ruled in her own right, not through marriage to a king), and Peseshet, a fourth dynasty doctor and the earliest recorded woman of that profession except possibly the even earlier Merit-Ptah who held the title of "Lady Overseer of the Female Physicians".

wings, though.

Enheduanna continued her senior role after her father's death when her brother Rimush became king. Eventually the siblings quarrelled. The priestess/princess was exiled, perhaps around the same time that the gods Enlil and his daughter Nanna[22] were temporarily banished from Sumerian religious life.

She may also be the first person to use literature as a form of P.R. The clay tablets on which she wrote *Exhalation of Inanna*, her autobiographical appeal to the gods against unfair exile, seem to have played some role in her reinstatement and that of her deity. This was a woman who *really* understood the power of words.

So, Enheduanna is one of the first women whose name had been recorded to history, and she is the most ancient author whose name is known. Her works include poems, epic narratives, an autobiography, and the first written attempts at systematic theology. She was daughter, brother and aunt to kings of Akkad and the High Priestess of the moon goddess Nanna in Ur. She seems to have been just as formidable and brilliant as one might wish the first writer to have been.

***

---

22 Enlil's origin myth story has been translated from a number of fragmentary tablets at the University of Pennsylvania, the Museum of the Ancient Orient in Istanbul, and the British Museum. Enlil ignores the laws of his homeland and seduces or rapes Ninlil, who bears him a child. When Enlil is banished to the underworld for his crime (which may have been ritual uncleanliness from pre-marital sex), Ninlil follows. Enlil disguises himself and when Ninlil asks him if he has seen Enlil he claims he has not – so she sleeps with the "stranger" instead. Three more children are successively conceived by this ruse, one of whom is the moon-goddess Nanna.

3.
On Heroes

WE LIVE in a cynical age where we've learned the hard way that people we're expected to look up to don't always deserve our respect. Presidents and monarchs have dirty secrets. Priests hide sex scandals. Captains of industry pilfer pension funds and sportsmen take drugs.

Not all of them, of course, but enough to disappoint.

Maybe they always did and we're just better at finding out now.

Anyhow, the point is that these failures have led us to be cautious about investing our adulation another time, like someone who's had a bad relationship and won't ever let themselves fall in love again.

And by some weird reverse psychology, that lack of trust gets turned into a "good thing". If nobody is a real hero then there's no pressure on me to be one. If nobody is extraordinary then it's okay for me to be ordinary too. If everyone cheats and lies and looks after number one...

Now our fiction, and especially our adventure and fantasy fiction, reflects two things: how we think the world is, and how we want the world to be. Sloppy lazy writers pander to the lowest denominator, peopling their world with the characters and situations that they believe their readership expects - venal shabby characters having easy sex and easy betrayals in a world where honourable people are fools and victims and where protagonists of stature must have some dark flaw to average them down to 'realism'.

Those writers betray their own insecurities in their work. They don't believe they can 'sell' a true hero. True heroes require some suspension of disbelief, and suspension of disbelief requires writing talent. They don't believe their audience has the imagination or nobility or character to accept such a hero.

There's a key passage in Terry Pratchett's excellent fantasy novel

Hogfather[23] where his hero, Death (the personification) prevents a plot to stop the sun from coming up. He's asked what would have happened if the mythological creature responsible for its rising hadn't been saved. "A mere ball of flaming gas would have lit the world," he replies. Events stripped of their meaning lead to a world stripped of any soul.

Asked why little fictions (such as Santa) should matter, Death answers, "You have to start out learning to believe the little lies." He explains that they to teach us how to accept the big fictions: "Justice. Mercy. Duty. That sort of thing..." And then he goes on to argue that unless we can imagine things that don't exist we cannot create them so they become real.

It's sophisticated, life-enhancing stuff for a humorous book, and Pratchett understands perfectly why we need to write about heroes. If we can imagine heroes then we can *be* heroes. If we have heroes amongst us then we're challenged to be like them.

There's a long-forgotten scene in an old Gruenwald issue of *Captain America* where Cap catches a kid shoplifting superhero comic books.[24] He asks how he can read those stories and still think it's okay to steal. And Cap is right. I once got in the way of some bullies at school just because I knew it's what Steve Rogers[25] would do.

Pulp fiction often specialises in tarnished heroes. These protagonists have character flaws - they drink, or gamble, or fall for the wrong girl, or carry some tragedy inside them. They've made some terrible mistake in their past. But the heroic part of them comes from conquering those flaws, from doing what's right despite their limitations. Many live in gritty sinful worlds but do the right thing at the last in any case. The more limitations, the greater the heroism to overcome them.

Put another way: a guy who runs a 20 mile marathon for charity is a hero. A guy who does it in his wheelchair's an even bigger hero.

I think that as a society we're starting to appreciate heroes again. It's a more mature understanding, perhaps, and it's slow to form. Maybe for America the turning point was the rescue services' sacrifice at the Twin Towers, reminding a nation what devotion and courage were about. Here in the UK we've been getting a fairly steady stream of military coffins back from Afghanistan and they're always flown back to the same air force base, RAF Lyneham. The nearby village is Wootton Bassett, a small place of 11,000 people. Every

23 *Hogfather*, by Terry Pratchett, Corgi, 1997, ISBN-10: 0552145424, ISBN-13: 978-0552145428
24 *Captain America* #425, Marvel Comics, March 1994, written by Mark Gruenwald.
25 The civilian identity of Captain America.

single time those coffins are brought through town those people line the streets in silence to pay their respects. They see it as their tribute to heroes.

Keep the faith, folks.

"Nurture your mind with great thoughts; to believe in the heroic makes heroes"

   Disraeli

"As you get older, it is harder to have heroes, but it is sort of necessary"

   Hemingway

***

4.
The London-stone

MANY GREAT CITIES have a central point from which all distances are measured. In 20 B.C., Emperor Augustus ordained the erection in Rome's forum of the *Millarium Aureum*, the golden milestone, to be the very centre of his empire. All Roman milestones were calibrated from that centre. Constantine the Great erected a similar column in Byzantium when it became the empire's capital.

London's centre is variously calculated as Piccadilly Square, Trafalgar Square, the Palace of Westminster, St Paul's cathedral or elsewhere. However, in medieval times there was no question. The centre was marked by one of London's now-almost-forgotten landmarks: the London-stone.

Take the Tube to Mansion House station. Walk east along Cable Street then turn left. Or get off at Bank and head down Whitechapel Road and New Road. You're on Cannon Street in the oldest part of London.

Look for 111 Cannon Street, beside what were formerly the offices of the Overseas-China Banking Corporation. It's a WH Smith's newsagent now. Examine the wall to the right of the main door. There's a barred glass screen. And inside that is a small block of shaped oolitic limestone, roughly twenty-seven inches tall, seventeen inches wide, twelve inches deep, originally from Rutland over a hundred miles away.

There's a small brass plaque that reads:

LONDON STONE

This is a fragment of the original piece of limestone once securely fixed in the ground now fronting Cannon Street Station. Removed in 1742 to the north side of the street, in 1798 it was built into the south wall of the Church of St. Swithun London Stone which stood here until demolished in 1962. Its origin and purpose are unknown but in 1188 there was a reference to Henry, son of Eylwin de Lundenstane, subsequently Lord Mayor of London.

That's the London-stone. It's been around a *long* time. It doesn't look as impressive now as it did in medieval times, when it was described by London historian John Stow in 1598 as "a great stone called London stone… pitched upright… fixed in the ground verie deep, fastened with bars of iron".

Two buildings down is the London Stone pub, where a slight dip in the road denotes the covered course of old Walbrook River, one of the city's 'lost' waterways.[26] The stone may move again soon; planning permission was sought in 2010 to relocate the London-stone to the retail frontage of a proposed new building on the same site.

Nobody is quite sure how long London-stone has been there. Like the sign says, the first Lord Mayor of London, sometime between 1189 and 1193, was actually called Henry Fitz-Ailwin de London-stone. He lived, as his suffix suggests, right at the London-stone on Ludgate Hill. He took office in 1189 and served for the rest of his life, to 1212. He's credited with setting up ordinances to deal with boundary disputes and for encouraging fire-prone London to be built up in stone.

Back in Henry's day the stone stood directly opposite the Guildhall, then the most important commercial building of the city.[27] Legend held that the Guildhall occupied the spot where Brutus, legendary founder of Britain, had once built his palace[28] and from where King Lud had raised up the city that took his name.[29]

---

26 Several rivers and innumerable smaller water-courses have been "lost" as London has expanded and developed. Each has been gradually paved over, reducing it to a culvert or a drain, or even a sewer. The route of some rivers and their continued underground existence are now purely conjectural, based upon imprecise representations on antique maps. Amongst the lost rivers on the Thames' north bank are the Fleet, the Westbourne, the Walbrook, the Tyburn and Tyburn Brook, the Mozelle, Hackney Brook, Muswell Stream, Counter's Creek, and Stamford Brook. Parts of the Brent and the Rom also run underground. In the south there are Earl's Sluice, the Pack, the Effra, the Falconbrook, the Graveney, the Quaggy, Beverley Brook (partly) and the Sudbrook. The names of some of these ancient features are remembered in street names such as the famous Fleet Street and in places such as the Walbrook Theatre.

27 The first written reference to a Guildhall is dated 1128, confirming the traditional use of the site long before the 13th century rebuild that vestigially endures as the current west crypt, or the 1411 rebuild that survived the 1666 Great Fire of London and still stands today behind an additional 1788 grand entrance in "Hindoostani Gothic". The building's name may come from *gild*, the Saxon word for payment, indicating the hall's function as a tax office.

At Henry de London-stone's time the vast old Roman amphitheatre behind the Guildhall was probably still visible and may even have formed part of the site. The positioning and unusual pre-Great Fire layout of adjacent 12th century church St Lawrence Jewry may well have conformed to the amphitheatre's curves. A portion of what was probably the largest amphitheatre in Britain is still preserved in the basement of the Guildhall Art Gallery.

The Guildhall remains the headquarters of the Corporation of London to this day.

28 See Chapter 18: "How the Americans Descended From Troy"

29 King Lud is probably also mythical, but the Saxon name for the settlement was Lundenwik, the domain of Lud.

Nobody really knew the origin of the London-stone. Some said the great block was the last dolmen from a pagan ring that had once topped Ludgate Hill before St Paul's cathedral had been raised.[30] Some claimed the Romans had set it to mark the highest point at which the Thames could be forded, and from there the distance to Rome was measured.[31] Others believed it the stone from which King Arthur had drawn the sword that proclaimed him rightwise born ruler of all England. Romancers claimed Brutus the Trojan had set it when he had settled Britain and given it his name, at the founding of New Troy, Trinovantium, the city of London.[32]

Everyone agreed that the stone was important. Mayors of London struck the stone to claim office. It was a site to pass laws, make oaths, pay debts, and make proclamations. Striking papers to the stone make them "official". Work contracts "for a year and a day" began at London-stone, and wages were paid off there at contract's end.

In 1522, printer Wynkin de Worde produced *A Treatyse of a Galaunt, with the Maryage of the Fayre Pusell the Bosse of Byllyngesgate Unto London Stone*, a satirical poem outlining the marriage of the London-stone to a well-known horse-trough in Billingsgate, describing the revels of the two monuments dancing at their nuptials. Implicit in the humour is an understanding that everyone knows of these two landmarks, and that they are known for their reliability and dignity.

The stone's other function was as a place to demand retribution. A grievance aired at London-stone must be redressed.

The Returne of the renowned Caualiero Pasquill of England, 1589, was the first sally in a war or words between critics and establishment of the Church of England. The pseudonymous writer announced his intention to post a list of his complaints upon the London-stone, and called upon all those who agreed with him to do likewise.

Jack Cade's popular rebellion against Henry VI travelled England to

---

30 The idea was repopularised by Elizabeth Gordon in her *Prehistoric London: Its Mounds and Circles*, 1914.

31 Such a stone would be a milliarium. The possibility was first raised by William Camden in Britannia, 1586. More recent archaeological study has suggested an alignment with the Roman Governor's Palace (now buried beneath Cannon Street station).

32 *Notes and Queries*, 1862, anonymous, recorded a supposedly-ancient saying that "So long as the Stone of Brutus is safe, so long shall London flourish," as support for the stone being a British version of the Trojan Palladium, its protective talisman. However, the book has since been attributed to Revd. Richard Williams Morgan, an eccentric who had stated in *The British Kymry or Britons of Cambria*, 1857, that the London-stone was the actual plinth of the Trojan Palladium; his work is not regarded highly by historians.

the London-stone, which Cade struck with his sword before passing on to Guildhall and the Tower of London to present his demands. The event is commemorated in *Henry VI part 2*, act IV, scene VI.

Queen Elizabeth I's mystic Dr John Dee wrote of the stone's occult properties. He allegedly took chippings of it to use in his alchemical experiments.

When the Worshipful Company of Spectacle Makers inspected their members' shops under their royal charter, lenses of an unsatisfactory quality were taken and shattered on the London-Stone to disgrace their erring creators.[33]

The London-stone haunted William Blake. In *Jerusalem: The Emanation of the Giant Albion* (1804), London Stone is a bloody Druidic altar. In *Jerusalem* and in *Milton a Poem*, it is the central marker of Blake's mystical city of London, Golgonooza. Here justice is delivered, where Los sits to hear the voice of Jerusalem and Reuben sleeps.

Eventually London-stone simply became inconvenient. Simply put, it blocked the road. Coaches kept on scraping it. Accidents happened. In 1742 the remains of the stone was moved across the street and reset beside the door of St Christopher's church. It was repositioned again in 1789 and 1820. Nathanial Hawthorne (he of *The Scarlet Letter*) visited in 1850 and mentioned in his journal how he had seen the marks on the stone's top, "said to have been made by Jack Cade's sword".

St Christopher's was bombed in the Blitz and remained a mere shell until its demolition in 1962. It was replaced by the present moderately unpleasant office block with shops on the ground floor and the London-stone was incorporated without ceremony into a small fenced-off alcove where it can be glimpsed today.

Nobody's allowed close enough to touch it or strike it though; perhaps at last the authorities have got wise!

---

33 The possibility of the stone being damaged in the Great Fire of London, 1666, is inferred from the 1671 account of spectacle-breaking on "the remaynyng parte of London Stone".

Frost Fairs

THERE ARE SOME times and places that just call out for stories to be written about them. Here's one:

The London winter of 1814 was bitter. The Thames froze that January, for the last time; a new version of London Bridge was erected shortly thereafter with thinner and less brick piles that no longer slowed and dammed the river. So 1814 saw the last and greatest of London's remarkable Frost Fairs, a festival and free market that took place on the ice of the river itself!

The Thames had frozen often before. The earliest recorded occasion was nine weeks in AD 250. The freezes in 1683 and 1715 lasted for at least three months each. In 1434, 1506, and 1575 the ice was strong enough for men to ignore the bridge and drive carts straight across the river. Henry VIII rode from Greenwich to London by sleigh along the Thames in 1536.

The first recorded Frost Fair was in 1564, when Londoners danced, feasted, held archery matches, and played football on the Thames. Queen Elizabeth I herself "shot at marks" (practiced archery) there. The second Frost Fair, in 1606, is described in Virginia Woolf's *Orlando*.

The third Fair, 1683, lasted from December to February and saw a whole village appearing on the ice, complete with booths, bars, and brothels. Whole streets appeared in an organised fashion, with different stalls arranged thematically. There was wrestling, bear-baiting, bull-baiting, and horse racing, all on the frozen river surface from Southwark to Temple. Those new-fangled printing presses were there too, creating Frost Fair souvenirs. Croom the printer made £5 a day (maybe $3000 in modern currency) selling personalised printed certificates of attendance. Even the royal court made an appearance; King Charles II and his retinue visited, and the printed souvenir he received is still on display in the Museum of London.

Diarist John Evelyn wrote of this occasion: "Coaches plied from Westminster to the Temple, and from several other stairs too and fro, as in the streets; sleds, sliding with skeetes, a bull-baiting, horse and coach races, puppet plays and interludes, cooks, tipling and other lewd places, so that it seemed to be a bacchanalian triumph, or carnival on the water."

Why the fuss? Because London is an ancient city with ancient ordinances and laws that prohibit or tax certain activities. Prostitution, gambling, and some gaming was illegal in the city proper; but the Aldermen's and Mayor's authority did not run to the Liberty of the Tower, no-man's land between the Tower of London's royal jurisdiction and the edge of civic control, nor to the Liberties of the manors across the Thames on the south bank. That's why theatres like Shakespeare's Globe were always built south of the Thames. Likewise, the city's ordinances did not cover the area usually occupied by the tidally-flowing river, so Free Frost Fairs were indeed truly free.

The 1814 Fair capped them all, though. When the water between Blackfriars Bridge and Three Crane Stairs froze for four days, thousands of citizens ventured onto the river. A great long street of booths and trestles, named City Road, ran the length of the frozen section. Simple stalls were soon replaced by more elaborate constructions, including no less than nine souvenir printing presses.

As this Fair progressed and the sale of items marked "Frost Fair 1814" and "Bought on the Thames" proliferated, one ambitious restaurateur slaughtered sheep then and there and began selling roast slices of "Lapland mutton". An elephant was led across the ice below Blackfriars. Music and dancing went on all night – and nothing could be done to stop it.

Eventually though the thaw had to come, and predictably some people underestimated the erosion of the ice. A waterman rescued two women who'd fallen through the weakening freeze. A plumber carrying lead pipes was less lucky and vanished to his doom. Tides returned and two men were swept away by the splintering crust. When the Thames melted it did so within a mere twenty-four hours, leaving only a bitter chill and a remarkable number of souvenirs from one of the first mass-marketing opportunities in history.

The Frost Fair was one of those odd, liminal places outside the usual laws and customs where anything might happen: affairs, weddings, births, unusual sales, remarkable stunts, shameless commerce, and abandoned pleasure. Surely somewhere there is a rich and fruitful basis for some kind of fiction?

A plan to freeze the Thames artificially for a millennium Frost Fair was quickly stamped upon by the Port of London authorities.

***

5.
On Heroines

PULP IS a very traditional storytelling form. It has deep roots, right back to the "penny dreadful" broadsheets, the popular middle ages ballads, and the bardic tales. It paints with broad strokes, intending to make the reader feel as well as think about its stories. Pulp can be a style, a genre, or a theme; but it's always an experience.

There are some experiences which go deep to our human cores. Death, violence, and sex are about as fundamental as it gets in human experience, so naturally those things are prevalent in much fiction and almost always in pulp fiction. These are the things that get our hearts thumping – and keep readers turning the pages!

It's been argued that there are really only three stories, and that they sum up every plot for every piece of fiction: A Man Goes on a Journey; A Man Learns a Lesson (or fails to); and Boy Meets Girl (or loses girl etc.). Fiction certainly devotes a substantial amount of time to telling stories of men and women relating romantically, not least because that's something that attracts an audience and makes the reader care about and pull for the protagonists.

So many pulp stories include a female character who is a potential romance or sex interest. She might be a virginal good girl menaced by her wicked uncle or a sinful bad girl seeking to manipulate our hero for her own devious ends, but she's prevalent in all kinds of variations; not just a female character, a female character with a relationship or potential relationship with the protagonist.

That's the sense in which I'm using the term heroine in this article. Sometimes heroine can simply mean the proper feminine of hero, the protagonist to whom the story happens; here I'm using the other definition, that of the female story lead with whom the hero must associate and who is often part of the hero's heroic mission.

Prior to our modern liberated era there was a general assumption that most female characters would be less capable of dealing with threat than male characters. If there's a plucky heroine, that's considered remarkable. She's an exceptional specimen of her gender, not the norm.

Reflecting societal attitudes, and perhaps a practical acknowledgement that when violence is involved women are at a physical disadvantage, the assumption has been that the female lead has eventually required some kind of help from the male lead. Let's not shy away from the truth that many pulp stories, especially older ones, hold this to be true.

Pulp can be a very honest storytelling style though, because that hero-saves-heroine trope goes way back in our society. It's probably engraved in our DNA. There is a very primal instinct in males to protect females from other males. It's probably about ensuring that our seed fertilises the woman rather than any other, but it's a very old urge. Protect the women and the children.

We've been telling stories about heroes who turn up to save the girl, often from death or a fate worse than death (impregnation by anyone other than the hero), for a very long time. How many fairy-tale princess and forest maidens are saved in the end by some handsome prince or burly woodsman? How many of our ancient myths include a damsel in distress being rescued? Hi there, Andromeda, Deianera, Sita.

From the Princess of Sana'a (*Arabian Nights*) to Canace (Chaucer's *A Knight's Tale*), from St George and the Dragon to Van Helsing's vampire hunters, the damsel in distress is hammered into our worldview as soon as we open a book.

Another very old assumption goes with that. When the hero rescues the heroine, she will fall in love with him. They'll marry and live happily ever after; or at least they'll have sex. Many older sources don't even question that her hero is entitled to the virginity he's just saved. To the hero the spoils. Only the brave deserve the fair.

We know, in our post-modern cynical diagnostic world, that the ability to kill ogres with a sword doesn't necessarily make one a perfect boyfriend – although a very useful one for an ogre-prone princess, I suppose. We know that men, however heroic and blood-stained, do not automatically qualify for a thank-you bedroom session. But when we allow ourselves to be drawn into the realm of fiction our expectations subtly change; our perceptions and values are dragged again into a world where the hero and heroine do find themselves compatible and attracted, and where a happy ending or a tragic loss are the two most likely outcomes.

That's not to say that there aren't plenty of stories that subvert these expectations. The most common is the one where the heroine turns out to be the villain after all. But these subversions only work because the expectation of how things should go is so ingrained into our reading experience.

Given that most pulp fiction was originally published to earn a living, its not surprising that it caters to the things that will most part a reader from his purchase money. Look at the covers of many old pulp magazines. A good percentage of them feature scantily-clad or naked women; that always sells. Of these, about half also feature the woman in bondage or immediate peril, requiring rescue or facing imminent destruction or ravishment. In about half of these the hero is also present, striving to save her.

Now go to the artistic depiction of heroines throughout history, back through the portraits of the Renaissance, the woodcuts of the Middle Ages, to the friezes and pottery of the Hellenistic period. See if the percentage of nudity, bondage, imminent peril and heroic rescuers is much different.

So what does this tell us? And what does it mean for modern writers and modern readers of adventure fiction?

Well, first off, it tells us that fundamental differences between men and women sometimes leak past our modern conceptions of equality meaning uniformity. Fortunately, society is past the days when gender equality meant that women should be just like men, so its not too hard for us to recognise that the sexes are physically different and that they have historically played different social roles. But when we settle into the world of fiction and fantasy, the masks come off and we allow ourselves a more guilt-free experience of the contrasts.

Second, it means that we have to buy in to the romanticised, sexualised way that men and women relate in fiction. In the same way as we allow that a protagonist may be more heroic, a better fighter, a smarter thinker as part of our suspension of disbelief, we have to allow his heroine to be more beautiful, more charming, and more available than we would give credence in "real life". That we consistently do make these allowances suggests how much we enjoy visiting worlds where heroes get the girl.

But because modern audiences tend to be more sophisticated and come to their reading with modern understandings of gender and morality, contemporary pulp writers have to be cleverer and subtler in how they apply the ancient tropes. Readers are still interested in boy-meets-girl, but they want another reason for why our protagonists hop into bed together at the end than "Oh thank you for saving me, my big strong hero!"

There are certain older assumptions and attitudes which writers can no longer get away with – thankfully. Depicting a Negro as naturally less smart or moral than a Caucasian might have been acceptable in 1920; now even stories set in that time that accurately depict discrimination of that era had better not try and suggest the view was justified. Likewise, the era when a hero could push a girl down on the bed, tear her clothes off, and ravish her until her protests end and she becomes an acquiescent passionate lover are past; now we call that rape.

But just because there are pitfalls, that's no reason for pulp writers or readers to shy away from one of the fundamental pillars of the genre. Boys still meet girls every day. People who are in trouble should be helped. Adversity forms strong bonds of fellowship, and sometimes of romance. All of these make for potent, visceral stories.

Heroes, of whatever gender, have to be heroic. Heroes rescue people. Heroines (also of whatever gender) tend to get into trouble; the best of them get into trouble because they're doing the right thing (c.f. snoopy reporter, princess defending her people, whore with a heart of gold). If the heroine has our sympathy, respect, or admiration then we're even more engaged rooting for our hero to get to her.

Pulp has traditions. Heroines are part of it. Go save one today.

Rescue Me:
A Meditation on Damsels In Distress
(If you're here for the serious analysis then my advice is to skip this one)

ONCE UPON A TIME...
"Is it dead?"

"As a doornail, milady. The fell wyrm is no more. You are saved."

"Whew. Thanks. Er, is there any chance you could cut these chains off me now, only my arms are going to sleep in this position?"

"Oh, sorry. Yes, there you are."

"Thank you again. I was feeling a bit... vulnerable all strapped up like that. Some people might take, you know, advantage."

"I assure you that the thought never crossed my mind. Well, not seriously. Really."

"Uh-huh. Well I guess you must be one of the good knights in shining armour then. I thought they only happened in storybooks."

"Well what exactly is one supposed to do when there's a maiden screaming and a very large winged lizard about to lightly toast her, if not charge to the rescue? "

"Well, I suspect the general consensus would be to run as fast as possible in the opposite direction."

"Surely not. Rescuing damsels is a major part of being a knight. We get special training, you know."

"Sure, just like us damsels take screaming lessons. Get real."

"Are you feeling alright? Only you seem to be a lot more… caustic than is customary after being saved from a horrible fate."

"Well, I suppose I'm just slightly worried by the fact you're a big shiny person who I don't know, with a sword, who's insane enough to charge dragons."

"Oh, sorry. I'll put it away shall I? You really don't need to worry about being ravished or anything. I'm quite harmless."

"Tell that to scaly there. Oh wait – he's dead."

"Besides, there'll be plenty of time for hanky panky after the wedding."

"The… the wedding?"

"Sure. Standard contract. Dead dragon, princess' hand and half the kingdom. Basic rates."

"Ah. Right. I see. And my father would agree to this why?"

"What?"

"Why? Why should my royal father agree to give away half his kingdom just because you spitted a big fire-breathing thingie? I mean, if he was that bothered about me do you think he'd have had me chained here as a sacrifice to appease the dragon in the first place?"

"Er…"

"Think about it. Just how does being able to stab wyrms make you a good husband and ruler? I mean, how many dragons do you think we get around here?"

"I'm guessing the answer is around one?"

"Yep. Spot on. The bottom has just dropped out of the local dragonslaying market. I don't suppose you have any experience in economics, or accountancy? You're not a secret expert on crop rotation or legal tort and stuff?"

"I can shoot a goblin through the eye at ninety paces if that helps."

"Not when you're ruling a kingdom that's just been artificially divided in two by an arbitrary royal edict to accommodate a sudden royal son-in-law, and you have to hammer out a working socio-political infrastructure, I'm afraid."

"Are you sure you're a princess? I thought you girls got etiquette instructions on being rescued. This doesn't seem like a proper damsel in distress response at all."

"Would you like me to faint? I suppose I could if it made you feel better."

"No, no that's quite alright. I'm just having to adjust to something of an unfamiliar situation, that's all. I never really expected a princess with an IQ, I suppose."

"Well I never expected a knight in shining armour to come and spoil my big plan to save the kingdom."

"Save the kingdom? You don't really believe that having fed the dragon one virgin you'd be able to keep it away from demanding more and more and more?"

"As a matter of fact that's exactly what I believe. After all, my dress has around twenty pounds of belladonna stitched into it. That should have been enough to poison even a dragon when he ate me."

"Clever. Very sneaky. I'm ever so sorry I stopped you getting eaten and spoiled your plan."

"No, no that's alright. I can't say I was looking forward to the being eaten part, so frankly I'd say your method was an improvement overall. And there was always the risk that the wyrm prefers his princesses crispy fried, in which case all the nasty poison gets well done along with me, and might have been useless."

"I can see how that would ruin your day."

"It's just that – and please don't take this personally – we never thought we'd find anybody stupid enough to charge a seventy-foot fire-breathing monster with nothing but a pointy stick."

"Well I'm glad I've been able to surprise you a little bit then. That way we can both say we've had an interesting afternoon."

"I suppose so."

"Yes."

"Absolutely."

"Indeed."

"Yes."

"Well… I've got to say that I'm a bit puzzled as to what to do next. I mean, custom dictates that I sweep you onto my horse, gallop off to your father, and pick up the reward. Since I apparently don't have the requisite agricultural or legal education for your exacting standards, I'm at a bit of a loss."

"Ah. Sorry. I didn't mean to spoil your rescue. It's just that I didn't want you to get the wrong idea. I didn't go to all this trouble to save the realm only to have some heroic imbecile take charge and run it into the ground. No offence."

"None taken. You have quite a good point. Never thought of it like that before."

"So… what happens?"

"I suppose… I place a single chaste kiss on your virgin cheek, leap onto the stallion, and ride off into the sunset leaving you wistfully wondering who the mystery hero was."

"It has a certain romantic rhythm to it, I admit, but that doesn't seem very fair on you after you got all scorched and sweaty saving my life. And who says I'm a virgin anyway?"

"Er, well, I just assumed. I mean, sacrifices to monsters are usually supposed to be…"

"It's a seventy foot long hungry reptile. It's not going to be bothered about my sexual history. Do you enquire after the marital status of your pork sandwiches?"

"You know, I think battling the dragon was the easy part of this rescue. Very well, milady, let me ask you a few questions. What are you going to do now?"

"Now? What do you mean?"

"What I mean is, you've just been miraculously saved – with a good deal of style and flair, if I say so myself – from a gory fate. Do you trot off back to the palace and say 'Hello everybody. Guess what? I'm not dead even though you were all perfectly happy for me to be left out to be eaten by a dragon to save your skinny butts. Hi, daddy, I'm back and ready for the next time I need to be sacrificed to save the day'. Or what?"

"That's not fair. I'm sure there was a good deal of soul-searching before they let me do this."

"So they didn't heave a huge sigh of relief that in feeding the alarmingly smart-mouthed princess to the dragon that they were killing two birds with one stone?"

"No. Of course not. No. Absolutely no."

"I thought so. And now that you're saved your father can line you up in some political marriage with the agricultural economist of your dreams."

"Look, the ability to hit things with a sword does not denote an aptitude for maintaining a stable relationship."

"Whereas the ability to operate a three-field rotation doesn't denote an aptitude for a romance filled with passion and fulfilment. But perhaps, not being a virgin, you already know that?"

"I never said I wasn't a virgin. I just said you shouldn't assume."

"You mean I should... what? Conduct practical tests?"

"No. I mean you should... not expect everything to be... what you expect."

"Are you trying to tell me that you're actually a prince in disguise?"

"No! What I mean is that... ooohh! You an be *really* irritating!"

"Heh. Now you know what it's like rescuing you."

"I am not like that."

"Oh, yes you are."

"Am not!"

"Are so."

"Not."

"So."

"Not."

"I rest my case. So seriously, what are we going to do? I mean, haven't you paid your dues to your kingdom now? You were willing to give your life for it. What else can they expect?"

"The rest of my life, I suppose."

"Oh, that's not fair. By that reckoning, you owe your life to me. So either I get to keep it, or else I get compensated for giving it back to your kingdom."

"What do you mean, keep it? You can't keep it – me."

"Why not? You're rather attractive in a sort of annoying nitpicky way. You'd be rather fun to keep."

"Well you can forget that idea right off, buster. Just because you saved my skin doesn't give you free access to it."

"Sad but true. And even if I was the liberty-taking type, which I trust you have noted I am not, I'm hardly going to annoy a girl who poisons her underwear and hurls herself into the maws of dragons."

"That's right. Don't forget my underwear."

"I'm thinking about it right now."

"That is not exactly what I meant. Kindly do not focus your attention upon my unmentionables. In fact kindly do not mention them."

"As you insist, milady. I am now concentrating my efforts on eliminating your underwear. Mentally, I mean. As requested."

"Not exactly, as it happens. Perhaps we should just recap at this point? I am very happy to be saved, but that does not give you free licence to picture my underwear or any possible lack thereof."

"Trapped or otherwise."

"In any variation, with or without lace, ribbons, silks, or gauzy see-through areas."

"Now you're just being unfair."

"*Nor* does it mean I have to grant you conjugal rights of either a temporary or permanent basis, *or* that the kingdom is necessarily liable to offer any compensation or remuneration for your unsolicited extermination of local vermiforms."

"I think that's absolutely clear now. However, likewise I reserve the freedom of thought to speculate upon the nature of any hypothetical belladonna-laced lingerie you may or may not be modelling, on the possibilities of any conjugal liaison of a temporary or permanent basis which you are under no obligation to grant, or about what a shame it would be if you didn't kiss me right here and now. Milady."

"You do not have carte blanche to go around randomly kissing princesses just because they happen to have had a recent draconic inconvenience."

"This is true. It is quite clearly an invitation-only event."

"And that is frankly not going to happen."

"Uh-huh. I see."

"What does that mean? Uh-huh what?"

"Oh, just uh-huh. As in, uh-huh, she's trying to pretend she doesn't want me to kiss her right now."

"Now that is just your imagination running wild. And also you being smug for no good reason."

"Hey, I killed a flaming huge flaming dragon. Surely I get to be very slightly smug for a limited time period? And if I'm just imagining an attraction then why are you blushing?"

"Because I'm shocked. I'm not used to such… boorish treatment."

"Uh-huh."

"Don't start that again. Look, you seem a nice enough young man apart from a tendency to wander round in a tin can doing monumentally suicidal things, but any inclination I might have to offer any kind of… lip contact… whatsoever can be clearly put down to post-traumatic stress reaction."

"So you admit to having an inclination, then?"

"I didn't say that."

"Yes you did. I heard you. 'Any inclination you might have', you said. So you do want me to kiss you."

"Might have. Not do have. Might have."

"I'm sure your father the king would be shocked if he found you were not being a wholly truthful princess. Perhaps you would care to clarify whether you are or are not secretly yearning for me to take you in my manly arms, fold you close, draw your head to mine and implement the kind of lip contact you referred to earlier."

"I don't see why I should have to supply any such clarification."

"I suppose not. It's pretty evident that you're dying for me to kiss you. Probably with tongues."

"Don't be absurd. You're going back to these fairy tale stories again. Nothing is going to happen."

"So you don't want me to kiss you, and you won't enjoy it if I do."

"Exactly."

"And you're willing to prove this?"

"If you insist. I expect I'll have to find some way of showing you that your ridiculous expectations are nothing more than absurd fantasy."

"You're going to prove you don't want to kiss me by kissing me."

"If that's what it takes to disabuse you of your absurd speculations about my emotional and psychological wellbeing then I am a princess who was brought up to do what is necessary for the common good."

"Right. Here goes."

"Right."

" . . . . . . "

"Well?"

"Nothing. Absolutely nothing. Not a thing."

"Really? Because I thought you were sort of kissing back there towards the end."

"Of course not. I was just trying not to choke on your tongue. Where did you learn to kiss like that?"

"Hero school. Standard heroine-kissing technique."

"You must have had great fun practising on your school-chums."

"I did not - and I wish to emphasise this - practise on my school chums. It was an all-squires school."

"Uh-huh."

"Now you're doing the uh-huh thing. I think we should have a sort of mutual uh-huh exclusion treaty. So you're saying that *you* got that good at kissing without practise, then, milady?"

"What? I certainly don't go around doing kissing practise. If I'm a good kisser it's an entirely natural talent."

"Not from doing what was necessary for the common good?"

"Absolutely not. And frankly I don't even see where you're getting that allegation about me being a good kisser from since I wasn't kissing you back at all. You're utterly imagining the whole thing."

"As previously described regarding the forbidden underwear topic, I have a very good imagination. I imagined that as I was embracing you, you were sort of pressing your whole body up against me and really quite enjoying the experience."

"Then you have a morbid, sick imagination. I was in no way either kissing or pressing. I was simply letting you get the thing out of your system and demonstrating that I was in no way aroused or excited by the contact, despite the adrenaline surge of escaping death by dragon."

"Really? I had a very different impression of the experience."

"Well you were clearly overcome by having the chance to kiss a stunning princess, so you probably weren't thinking clearly."

"But I was definitely paying attention, milady. In the interests of fairness I think we owe it to ourselves to repeat the experiment and find out which of us has the proper perspective on this."

"Oh, you do, do you? And you think I have nothing better to do than stand here while a sweaty knight paws me and pulls me close to him and…"

. . . .

"That… was cheating."

"Cheating? What do you mean?"

"You cheated. I was letting you kiss me and then you… tickled."

"I was just making sure I had a firm hold on you for the purposes of the kissing, milady.

"Oh, you got a firm hold alright. You might possibly want to remove your hand from its current firm hold, if you please."

"I might, but in a full and measured judgement about the situation I'd say on the whole I'd probably prefer to leave it where it is."

"Ah, perhaps I should clarify my statement. Get your hand back on my waist or we'll be finding out just how good that shiny codpiece thing of yours really is."

"An admirable clarification, milady. Since you seem so good at expressing your views, you might perhaps want to admit now that on that occasion you were most definitely both kissing and pressing. In fact I might go so far as to say that you also gave the impression of melting."

"Rubbish. If I appeared to kiss and/or press I was merely being polite since you seemed to be taking the whole thing so seriously. As for melting, I can assure you that at no point did I allow myself... that is, at no point did I do anything which could possibly be construed as melting."

"You realise that if we hadn't banned uh-huhs I'd be doing one just about now, don't you?"

"Yes, but we did ban them, so I'll thank you to accept my word when I say I felt absolutely nothing as you kissed me. Except for a tickle. And your hand going where it shouldn't."

"I can only apologise for my forwardness in that matter, milady. I can't help but notice however that it took you the better part of ten minutes before you drew your objections to my attention."

"I was too shocked to say anything."

"Except press. And melt."

"I did not melt. I may have swooned slightly. As soon as I came to my senses I immediately reported my concerns."

"I only mention it because you have so far in the course of our relationship not felt particularly constrained to withhold your objections on a wide variety of other topics."

"Speaking of feeling constrained, may I draw your attention to the fact that you hand has not in fact been relocated from the position which prompted our current conversion, and in fact appears to be what I can only describe as cupping and kneading."

"Ah. Well feel free to speak up anytime during the following embrace if you want to lodge some kind of complaint."

. . . .

"I think I was safer with the dragon."

"So was I, milady."

"It was fairly evident during our most recent... experiment that you are not, in any way, threatened by belladonna-d underwear."

"That kind of padding cannot be hygienic or healthy."

"Your vigorous attempts at ensuring my wellbeing did not stop at impaling wyrms, I note."

"I try to be a full service knight."

"I have no intention of being a full service princess."

"You know, there's no witnesses to you not being eaten by the wyrm. If you vanished – say with a passing knight, on to adventure and romance in a world you never made - nobody would know you hadn't just been digested."

"I couldn't do that."

"Really?"

"Really."

"Uh-huh."

"You said no more uh-huhs!"

"Well that was such a blatant asking for an uh-huh that I couldn't resist it. Of *course* you could do it. All you have to do is hop onto the four legged thing over there eating the grass, follow the straight muddy track thing we call a road, and keep going."

"And what happens then?"

"The usual expectation is that we live happily ever after."

"Uh-huh."

"Uh-huh."

"That sounds very irresponsible."

"I'd have chosen the word *romantic*. Or possibly *fun*."

"I am clearly suffering from post-traumatic stress syndrome to seriously consider this."

"You should be very flattered. I'm forgoing the fifty percent kingdom deal and just seeking the princess' hand."

"It wasn't my hand you seemed to be paying particular attention to just now."

"It wasn't your hand you were squirming up against me when you were melting."

"I was not, and I wish to emphasise this, melting."

"Well I have to say that from where I was it gave a very good impression of…"

"Shut up. *This* is melting."

***

6.
Bad Girls of Myth

THE BAD GIRL. We writers love 'em. She's the dangerous woman, often a sexual predator, almost always a sensual exotic, who comes into the hero's life and turns it upside down. She makes him question his choices, tests his loyalties, sometimes makes him doubt his sanity.

She's the cool brunette in the tight red number who sashays into the broken-down 'tec's office with a hazardous case for his attention. She's the villain's wicked daughter who has her own agenda for the hero. She's the svelte foreign spy who manipulates men as easily as she murders them. She's the femme fatale.

Brigid O'Shaughnessy killed Sam Spade's partner.[34] P'Gell beguiled and betrayed the Spirit.[35] Fah lo Suee plotted against her father Fu Manchu while seeking to manipulate Nayland-Smith and Petrie.[36] And for Sherlock Holmes, the divine Irene Adler was always The Woman.[37]

But seductive, assertive bad girls aren't anything new in literature. Morgana le Fay pursued Sir Lancelot and sought her half-brother King Arthur's downfall.[38] Salome dropped seven veils and demanded John the Baptist's head on a dish. Clytemnestra and her lover accomplished the murders of her husband King Agamemnon and his new bedfellow, Trojan slave-princess Cassandra. Odysseus had some dinner-party trouble with Circe the Enchantress.

34 *The Maltese Falcon*, Dashiell Hammett, *Black Mask* magazine 1930, most famously adapted to the big screen in 1941 with Bogart, Aster, Lorre, and Greenstreet.
35 Will Eisner's seminal *The Spirit* comic strip was circulated in the newspapers of the Register and Tribune Syndicate from 1940 onward, reaching five million readers. P'Gell is a serial husband-murderess who recurrently disrupts the crimefighter's work.
36 From Sax Rohmer's *Fu Manchu* series.
37 "A Scandal in Bohemia" by Sir Arthur Conan Doyle.
38 Modern versions often conflate Morgana with her older sisters Margawse and Elaine, so that Morgana, not King Lot's queen and Gawain's mother Margawse, is the half-sister upon whom Arthur fathers Mordred.

And it goes back even before that. It goes back to Lilith and Eve.

But by the time we're back to Greek myth there's another aspect to bad girls; they're girls who've been done wrong.

Let's take Medea, Circe's niece, princess of distant exotic Colchis, priestess of Hecate, keeper of the sacred serpent grove where the holy treasure was preserved. In a movie-style romance she's swept off her feet (or at least swept to sea) by accomplished seducer Jason of Iolchis, of Argonaut fame. He runs off with her, but the ancient sources make clear that what he's really after is the sacred treasure only she can get him to, the gold-fringed purple fleece of the divine ram of Zeus. Jason convinces Medea to turn on her family, to steal the fleece, and to elope with him.

There are two different versions then. In one, Medea's brother is a full-grown man who is sent to stop the Argo with a fleet of warships. Medea guides Jason in ways to elude and then defeat and kill her brother - she chooses her man over her past family. In the other story, Medea kidnaps her infant brother, sacrifices him, and tosses him from the ship or else hides his dismembered pieces, to slow pursuit because the Colcheans have to stop and retrieve their prince's body.[39]

This being ancient myth, Medea's motives aren't as spelled out as in a modern narrative. We don't get her inner monologue or even conversational exposition. Different commentators have drawn different conclusion. Some, like Graves,[40] point out that Medea was likely to be betrothed to a savage Molochian prince (the Molochians were notorious for their anal intercourse, to which Hecate's priestess objected), and that Medea was therefore a classic heroine escaping a horrible arranged marriage. Others take a more metaphysical view that, as a servant of the dark aspect of the moon-goddess, Medea had a right or duty to render sacrifice when she took a sacred object from Hecate's grove. Yet others portray her as a young woman head-over-heels in love with a dangerous stranger, willing to do anything to be his.

Medea is one of only two women to travel on the Argo as 'crew' not 'guests'. The other was Atalanta, a warrior who had pledged her continued chastity to her patron goddess Artemis the huntress. Atalanta's bench-mate was the man with whom she was passionately in love. Ancient writers had great fun describing how the rest of the crew had to continually keep these two from breaking Atalanta's vow and bringing the wrath of Artemis down on their mission.

39 The principal variant sources begin with Apollodorus i.9.24 and Apollonius Rhodius iv.212-502.
40 *The Greek Myths* volume 2, Robert Graves, 1955. This work in two volumes is invaluable to the scholar and to the myth-lover.

Back to Medea. Her next 'bad girl' act is when Jason gets home. His wicked usurping uncle Pelias still sits on Iolchis' throne, despite agreeing to step aside if Jason retrieved the fleece. While the hero was away Pelias has executed Jason's parents, the dispossessed former king and queen,.

Medea now acts on behalf of her new husband to secure him a throne. She convinces the tyrant's daughters that she has the power to regenerate old men to youngsters. By means of a demonstration she cuts up an old sheep, throws it into a pot with sacred herbs, and produces from the interior a new-born lamb. This is sufficient to prompt the girls to cut up their aged kingly father and put him in the pot for renewal. Alas, Pelias is not reborn, and the Furies curse falls not on Medea and Jason but upon his blood-stained daughters.

Jason becomes king - but then he does Medea wrong! As always his eye wanders. Yet again, Jason isn't just playing away for fun. He's been run out of Iolchis, but his new squeeze is another princess whose father has a kingdom to bestow. Jason decides to replace Medea as his queen with Glauce, the new mistress who has his attention (and other parts).

It's interesting and sometimes tragic when the hero of the story doesn't measure up to the heroine. Nearly all the Greek heroes are like that. Theseus was saved by Adriane then abandoned her afterwards on a deserted island. Hercules went mad and slew his children by his first wife Megara. When his bride got a bit too old for the big leagues he passed her on to his herald. Agamemnon's wife Clytemnestra was excited when her husband sent word he'd fixed their daughter up as bride to the mighty Achilles, she packed Iphigenia off to the Greek army camp for the wedding, then discovered that the girl was actually required as a human sacrifice to gain good weather for the sea voyage to Troy (hence the aforementioned revenge murder). And so on.

When Jason dumps her, Medea goes *totally* bad girl. After all she's done for him...!

So Medea does what every self-respecting ancient Greek princess with access to the dark arts would do: she sends Jason's new wife a poisoned robe that kills both Glauce and her royal father. Medea chops up her own two children by Jason into a stew and feeds it to him, seriously messing with his afterlife karma. Then she escapes in a fiery chariot pulled by dragons.

Medea's second husband turns out no better, leading to a plot to murder his unknown son Theseus. Thereafter she returns to Colchis to wreak vengeance on her usurping uncle and place her father back on his throne.

And so on.

The point is that the tropes of 'bad girl' are pretty much all there. She's not just bad, she's bad for a reason. That reason usually a man. Her motivations are passion and vengeance. Her methods are trickery and seduction. She can be both cruel and enchanting. She is misunderstood. She is bad news.

Medea would translate to a modern pulp without any alteration at all.

The Lesson of Inanna

REMEMBER NANNA, Enheduanna's moon-goddess? She also went by the name of Inanna, Sumerian goddess of love and war, as Ishtar or Belili to the Babylonians, and later as Astarte to the Greeks. She is the bringer of fertility, the personification of the morning and evening star (the planet Venus). She was worshipped by sacred prostitution; every young woman of Babylon had to serve as a prostitute at the holy Blue Gate in her honour before they could marry.

Ishtar gets a more prominent role in myth than her counterparts like Aphrodite, being involved in adventures which are more than "then she had an affair with Ares and as they copulated they were caught by a net-trap set by her husband Hephaestus." In fact she's a heroine in her own right, starring in a number of stories. She even has a walk-on part in the *Epic of Gilgamesh*, and her big starring role comes in something of a sequel to it.

In his epic, Gilgamesh slays the Great Bull of Heaven, Gugulanna (the original bull associated with the constellation Taurus and the zodiac sign). Gugulanna is the husband of Ishtar's sister, the death-goddess Erishkigal, and his loss has cosmic consequences that have to be put right. In other versions it is Ishtar's own lover who dies. In either case, Erishkigal must be made to relent and return death back to its boundaries, so Ishtar descends into the underworld for love's sake to plead with the goddess of death.

This isn't easy. At each of the seven gates to hell Ishtar must surrender something. She performs a kind of striptease, sacrificing one of her jewels or garments each time - a lapis lazuli measuring rod, a golden ring, a turban, a wig, her pectoral, her "ladyship garment", her necklace, the jewels at her breast, even her mascara. Each of these items symbolises some aspect of her power or authority. If she is to brave Absolute Death "she can't take them with her".

Naked and helpless, Ishtar pleads before Erishkigal. The death goddess will not relent. She wracks Ishtar with plagues and pain, turning her into a living corpse for her presumption. As the story goes: "The seven judges rendered their decision against her. They looked at her -- it was the look of death. They spoke to her -- it was the speech of anger. They shouted at her -- it was the shout of heavy guilt. The afflicted woman was turned into a corpse. And the corpse was hung on a hook."[41]

Of course, now that the goddess of sex isn't on Earth, sex is no longer possible. The various gods who had previously been indifferent to Ishtar's concerns realise that the world will end without sex. Enlil and Nanna refuse to help, but Enki, god of crafts, mischief and intelligence, shapes one or two genderless beings that he sends down to Erishkigal to bargain for Ishtar's release.

When they get there, Erishkigal isn't in a good way, wracked by cramps and wounds; even death can't survive without life to feed on, and life needs sex!

Ishtar is released. She passes through the seven gates, regaining her clothes (and power). But there is a price. Another must take her place in death. Ishtar refuses to sacrifice the friends and allies she meets, but her lover has not mourned her so she renders him to death. The compromise is that he and she (or he and his sister) will each spend six months in turn in the underworld (c.f. Persephone), provoking the turning of the seasons.

There's plenty of varieties of this story and as many interpretations. I adduce it because it demonstrates a rather gutsy woman - or goddess - taking charge to handle a problem nobody else dared tackle, making Christ-like self-sacrifices, suffering for love, and finally being proved right.

One can imagine Babylonian grandmothers tucking their grand-daughters into bed with the story and saying: "And the moral is, my dears, that you can achieve anything and get anything as long as the sex is good enough. Night night!"

***

---

41 *Translated source: The Electronic Text Corpus of Sumerian Literature*, University of Oxford, online at http://etcsl.orinst.ox.ac.uk/section1/tr141.htm The text is reconstructed from numerous ancient sources.

7.
Chapters

NOTE TO WRITERS: anyone in a historical story who quotes the Bible using chapter and verse before A.D. 1553 is an anachronism. That was the year that the *Geneva Bible* first included both chapters and verse numbers to help identify places in the text.[42]

Chapters really became fashionable in the 13th Century. Before that the main large division of text was "the book", as with the works of the Greek and Roman classics. A "book" of Pliny or Ovid might equate to a modern chapter, and often does in published volumes, but originally it was a very practical division. Each book was the length of a typical parchment scroll.

With the development first of the bound book of page-leaves and then of the printing press, scroll length was no longer an issue by the late middle ages. New formats of publishing meant new mechanisms, and that included chapter and sometimes verse. By the 1500s they had been joined by the contents page, the index, and the page number. The footnote was not far behind.[43]

Chapters were quickly "backdated" into older works, breaking up the lengthy homilies and monologues of the historians and philosophers into chunks so that key passages were easier to locate. That in itself sometimes caused controversy. Labelling a section of the Bible "Jesus Promises Redemption For All" was itself a theological assertion that weighted the original text it headed and might be seen as adding to Holy Scripture.

Today, chapters are a tool in the writer's box. Some authors use them; other times its better to do something else. Chapters are the next break point

---

42 There had been previous attempts. Verses date back to Dominican scholar Santi Pagnini (1470–1541), although his system was not adopted. Chapters were pioneered separately by Archbishop Stephen Langton and Cardinal Hugo de Sancto Caro in the early 13th century. Langton's system prevailed. Before that ancient Hebrew texts had been divided by the letter *Pe* for an open paragraph and *Samakh* for a closed one.
43 Because footnotes are good.

up from section breaks and scene changes, and generally when I use them its because I want my readers to pause and consider what's just happened and come to the next bit fresh. It's like clearing the plates away and serving the wine for the next course of the banquet. I'll sometimes treat chapters like episodes, finishing on a cliffhanger or with a revelation, or else offering some kind of closure before moving on to the next plot point.

For pulps, which tend to be visceral, immediate, plot-dependent and pacy, chapters can be a real boon. They can be the equivalent of the dotted line on the map in the Indiana Jones movies. They can be the "tune in next week folks..." ending to a serial-style action sequence. They can be the sledgehammer silence that comes after a shocking event or revelation. And of course they can simulate the format of many early serialised pulp stories.

In fact chapter breaks in literature have many of the same practical functions as act and scene breaks in theatre: pacing, scene changes, theme changes, and toilet breaks.

Pacing: Chapters are important for pacing. Want to draw a line under something and give the reader time to think about it? Put in a chapter break. Even if the reader turns right on to the next page there's that psychological pause to absorb what's just been read.

Want to leave in the reader, just for as long as it takes to flip the page – or these days scroll the page - asking, "How can he get out of that?" Or perhaps give the audience a moment to breathe out, a "moving on now that's done" moment? Does the story require a mental pause to consider the consequences of recent events? These are all effects of the chapter break.

Scene Changes: A book doesn't need physical time to shift the backdrops and props like a stage production, but that little mental discontinuity between chapters allows for mental images to be reset, for moods to be changed. It can give the impression of time or distance travelled. Readers have been educated to know that things can move on between chapters, and the story starts again with each new section.

Theme Changes: Some writers like to offer mini-themes within their larger narrative, and chapters are an ideal vehicle for that. One chapter might be set in spring, full of hope and new promise. A later one is winter-bound, full of death and regret. Chapters act like the picture frame that distinguishes one piece of work from another while keeping the collection unified into a greater whole.

Toilet Breaks: Readers have to stop reading sometime. An author, hoping for the best effect from his efforts, may want to direct the likely times when those choices to put the book down happen. Chapter ends are a natural closure point, a planned pause. Likewise, chapter beginnings offer the best chance to re-engage a reader who returns to the story after some time away.

Closing lines have special impact. They are the last note that stays in the reader's head, the last hammer-blow that knocks down the adversary, the shock or closure the story section requires.

Chapter openings are also important. Everyone knows that the first line of a book has to sell the story and hook the reader. Chapter openings have to do that in miniature; what's written in the first paragraph goes into the reader's head deeper than what's in paragraph thirteen.

Chapter Titles are the next rank up from numbered chapters themselves. A chapter title halts the reader that one beat more, emphasising that something different is about to happen now, or giving them a moment to savour the situation if the story carries right on from before. It also shapes the reader's anticipation of what's to come.

Basic information chapter titles that offer place and date are practical shorthand ways of scene setting, avoiding "Three days later they were still in the black swamp…" and the like. More colourful titles are an announcement of the content to come ("The Enemy Attacks"), a foreshadowing of plot ("The Enemy Within"), a reference to theme ("Enemies"), or even information offered by the omniscient narrator ("Her Greatest Enemy").

The purpose of these title headers is often to tease, to draw the reader into the narrative again. They're the shiny gold wrapping on the chocolate bar. But they can also set a mood ("Into the Caverns of the Dead"), worry the reader ("A Hero's Death"), emphasise a key development ("The Sword Is Drawn"), even spell out the "message" of the story ("The Price of Treachery").

Sometimes chapter titles are artsy. I once wrote a whole book where the chapter headings were all Shakespearian quotations. Sometimes titles can be fun, mischievous like the book where the first letter of each chapter title spelled out the name of the murderer. They can be retro ("On the Discourse between the Elves and the Dwarves and What Came After"). They can have a continuity ("Chapter One: As I was Going Up the Stairs" "Chapter Two: "I Met a Man Who Wasn't There"). They can even deliberately misdirect the reader; my favourite title was "The Happy Ending", which I used four chapters off the end of the book so readers would just know that this wasn't the happy conclusion the cast members all expected, and would dread things going wrong.

Those authors who want even more of a mental break than a mere chapter title could even go for the very old method as follows: "Chapter XVI: The Summoning of the Heroes - in which we are introduced to the knights of the realm and learn somewhat of their strengths and failings, the Princess makes a remarkable promise, and the mystery of the silver egg is unfolded."

I would neither exclude nor insist on chapters or chapter titles. Just because they can be effective methods doesn't make them the only effective methods. There's not just one right way or writing. Sometimes less is more and it's better to cut out the breaks and the headers and all the frills. Best to leave in the punctuation though.

Next chapter.

***

8.
Updating Pulps

I WAS PROVOKED by a review I read recently that slated Doc Savage for "running around with five white men". It made me consider how society's expectations of pulp fiction have changed in the last century – and how that affects modern iterations of classic pulp characters.

A century ago it was okay for Alan Quartermain to go to what we'd now call third world countries (or developing nations) and triumph over mad, cruel, superstitious native witch doctors or sinister cunning Asiatic masterminds just be being more British than they were.

Eighty years ago it was okay for the hard-boiled detective to slap around a dame who was giving him the runaround or who got too hysterical.

Sixty years ago it was fine for mystery men to have a comedy Negro or Chinese sidekick or servant, or else a silent ethnic minority strongman.

Forty years ago a spunky wildcat girl would keep saying "No" while the hero pressed his advances then suddenly turn into a raging sexual spitfire when he showed her what a real man could do in bed.

But now when we come back to write stories featuring those characters it becomes an embarrassing problem to have to write around attitudes and practices which were considered just fine by the standards of their original time – at least by the standards of the white Western pulp fiction audience. But when we shy away from them we lose some of the flavour of the period and we're not being true to the original continuity.

From the 80's onwards, every adventurer had to have a feisty female romance interest who gave as good as she got and a non-white friend to prove how open our hero was to ethnic harmony. That sometimes backfired; a lot of best friends and girlfriends end up dead in pulp fiction, so the death, torture, or even just the constant capture of these supporting characters seemed misogynistic or racist. Unfortunately the role of supporting characters in adventure fiction is often to need help or avenging from the hero – it's the hero's story.

All fiction says more about the time it was written than the time it is set. Even deliberate pastiches in the style of earlier eras tend to reflect the mores, customs, taboos and concerns of the present age.

For example, there was a time when the hero was rewarded by a kiss from the heroine and he rode off into the sunset - or married her. Nowadays if there isn't graphic sex the audience seems to feel the story's not complete. There was a time when the heroine was expected to be chaste and virginal - unless she'd been done a terrible wrong or was a 'bad girl' character (perhaps from Chapter Five). Now the assumption is that if she's not sexually active then there's something not right with her. She's not "realistic". Stories set in the past tend to reflect our changing contemporary sensibilities and social expectations.

Perhaps foremost in our changing social understanding are contemporary views on gender, race, and sexuality. Our society has become very sensitised to these things. A writer has to thread the narrow path between being fair to the genre, era, and continuity of their story's source material of on one hand and an appreciation of the audience's sensibility and of his or her own ethical beliefs on the other. It's all about where the line is drawn.

How much should a writer allow modern sentiments on race, gender, sexuality, creed and so on impinge on stories set in older times (say the 1920s)?

THERE HAS TO BE a distinction between the author's voice, the hero's voice, and the rest of the cast's voices.

The *author* can never suggest that racism, or sexism, or fascism, or domestic violence or lots of other nasty things are actually okay. That's not to say that the *story* can't depict them; pulp fiction often draws on absolutes of good and evil and those are some pretty nasty evils.

The hero has to be carefully handled. On the one hand he or she can't become so anodyne as to be uninteresting, or so politically correct as to break suspension of disbelief. The hero can't stop the action to preach for three pages on the evils of child abuse or whatever. The "friend of the Native American" can be as insulting and cliché as the redskin-fighter. On the other hand, the days of showing the hero beating his 'nigger servant' for being lazy and cowardly while the black man cowers begging. "Please massah, I's be good now!" are long gone. Hopefully.

The other cast should be as varied in their responses as the story demands. In fact their responses will help define them. If we see a character bullying his wife we know him to be someone unpleasant and wait for the moment when the hero leaves a spider-shaped mark on his face.[44] As long as characters are written well then I don't have a problem with them expressing contemporary values.

It's all in the treatment, I suspect. For example:

A massive staple of *Weird Tales*-type anthology tales was the idea that They were after Our Women. How many covers show the scantily-clad heroine being menaced by the pirate/Martian/monster/gangster/robot/Nazi with the implication that rape and ruin were to follow? The hero saving the heroine from a ravishing rival is a very old trope hardwired deep into male reactions, which is why it appears so much in pulp fiction (there's not much more visceral for males than fighting to save the woman; see Chapter 5 again).

The key to covering this stuff tastefully and appropriately is to ensure that neither the writer nor the hero ever endorses what is really a truly horrible act. That means not offering graphic titillating portrayals, nor using it as a way to demean or diminish a character, nor suggesting that there are genuine justifications ("The frail was asking for it").

Is there a difference if the modern author is continuing a body of work that already has established canon, such as with Doc Samson or the Spirit?

THERE'S AN ADDITIONAL responsibility to respect the work done by an earlier writer who has, after all, laid the foundations of a character that has endured for many years. If people don't want to respect the original in its setting and context then why use him? I've got little time for politically correct revisions that need to replace characters with ethnically acceptable gender-balanced cyphers. Create a new character in a similar setting who won't be a misrepresentation.

Care needs to be used when an established character has previously been portrayed less than sensitively; Ebony White[45] comes to mind. Eisner himself

44 A reference to Harry Steeger's popular 1930s pulp character the Spider, a crimefighter whose ring punched red spider-shaped marks onto the faces of his adversaries.
45 Ebony White appeared regularly in *The Spirit* comic strip from June 2 1940. He was the hero's black juvenile sidekick and go-fer. He was drawn as a picaninny with large white eyes and thick pink lips. However, within the story writer/artist Will Eisner according Ebony a good deal of respect. *The*

sorted out that problem though, fleshing the character out as time went on. He also introduced other black characters of very different kinds, including the ahead-of-his-time Detective Gray.

And I don't have any problem at all with fleshed-out funny companions like the Saint's Hoppy Uniatz.[46]

Are there any classic pulp situations which are no longer tasteful to use that have to be quietly retired?

IT WOULD AND SHOULD be abhorrent to modern audiences if the hero did certain things like flogging a servant or beating a woman, or if he made sweeping racial statements like "greedy as a Jew". Apart from being in very poor taste, it also demonstrates a shocking naiveté on the author's part. If those things happen then that's what the story becomes all about, intended or not.

Care also needs to be taken about the "treat 'em rough and they'll come round" school of romance. And the days when the leading man could put an uppity dame over his knee and give her a good spanking to remind her of her place are probably over.[47]

Mostly though I think the treatment is far more important than the content and good writing trumps bad political correctness.

One last thing - I once had a story set in the 40s edited because it depicted the characters smoking! And Smoking is Bad.

***

New York Herald Tribune quoted Eisner's former office manager Marilyn Mercer's defence: "Ebony never drew criticism from Negro groups (in fact, Eisner was commended by some for using him), perhaps because, although his speech pattern was early Minstrel Show, he himself derived from another literary tradition: he was a combination of Tom Sawyer and Penrod, with a touch of Horatio Alger hero, and color didn't really come into it."

46 Leslie Charteris' outlaw adventurer the Saint first met womanising, hard-drinking met New York hoodlum Hoppy Uniatz in "The Simon Templar Foundation" in *The Misfortunes of Mr Teal*, 1934 (also released in the US as *The Saint in London* and *The Saint in England*). The character returned in many subsequent chapters of the Saint series as the hero's occasional assistant and partner in crime.

47 The practice could still be used without irony as late as April 1980, when Ben Grimm, the Thing from the Fantastic Four, delivers a 'well-deserved' bottom-spanking to the interfering and elitist Moondragon in the all-ages comic *Marvel Two-In-One* #62 by Mark Gruenwald and George Perez.

9.
William the Conqueror – Conan or Attila?

KNOW, O PRINCE, that in the years after the fall of Rome and the rise of the sons of Henry II there was an age undreamed of... Thither came William the Bastard, mighty in war, great in mirth, massively annoyed if you reminded him of his humble beginnings, to tread the throne of England beneath his booted feet.

The one date every English schoolboy knows is A.D. 1066, the year that William of Normandy invaded and conquered. Like 1776 for Americans, it is the year from which our nation is counted to have begun.[48] But William himself remains something of a legend, depicted on the world's most famous not-actually-a-tapestry at Bayeux, France, ancestor of pretty much every British monarch up to today (by some pretty twisty family trees).

Unlike the American founding fathers, William hasn't appeared much in fiction – which is strange considering that he could be accurately portrayed either as a Robert E. Howard hero or as a Robert E. Howard villain.

In the ninth century, Viking holiday plans were always the same. Between planting the fields and harvesting the crops there was time to pack the longboat and raid England for treasure, slaves, or pay-off protection bribes. Then the English gained Alfred the Great as king, a ruler who cheated by organising resistance in the form of coastal watchtowers, a navy, a road system, education, laws and courts, and generally made it horribly dangerous and unprofitable to nip across the North Sea for a bit of English plunder. So like all bullies faced with strong resistance, the raiders looked elsewhere.

The northern coast of France looked good. The Franks, Bergundians, Lorraines etc. (the nation of France was no more established than the final boundaries of England then) didn't have an Alfred. They were easy meat. In fact they were so scared of the Vikings (or *Normans* as they were by then

---

48 From which discerning readers will surmise, if they have not already gathered from the language of this document, that I.A. Watson is a Briton.

terming these southern-bound holiday-makers) that they gave them the top third of what we'd now call France as holiday villas, a nation of their own. This was the kingdom of Normandy, and the Normans became rough, dangerous neighbours.

William was born in Falaise, Normandy, of a tanner's daughter variously chronicled as Herleva, Harlotta, Herlette, Arlot, Alleiva, and Berlon. I suspect Robert, younger son of the Duke of Normandy, didn't stop to enquire properly before he took the girl in a "Danish marriage" – that is, one that didn't require priests, churches, commitments longer than breakfast the next morning, or consent of the female involved. In fairness to Robert he did go and announce his intentions beforehand to the girl's father, who made no objection given that Robert was a nasty piece of work known for flaying people who got between him and what he wanted. In fact Robert's older brother was between him and the Earldom, and Robert's brother suffered an unfortunate and mysterious death.

Unlike the French, who sniffed at bastards (especially bastards of a tanner's daughter, given that tanning requires soaking bits of rotting cow in urine and makes for very smelly peasants), the Normans had no problem with recognised sons from "Danish marriages", so William grew up just like his father, only a little bit harder. William was groomed for power and gained a reputation for being serious about it. He hunted well, fought better, never drank more than three glasses of wine (remarkable enough to be chronicled as an eccentricity), and stabbed people who sneered at his origins.

William decided the answer to his social mobility problem was to marry well. He picked Maheut (Matilde), daughter of the Count of Flanders, grand-daughter of the King of the Franks. Maheut wasn't as keen, noting that William was (a) a Norman, (b) a bastard, (c) a complete bastard, and (d) two hundred miles away with plenty of her father's armies between them.

What would Conan do, by Crom? William rode off into enemy territory across the Seine and the Somme, all the way to the Count's stronghold at Lille. Here he broke in, interrupted the Count's court, approached Maheut, and, so the chronicle relates, "tore her robe open with his spurs" and convinced the lady – in front of the court and her father – to consent to his suit. According to the monkish account, Maheut "recognised that she had met her master" and subsequently became the mother of English monarchs. In their 36-year marriage she bore William six daughters and four sons.

But what would Attila do? By 1050 William was Duke of Normandy, having delivered proper kickings to rebel Normans, invading Bretons and

Franks, and done it with sufficient venom and brutality to discourage anyone else from trying it again, ever. William was not a big believer in the doctrine of proportional response. So he looked across the water to the land of the Anglo-Saxons, who had a weak king now; Edward the Confessor might later go on to be sainted, but he was led around by his barons, was unpopular with his people, and really looked like the sort of kid who gets his lunch money taken. William made a friendly state visit to England, got pally with the snotty little saint-to-be, and convinced Edward that an ideal person to get named as his successor as King of England was... William.

There were problems with this. For starters, while Norman law allowed a ruler to name his successor – which was how William was now ruling Normandy – Saxon law didn't. When a new English king was needed, a Witangemot or Parliament met to consider the claims of self-nominated candidates then picked one by election. The recommendation of a predecessor might be considered, but was by no means binding. Secondly, and more practically, England was really being ruled just then by a bunch of barons who had different ideas. The Tony Soprano of the lot was Godwin of Essex, and he had plans of his own.

Godwin had married his daughter Edith to King Edward. Commentators differ on how or why, but about half of them suspect that the marriage was never consummated. Edward really yearned to be a monk and wanted to live a chaste life. Or else he preferred men – which was okay, because one of Godwin's sons became "his close companion". And Edith managed to get pregnant anyway; some suggest with the active assistance of her father and brothers. Godwin was *really* keen to control the crown.

After Edward died young and pious and went on the waiting list to be canonised, the Witangemot met and decided that William wasn't in the frame. They elected Harold Godwinson, Godwin of Essex's youngest, as king.

William was not amused. Apart from anything else, he'd captured this Harold a year or two earlier and had made him swear an oath on holy relics never to be King of England. But happily William happened to have an army and navy massed and was ready to cross the English Channel and discuss the decision like a calm responsible adult who has 8,000 screaming profit-hungry marauders alongside him.

Harold turned out to be a remarkably effective king. Almost as soon as he'd got the crown, England was attacked in the north by Harald Hadrada, the undefeated-in-battle Scandinavian monarch who was as major-league-enemy as you could get. On his first outing young Harold was up against the 9th century equivalent of Dr Doom.[49] Somehow newly-kinged Harold managed to claw an army together, head up to York, and take on Hadrada's seasoned raiders across unfavourable terrain – and win. Harald Hadrada was killed, the invasion smashed. It was an amazing result for the plucky newcomer!

That was pretty much on the day that William landed his forces in the south.

So Harold had to bring the remains of his beaten-up army on a ten day hike south, leaving the wounded to follow as best they could. He couldn't delay. William was being his usual charming self and burning towns while he waited for a chat. As Halley's comet lit the skies, King Harold went to meet the invaders with his 7,500 exhausted men at a little seaside resort called Hastings.

The problem was that when Harold and William met they were *both* heroic figures, both brave canny fighters, both inspiring capable leaders, both ruthless rulers. It was one of those fantasy "who'd win" clashes like Superman vs. Thor. William had slightly more men, including a cavalry which was unheard-of in Saxon warfare. Harold had a ragged exhausted army but had learned enough from fighting Hadrada that he seized the high ground and held it well.

In the end it was probably battle styles that decided winner and loser. William kept his Normans in formation and disciplined. He tempted the personally-brave Saxons to break ranks and charge a retreating enemy, then closed his trap. At some point Harold went down – legend says with an arrow in the eye – and then it was all over except for the mass slaughtering.

William was crowned on Christmas Day 1066 in Westminster Abbey. He was king, whether the Anglo-Saxons liked it or not. They didn't like it. When London resisted, William burned it to the ground and destroyed all the crops for twenty miles around so the survivors would starve. When the North resisted he undertook a campaign of what we'd call ethnic cleansing that depopulated the top half of England (estimates vary between a 50% and a 75% population drop in three years). William was never that big on seeing the other person's point of view.

Norman law replaced Saxon law. The feudal system of the middle ages began. Freemen became serfs, tied to their lord's land without rights to own property, to move away, or even to marry without permission. The Catholic

---

49 Marvel Comics' archetypal archvillain, who first troubled the world in *Fantastic Four* #5, 1961, and set the benchmark for megalomaniac all-conquering supervillains. We'll be footnoting him again later.

church replaced the old Anglo-Celtic faith. Norman castles sprung up all around the nation, the first stone-built keeps in England. Mounted lords clad themselves in armour and called themselves knights.

William ruled for twenty-six years before he fell off his horse whilst on a trip back home to Normandy to kick the Franks again for insulting him. King Philipe I, thinking William was safely a long way off, had joked about the now-somewhat-plump Conqueror, "When is the fat man's baby due?" William replied by burning Mantes, but his fall injuries caused internal bleeding, six weeks of excruciating pain, and his eventual death.

So, William the Conqueror: pulp-fodder for sure – but as good guy or bad guy?

***

10.
Writing Historicals

I'M TALKING HERE about stories that were written after the time they are set in. The Scarlet Pimpernel, Robin Hood, Treasure Island, Solomon Kane, and Horatio Hornblower all count. Sherlock Holmes, Dick Tracy, James Bond, and the Shadow don't because they were intended to be contemporary at the time of their first writing.

I seem to get commissioned to write a lot of historical stuff. I've published three volumes of Robin Hood stories, have contributed to six Sherlock Holmes anthologies (they're historical *now*), and have written tales covering periods from Babylonian and Greek eras to World War II,[50] so there are some questions I have to think about a lot. What are the choices a writer has to make every time he or she sets a tale in some historic setting?

Where does one draw the line when writing about olden times? Historical accuracy or a more impressionistic montage background? Weed out anachronistic language and concepts or not? When writing about characters created by someone else, how important is it to respect previous 'canon'? I'm not the only one who gnaws at these questions.

The first choice for an author preparing a story set in the past is deciding where on the axis between absolute historic accuracy and popular culture history the story-world is set. Will a 1930's novel take place against a backdrop of gruelling realistic great depression poverty with desperate characters eking a living in dustbowl shanties, or perhaps happen in the Indiana Jones-style pastiche of the icons of the era, the kind of setting a casual reader might immediately identify? I suggest that most authors find a position between the two extremes where they're comfortable.

That in turn sets up the next set of decisions about how close to the behaviour, prejudices, and beliefs of the time will the characters conform.

50 I.A. Watson's publications are listed online at http://www.chillwater.org.uk/writing/iawatsonhome. htm

We've discussed earlier how far outdated attitudes to race, women (and violence to women), sexuality, religion etc. can or should be reflected in historical fiction written now. Choices about realistic vs. iconic settings inform choices about realistic vs. iconic (or idealised) characters.

The further back the tale takes place the more important these decisions become. King Arthur's legends are generally set around the 5th or 6th century, a hundred years or less after the Roman withdrawal from England; but historically at that time there were no medieval stone castles as we now imagine them, no battlements, no mounted armoured knights, no great cathedrals with cloistered monks, no code of chivalry, and no unified nation of England for one king to rule over – and there wouldn't be for 500 years. A totally "authentic" Arthur would be ruling from a hill fort with round huts inside a ditch and bank defence, fighting with spear and sword from a chariot, trying to stem an overwhelming tide of Saxon raiders from Germany who eventually overran and conquered the country.

Of course, King Arthur's stories were mostly written down in the eleventh and twelfth centuries, as tales from "long ago", so they count as historical fiction (and by most definitions pulp fiction). The writers of that age imagined Arthur and his court as being very similar to the contemporary knights and castles of their own era and wrote them with similar customs and manners. That's why we associate Arthurian tales with ladies with cone-hats in stone towers and men in full plate mail trying to knock each other off warhorses.

Novels have been written at both extremes of accurate vs. conceptual Arthurian stories. These days the trend seems to be towards "realistic" Arthur, deconstructing the myth to get to "the real man". My own preference tends more towards the traditional Arthur of Camelot, with the jousting, mounted knights and Norman castles, so I pitch my stuff towards that end of the scale; but I accept that others have different tastes.

I'm liberated by how the older creators like Sir Thomas Mallory and the anonymous authors of the French Vulgate cycle happily chose and revised their material to suit their story needs. Apart from anything else it offers a variety of choices in retelling or referencing events from their books, so I can follow my usual "game" of trying to reflect as much of the original mythical source material as possible in my own stories.[51]

---

51 For more on King Arthur and his legend vs. his historicity see Chapter 32: "The Once and Future King". King Arthur will be back. But everyone knows that deep inside, don't they?

Writing Historical Pulp Fiction

PULPS WORK BEST in any era that is turbulent, atmospheric, and has a strong mood. Pulp tends to use stereotype to shorthand things, so as to emphasise other elements of the story. Periods that are well known and have distinctive settings are another way of doing that. Most people can picture 1938 Berlin, or Victorian England, or the age of the Barbary Pirates, or even a Buck Rogers future. There's no reason you can't set a story in 1806 Bavaria during the reign of King Maximilian I Joseph, but you're going to have to work that much harder to get the scenery right.

With existing properties from earlier eras, for example with new Shadow stories or Sherlock Holmes stories, the advantage of keeping the tales in period is that the setting works for the author, and generally well suits the character too.[52] Displace the character in time and the story generally becomes about what's different now, like how Margo Lane can call the Shadow up on her mobile when she gets into trouble. That's not to say that there can't be great stories told where the characters either travel from their original time or are assumed to have always been contemporary, but mostly its another uphill challenge to sell a "genuine" version of the character; even the very successful B.B.C. TV show *Sherlock* has fun riffing on what's similar and what's different to the original.

That said, there are some characters with long publication histories that have been the same age all their career. Simon Templar's only concession to time was to upgrade the car he drove from a Hirondel to something more modern. Clark Kent is no longer a former World War II battlefield reporter. James Bond has had to trade in his Walther PPK for something that's not an antique in 2013.

A disadvantage of using original time periods is that our knowledge of them is much more imperfect than the writers who lived in those times, so we have to work a lot harder to fact-check. And readers know a lot less too, so we have to explain references that the original audience would have got right away. Victorian Sherlock Holmes readers had no need to be told in-story what a gasogene was, any more than readers today require a footnote on the workings of an iPad, but twenty-first century Holmes fans *may* need

---

52 I.A. Watson is a contributor to the anthologies *Sherlock Holmes: Consulting Detective* volumes 1-7. He won an industry award for his volume 2 story "The Last Deposit" and four others have been nominated.

enlightening about a long-forgotten device designed to put carbon bubbles into alcoholic drinks.[53] A certain effort to guide our audience through unfamiliar terrain is necessary.

The other change is our developed sensibility about some ethical things that weren't understood in, say, the 1930s period. As noted in previous essays, we can't reflect attitudes to race, gender, and sexuality that were common and acceptable then. We just have to remember that what the original writer wrote as contemporary fiction we're writing as historical fiction, and make adjustments accordingly.

Some classic pulp characters suit a modern age better than others. Tarzan might as well battle logging companies or oil drillers as ivory poachers. On the other hand it may be less acceptable for African tribesman to recognise that the Lord of the Apes should be their natural leader because of his superior white traits. Other heroes are impossible to transplant; the Three Musketeers, the Scarlet Pimpernel, or Horatio Hornblower, for example, whose whole set-up revolves around a particular situation in history.

If there is an advantage to modernising settings it's that one has to distil the core of the character and what his or her stories are about rather more thoroughly. A contemporary Philip Marlowe can't hide behind the gin-joint trappings and stock cast of the pre-war era, so he'd better damn well be the Marlow-iest Marlowe there ever was! He can still be tough, cynical, two-fisted, street-smart, down to earth, and tormented by lethal women - but without the "wallpaper" of his original period more effort needs to go into getting our hero exactly note-perfect.

However, the reason for using an established character is presumably either (a) because there are fans out there who know and like him and his world, or (b) because the author thinks the character and his concept as interesting and exciting. So taking the character out of that world the fans like and expect would alienate the most loyal readers right from the start - think of all the flak the *Green Hornet* movie took for not being "canon".[54] And if the point of doing the character is because the author likes the property, why then change it to something else?

---

53   In the same educational spirit, it might be noted that a tantalus was a lockable drinks-stand designed to keep servants from pilfering the good stuff.

54   The *Green Hornet* film was released in 2011 to mixed reviews and uninspiring box office. The producer has announced that no sequel will be commissioned. A common criticism was that the tone of the film did not match well with the source material. The "comedy-isation" of originally serious pulp style properties seems to be an error Hollywood commits regularly. Ask *Dark Shadows* (2012) or *The Lone Ranger* (2013).

The Telephone Exchange

THE ADVENT of the mobile phone is a narrative game-changer. In fact the mobile phone revolution has perhaps done more to move contemporary adventure storytelling away from that of even twenty years ago than anything else. My son reads a *Three Adventurers* or *Hardy Boys* story and wonders, "Why didn't they just use their mobiles to ring for help?"

A new generation of readers fully expect to be in constant or readily-available communication with others at all times. Any thriller set in the present day needs to account for the phone problem; that is, the existence of a telecoms network that could summon help, instantly transmit vital information, allow movement to be tracked; things which can easily defuse suspense.

Of course there are ways around it – but the author has to trouble himself *explaining* why the phone can't save the day or it looks like a plot oversight.

So much of dramatic fiction depends upon characters being out of touch with each other that the existence of the mobile phone has changed the expectations and rules of adventure stories set in the present. Given that phones are now also cameras and GPS devices and web browsers, we're going to see even more changes required to the old situations as time goes on. No technological advance has made such a difference to a writing genre since fingerprints made detective fiction forensic.[55]

Telecommunications can be used to good dramatic effect. I first noticed mobile phones being used as story drivers on *The X-Files*. Probably the first TV series to grasp some implications for instantaneous and readily available long distance social communication was *Star Trek: the Next Generation*, with their chest communicator badges.

A phone conversation is a great way of introducing information without having to cut away to another scene. The detective doesn't need to head down to the path. lab now. He can get straight on with the hunt while getting his forensics report on his mobile.

And of course there's plenty of dramatic potential in the interrupted phone call or the sudden loss of signal.

I'm not arguing that phones ruin stories. I'm asserting that any story set

---

55   Eccentric French policeman Alphonse Bertillon identified thief and murderer Scheffer from prints on a broken glass case in 1902 and secured the first conviction on fingerprint evidence. In *The Hound of the Baskervilles*, Sherlock Holmes is referred to as "the second highest expert in Europe" after Bertillon.

in the twenty-first century has to deal with the great prevalence of mobiles and internet in the same way that an adventure set in 1882 has to factor in horse and train travel times.

The Language Barrier

AN OLD CONVENTION of written stories, carried over to movies and TV, is that everybody speaks the same language as the reader or viewer, unless some character is deliberately foreign or alien. If the tale is set in ancient Rome, we assume that the kindly author has translated the Latin text for us. If the story is set on futuristic Mars there's clearly some technological innovation enabling the exchange of words.

This is a necessary compromise between reality and readability. A story around the pilgrims of the Mayflower that reported their dialogue in accurate fifteenth century English would be incomprehensible to most people.

All a writer can do is compromise between the patois of the time and place and recognisable modern English, and expect the reader to allow that we're translating for their benefit. We often do that with dialogue for foreign characters anyway; historical or future ones are only one step further.

How much modernisation? I'll often allow some anachronistic phrases to crop up if they help express a sentiment in a way the reader will appreciate. For example, "Give me a minute" is a relatively modern term, popularised when the clock became a common household item, but I'd probably allow it to be voiced in dialogue before that era since its not too obviously out of place. On the other hand, "Okay" only rose to prominence during the twentieth century, so I cringe when modern writers have Victorian heroes asking their rescued damsels, "Are you okay, milady?" She might as well answer, "Sure, I'm totally jerkin', dude!"

Likewise, it jars when an historic character express his views of another cast member by saying, "He's so paranoid" or some other modern analytical diagnosis.[56] On the other hand one, one doesn't want to write something in middle-English or cod-Shakespearian (yes, Thor, I dost look at thee).

SF language dates quite quickly, and most often when it tries to be contemporary. All those 60's stories where everyone in the 40th century calls each other "man", for example. Technobabble can sometimes seem awfully old fashioned too. Think on that as your advanced transistorised diode tubes are activating on your futuristic 200 megabyte computers.

---

56   The author is fully aware that the short story "Rescue Me" in this volume features a hero using the abbreviation "IQ". The rules are different for humorous fiction.

In another century I expect we'll see a more homogenous speech relax rules of grammar, append even more words from other languages, and be given common international currency through TV, movies, or whatever entertainment media has replaced them.

But beyond language a lot of our classic SF suffers from the fact that the world has just developed in different ways. It's hard now to envisage any technological future that doesn't involve some version of the internet or of mobile phone communications, for example, and both of these are absent from the classic years of SF writing.

The other historical dialogue pitfall is to spend all one's time trying to make speech seem authentic based on our understanding of how characters spoke then. It's like writing 20's US crime fiction and having everyone call each other "mugs and mooks" then "rub people out" all the time; it's become cliché and probably isn't too period authentic anyway. Medieval cries of "zounds" (a contraction of the blasphemous cry "God's wounds!") or "varlet" have to be used just as carefully and scarcely.

That said, I'm determined at some point to work in the insult "tattered seeping merkin", a fine middle ages crudity given that a merkin was a pubic wig often worn to hide V.D. sores.

My mother's comment on proofing "The Western Mail", my story for *Sherlock Holmes, Consulting Detective* volume 2: "I'm sure I've read this somewhere before. Only it was better then."

"Thanks, mum."

***

PART TWO: MYSTERIES
In which we consider enigmas and conundrums literary and historical

11.
Whatever Happened at Eilean Mòr?

WHEN MONDAY MORNING work beckons, quite naturally I therefore want to review a 113-year-old mystery with a view to literary endeavour. In case readers of this book have Mondays too, here are the facts of the case:

The Flannan Isles, or the Seven Hunters, are a bunch of rocks in the Outer Hebrides, north and west of the top of Scotland. Eilean Mòr (Gaelic for *Big Isle*) still contains the ruins of a seventh century chapel dedicated to St Flannan.[57] A 1703 book by Martin Martin calls the place "the seven Haley [Holy] Isles" and describes strange customs such as removing one's hat and upper clothing and turning sunwise when achieving the plateau of Eilean Mòr. The desolate lonely weatherswept islands have probably been unoccupied since Viking depredations of the ninth century. Inhabitants of other islands visited by day to graze sheep and raid bird's nests but thought it unlucky to stay overnight.

Until the Victorians. As Britain's wealth from shipping reached its peak, the record of vessels lost and threatened around the archipelago was a concern to the Northern Lighthouse Board. Serious men in George Street, Edinburgh, met and determined that a light must be set on Big Isle for the preservation of life and property. In 1896, the NLB commissioned David Alan Stevenson of the famous Stevenson engineering family to design and build it; writer Robert Louis Stevenson, who had died the year before, was the engineer's cousin.

There were some particular problems to this lighthouse's construction. All supplies, including the tower's stone, had be lifted by rope up 148 foot cliffs from supply boats in churning seas. Builder George Lawson of Rutherglen

---

57   Flannán mac Toirrdelbaig (or Turlough) was a son of the king of Thomand (a part of Ireland covering most of North Munster). He returned from a 7th century pilgrimage to Rome to become the first Bishop of Killaloe (the greater part of County Clare). His feast day is 18th December.

installed a temporary railway track to shift materials to the chosen site on the mysterious plateau. Eventually a new iron landing jetty had to be constructed. The total cost of the completed project was £6,914, which would equate to roughly £1.3 million or $1.9 million in today's money. An additional £3,526 was spent on a shore station at Breasclete on the Isle of Lewis. Work was completed and the light first lit on 7th December 1899.

Four men were appointed to keep the Eilean Mòr light. At any given time three of them resided at the tower on 14-day shifts, while the fourth took shore leave on Lewis. On December 14th 1900 the three men on duty were Head Keeper James Ducat, appointed for his more than twenty years experience, First Assistant Thomas Marshall, and Second Assistant Donald MacArthur (or McArthur); these latter two were both seamen.

That day a tremendous storm battered the coast and islands of Scotland. The poor weather persisted for many days, making relief of the keepers impractical and obscuring the semaphore balls on posts that were their only means of communicating with passing ships. On the 15th, the captain of the *Fairwind*, struggling in bad seas, made an angry log entry that the Eilean Mòr light was extinguished. Captain Holman of the steamer *Arctor* from Philadelphia to Leith put in at Oban with the first official report of the lamp being quenched.

The Northern Lighthouse Board seems to have taken no immediate action. The relief boat with fourth crewman James Moore was due at the island on 20th December; presumably that was considered a sufficient response, or perhaps Captain Jim Harvie who commanded the lighthouse tender vessel *Hesperus* was not optimistic about reaching the island in the continuing squalls.

In fact the bad weather prevented any visit to Eilean Mòr until noon on 26th December. At that time, the *Hesperus* observed that the lighthouse's flagstaff was bare, that no empty supply boxes had been set out on the jetty for loading, and that no men waited to greet the ship's arrival. A flare and a blast of the boat-whistle attracted no attention from shore.

The lamp remained extinguished, something that worried Moore. Allowing the light to fail was anathema and virtually unheard of in the lighthouse service. It was reported afterwards that Moore had been anxious all the journey from Breasclete, refusing breakfast and pacing the deck with foreboding. At Eilean Mòr, a small boat was launched from the *Hesperus* and James Moore was put ashore on the east landing – alone.

Moore headed to the lighthouse compound. He found both gate and tower door closed. Inside the building clocks were stopped, beds unmade, and there were cold ashes in the grate; but lamps were trimmed and, apart from one overturned chair, there was no disorder. There was no sign of the three keepers.

Moore returned to the jetty and shouted his findings to the *Hesperus*. The ship's second mate and another seaman joined him for a more thorough search. This check discovered further evidence of extraordinary weather. The west landing pier was severely storm-damaged, its steel twisted by the force of the squall. A box 128 feet above sea level had been smashed by waves and its contents scattered. A rock weighing more than a ton at an even higher elevation had also been shifted. Turf up to ten yards from the edge of the 200 foot high cliff top was stripped away. Ropes and jibs of the cliff hoist were broken. The iron staircase stapled up the cliffside was deformed and wrenched from its concrete foundations.

This damage had been recorded in the lighthouse log. The last entry was at 9am on 15th December.

In the lighthouse, the investigators found that a toolbox, boots, and two of the three sets of oilskins were missing, suggesting that two men had deliberately left the tower during bad weather and a third – presumably MacArthur since his oilskin remained - had quit it without precaution. It was against NLB regulations for all three men to leave the tower at once.

Here the mythographers begin their work. Other, probably secondary, sources claim a half-eaten meal of salted mutton and potatoes on the kitchen table, but that gibes with Moore's written account that states, "The kitchen utensils were all very clean, which is a sign that it must be after dinner some time they left". Another report said that mysterious traces of seaweed were found on the tower's stair and in a lamp locker.

A much-circulated and repeated account claims to quote entries from the lighthouse log. These are now generally debunked as additions from an American pulp story, but I've been unable to trace it. The logs are supposed to have said:

December 12. Gale north by northwest. Sea lashed to fury. Never seen such a storm. Waves very high. Tearing at lighthouse. Everything shipshape. James Ducat irritable.

Later that day: Storm still raging, wind steady. Stormbound. Cannot go out. Ship passing sounding foghorn. Could see lights of cabins. Ducat quiet. Donald

McArthur crying.

December 13. Storm continued through night. Wind shifted west by north. Ducat quiet. McArthur praying.

Later: Noon, grey daylight. Me, Ducat and McArthur prayed.

On 14 December there was no entry in the log.

The final entry was made on a slate, which under normal circumstances would have been transferred to the logbook proper later on:

December 15. 1pm. Storm ended, sea calm. God is over all.

Sceptics note that these would be very unusual entries for an official record. Marshall's written comments about his superior Ducat would have been unlikely; Ducat was usually known for his good nature and MacArthur was a tough and seasoned keeper.

Moore and three volunteer seamen remained to tend the light – brave men. The *Hesperus* returned to shore, where Captain Harvie telegrammed the NLB: "A dreadful accident has happened at the Flannans. The three keepers, Ducat, Marshall and the Occasional have disappeared from the Island. The clocks were stopped and other signs indicated that the accident must have happened about a week ago. Poor fellows must have been blown over the cliffs or drowned trying to secure a crane or something like that."

On December 29th, NLB Superintendent Robert Muirhead arrived to investigate. There were already plenty of theories and some wild speculation about what had happened. Rumour had it that a ghostly Viking longship had been seen by the *Fairwind*, "crewed by warriors with faces the colour of bone". Others interpreted the sighting as the three keepers escaping some horror by rowing boat. Wild speculation ranged from a giant bird to a sea monster claiming the lives of the missing men. Some armchair detectives preferred a solution of murder and madness between three keepers in close quarters under mounting stress. Locals blamed "the Phantom of the Seven Hunters".

Muirhead, who noted in his report that "I visited them [the lighthouse crew] as lately as 7th December and have the melancholy recollection that I was the last person to shake hands with them and bid them adieu", offered a more prosaic answer: "From evidence which I was able to procure I was satisfied that the men had been on duty up till dinner time on Saturday the 15th of December, that they had gone down to secure a box in which the mooring ropes, landing ropes etc. were kept, and which was secured in a crevice in the rock about 110 ft above sea level, and that an extra large sea had rushed up the face of the rock, had gone above them, and coming down with immense force, had swept them completely away."

Muirhead's findings have never quelled popular imagination about the case, of course. Wilfred William Gibson's 1912 Ballad *Flannan Isle*,[58] told:

Aye: though we hunted high and low,
And hunted everywhere,
Of the three men's fate we found no trace
Of any kind in any place,
But a door ajar, and an untouched meal,
And an overtoppled chair.

Amongst many other creative works, Eilean Mòr inspired the Genesis song *The Mystery of Flannan Isle Lighthouse*, Peter Maxwell Davies' opera *The Lighthouse*, and the Doctor Who story *Horror of Fang Rock*. The incident has been co-opted to support alien abduction, fairies, giant squids, and Lovecraftian terrors.

I think Eilean Mòr is a fine topic for pulp fiction. Maybe one dark and stormy night I'll take on what "really" happened to storm-lashed Ducat, Marshall and MacArthur on 15th December 1900, and why the light went out.

***

---

58 Full text at http://www.potw.org/archive/potw230.html

12.
Famous Monsters of Pulpland

WHAT MAKES a "pulp" monster? How is it different from a non-pulp one? Are there any empty niches out there for great new pulp monsters, or has the golden age well and truly gone?

Pulp fiction tends to go for a gut response from the reader. It often mines the most primal human urges, and that includes survival instincts and protective feelings for others. It seeks an emotional reaction: foreboding, excitement, tension, fear.

Fear of monsters runs pretty deep in us, lurking somewhere in that primitive hindbrain that says, "Watch out for the dark, there are things in it that want to eat you". Five thousand years ago our ancestors were the ones smart enough to listen. So when pulp writers hoist pen or keyboard to connect with their readers there are plenty of back-doors into the audience's heads that a good monster can exploit.

So who are the pulp monster stars? Those earliest of pulps, the "penny dreadfuls" notoriously featured *The Castle of Otranto*[59] and *Varney the Vampire*.[60] Poe gave us the Murderer of the Rue Morgue.[61] Lovecraft bequeathed an entire pantheon of loathsome squamous rugose elder gods. And there's a lot of "classic" monsters running round pulp stories, be they bandage-wrapped pharaohs, moon-cursed werewolves, brain-eating zombies, body-probing aliens, or plain old psychotic serial killers.

Count Dracula? Bram Stoker might not count as a pulp author. *Dracula*

59 Originally published anonymously in 1764 under the title *The Castle of Otranto, A Story. Translated by William Marsha, Gent. From the Original Italian of Onuphrio Muralto, Canon of the Church of St. Nicholas at Otranto*, subsequent editions identified the author as Thomas Walpole.

60 *Varney the Vampire; or, the Feast of Blood* first appeared in 220 chapters from 1845-47. The 667,000 word story is usually attributed to James Malcolm Rhymer, with a dissenting minority crediting Thomas Preskitt Prest.

61 "The Murders in the Rue Morgue", by Edgar Allen Poe, first published in *Graham's Magazine* 1841, is often credited with being the first detective story. It probably is, but see Chapter 15.

was written primarily to pay the bills and it was sold as a mass-market work, but it doesn't have the hallmarks of later classic pulp-era pacing. But then, the Count has probably escaped his original story by now and has gone on to become an archetype. If Stoker's *Dracula* isn't pulp, the various other versions of him from Lugosi to the modern day probably are. Likewise if Sheridan Le Fanu's *Carmilla* wasn't strictly in the genre,[62] the various later outings for the mysterious predatory "Mircalla, Countess Karnstein" certainly have been.[63]

Quite a few of the early monster stories go at a pace we'd probably consider slow today. On the other hand, Lovecraft's works were actually published in pulp magazines and they too tend to be "slow burn" stories that don't feature slam-bang action and rapid plot turns. Dracula's no slower than Lovecraft's novellas like *At the Mountains of Madness* and *The Case of Charles Dexter Ward*.

Frankenstein's monster as depicted by Mary Shelley probably doesn't count, but has been co-opted later. Bertrand Caillet, *The Werewolf of Paris*[64] and Erik, *The Phantom of the Opera*,[65] probably do.

Other monsters have been popularised into common culture through their use and reuse in pulps. The "disfigured madman", the "swamp monster", the "zombie that walks", the unquiet mummy, the wax dummy, the possession and so on are steady staples of the pulp genre. I don't know if their literary origins predate their celluloid ones in every case but pulp is in their blood – or lack of it!

Does a character have to have originated in a pulp story to count as a pulp monster? What about Freddy Krueger or Jason Voorhees or Leatherface?[66] What about the Bride of Frankenstein?[67] What about Hellboy?[68] If the Phantom of the Opera is a pulp monster then why isn't the equally disfigured

---

62 Although *Carmilla* first appeared in serial form in the magazine *The Dark Blue* in 1871 and 1872, predating Dracula by some 25 years. It was reprinted in Le Fanu's anthology *In a Glass Darkly* in 1872.

63 Carmilla's first screen appearance was in *Vampyr*, 1932. Roger Vadim's 1960 *Et Mourir De Plaisir* was the first to make explicit the lesbian undertones of the original story. *Crypt of the Vampire* (1964) starring Christopher Lee, and especially the Hammer movie *The Vampire Lovers* (1970), the first of "the Karnstein trilogy" secured Carmilla's place in the pulp monsters hall of fame.

64 Guy Endore's 1933 *New York Times* bestseller

65 Gaston Leroux's lurid serial for *Le Gaulois*, 1909-1910

66 These are the antagonists of film series beginning respectively with *A Nightmare on Elm Street*, *Friday the 13th*, and *The Texas Chainsaw Massacre*.

67 Technically, this would be the Bride of Frankenstein's Creature. Taking inspiration from a brief part of Mary Shelley's original book, the 1935 movie sequel to *Frankenstein* (1931) introduced another icon into the monster pantheon.

68 Mike Mignola's comic-book creation debuted in *San Diego Comic-Con Comics* #2 (1993) and has gone on to spawn a small industry of publications, two movies, two animated DVDs and two video games to date.

and insane Red Skull?[69]

Anyhow, the "definition of what is pulp" debate is well documented so I won't dwell on that.[70] Instead let's think about what makes a pulp character a *monster* rather than just a villain or protagonist. I'd suggest that a pulp monster must have some of the following characteristics:

1. There is some element of the horrific about the character; appearance, behaviour, circumstance;

2. The character would be considered monstrous in the society in which he dwells;

3. The character behaves in a manner which would be considered horrific; or rarely goes against type and does not behave as he 'should' given his condition;

4. The character's nature or circumstance is portrayed as unpleasant and unenviable; it's the difference between a monster and a superhero;

5. There is something tragic about the creature or the circumstances surrounding it;

6. The entity possesses the ability to return in a sequel or series, even from beyond the grave; a modern example might be a T2000 from the Terminator movies.

It's impossible to deny the interaction between pulp literature and the equivalent-of-pulp movie industry in developing monsters for popular entertainment. Universal Studios was probably the first filmmaker to understand the sales potential of their horror stable. What made the Universal creatures formula work tended to be:

1. A recognisable and distinctive visual; ask people to pick out Universal monsters by silhouette and pose and nearly everyone can.

---

69 Captain America's twisted and disfigured Nazi archenemy debuted in *Captain America Comics* #1 (1941), created by Joe Simon, Jack Kirby, and France Herron.
70 For example, in April 2011 the Pulp Defined writers group argued that "PULP IS -fast-paced, plot-orientated storytelling of a linear nature with clearly defined, larger than life protagonists and antagonists and creative descriptions and clever use of turns of phrase, words, and other aspects of writing that add to the intensity and pacing of the story." And I mean *argued*.

2. A clear and distinctive backstory, often based on traditional folklore: a vampire count, a reanimated creation of science, a man cursed to transform to a monster etc.

3. Powers and limitations and a specific set of motives and methods; each had a weakness and a particular way of posing a threat.

4. Many provoked some degree of sympathy.

Can "new pulp" creators ever hope to find any new creature that can match the greats of the past? Are there techniques or insights available to us that might let us do something not previously possible? Frankenstein was about the fear of science replacing God and Dracula was about the foreign invading the domestic, so what are the contemporary fears we might exploit to birth new horrors? Global warming? Ecological disaster? Internet spam? What new primal fears prey upon modern society?

There's plenty of contemporary nightmares out there to exploit: GM crops, sentient computer virii, body modification, electromagnetic pollution, deforestation; but I don't know if there's any current universal fear that matched the cold war / nuclear age paranoia that gave us so many memorable creatures.

Or, a less cognitive way to assess the new crop of horrors: what would be the next creature in the Aurora kits range?[71]

***

---

71 For our younger audience, from 1961 to the '70s, Aurora Plastics Corporation manufactured a classic series of self-assembly model kits based upon the old Universal movies monsters and a few others (plus, of course, "Girl Victim"). They managed to put out versions of almost all the pulp staples, from The Creature From the Black Lagoon to Jack the Ripper.

13.
The Horrific Exploits of Spring-Heeled Jack

EVERY PULPSTER SHOULD know about Spring-Heeled Jack. He inspired the rise of the shock newspapers like *London Illustrated Crime Weekly* and the Penny Dreadfuls, forerunners of the pulp magazines. And he's a great bogeyman.

According to the broadsheet newspapers of October 1837, a house servant called Mary Stevens was returning from visiting her parents in Battersea to her employers' house in Lavender Hill. At that time the sprawl of London hadn't yet engulfed these villages so she'd be travelling along winding hedge-lined country paths. She cut across Clapham Common and was grabbed by a dark figure that leaped from an alley. He pinned her, kissed her face, and tore at her clothes and bare flesh with "claws" that were "cold and clammy like those of a corpse". The girl screamed, people came running, and the assailant fled.

The next day the same man struck again at another maid quite near to Miss Stevens' Lavender Hill address. This time his escape included impossible leaps, including vaulting a nine foot high boundary wall. He was laughing manically. At some point during the chase he bounced in front of a horse and carriage, causing it to swerve and crash, seriously injuring the driver. The press took up the description of him leaping as if he had "springs in his heels" and Spring-Heeled Jack got his name.

Sightings and attacks continued and fear spread. A written complaint submitted by "a resident of Peckham" to Sir John Cowan, Lord Mayor of London, brought the matter to official attention and has become the much-quoted staple of Jack-lore:

"My lord - the writer presumes that your lordship will kindly overlook the liberty he has taken in addressing a few lines on a subject which within the last few weeks has caused much alarming sensation in the neighbouring villages within three or four miles of London.

It appears that some individuals (of, as the writer believes, the highest ranks of life) have laid a wager with a mischievous and foolhardy companion (name as yet unknown), that he durst not take upon himself the task of visiting many of the villages near London in three different disguises - a ghost, a bear, and a devil; and, moreover, that he will not dare to enter a gentleman's gardens for the purpose of alarming the inmates of the house. The wager has, however, been accepted, and the unmanly villain has succeeded in depriving seven ladies of their senses. At one house the man rang the bell, and on the servant coming to open door, this worse than brute stood in no less dreadful figure than a spectre clad most perfectly. The consequence was that, the poor girl immediately swooned, and has never from that moment been in her senses, but, on seeing any man, screams out most violently, 'Take him away!' There are two ladies (which your lordship will regret to hear) who have husbands and children, and who are not expected to recover, but are likely to become a burden on their families.

For fear that your lordship might imagine the writer exaggerates, he will refrain from mentioning other cases, if anything more melancholy than those he as already related.

The affair has now been going on for some time, and, strange to say, the papers are still silent on the subject. The writer is very unwilling to be unjust to any man, but he has reason to believe that they have the history at their finger-ends, but, through interested motives, are induced to remain silent. It is, however, high time that such detestable nuisance should be put a stop to, and the writer feels assured that your lordship, as the chief magistrate of London, will take great pleasure in exerting your power to bring the villain to justice."

The Times reported the case on 9th January 1838, elevating Jack's profile to a national level. The same article indicated that the Lord Mayor had indeed made investigations, and that:

"A gentleman stated to his Lordship that the servant girls about Kensington, and Hammersmith, and Ealing, told dreadful stories of a ghost, or devil, who, on one occasion, was said to have beaten a blacksmith and torn his flesh with iron claws and in others to tear clothes from the backs of females. Not one of the injured people had been known to tell the story; perhaps they didn't like to tell it."

A flood of claimed sightings followed from all parts of London. Some women were said to have been driven to fits and others to have died of fright, although no names were given for the latter. Vigilante patrols began to search for Spring-Heeled Jack after dark; several "suspicious characters" were beaten within inches of their lives. When the *Brighton Gazette* reported that a Sussex gardener had been terrified by "a four footed apparition" that had escaped over a high wall, the papers were quick to proclaim that Jack was now roaming the country at will.

On February 19th of that year pretty Jane Alsop answered urgent knocking at her father's door to someone claiming to be a policeman, who shouted, "Bring a light! We have caught Spring-Heeled Jack here in the lane!" When she hurried out with a candle, the visitor cast off a dark cloak to reveal tight-fitting "oilskin" clothing, a helmet, and eyes like "red balls of fire". He vomited blue and white flame into the girl's face then tore at her with iron claws. She struggled free but he caught her again at her doorstep, tearing her gown, arms, neck, and breasts. When Jane's sisters answered her screams the attacker raced away. A subsequent search did not locate him.

On February 28th, 18 year old Lucy Scales and her younger sister cut down Green Dragon Alley on their way home from visiting their married brother in Limehouse. A stranger in the alley blocked Lucy's way and breathed blue fire into her face, blinding her. Lucy fell to the floor in a fit that lasted for hours. Her sister screamed and her brother responded. The stranger, dressed like a gentleman and carrying a bulls-eye lantern, slipped away.

Police treated these cases very seriously. A self-confessed Spring-Heel Jack was tried at Lambeth Street Court then acquitted.

Some linked him with the mysterious "Devil's Footprints" in Devon in February 1835, where miles-long tracks of bipedal hoof-marks snaked over the snow-covered landscape, including passing across rooftops and over high walls. In 1843 he was reported in distant Northamptonshire. Later that year he was attacking lone coachmen in rural East Anglia.

What we would now call the popular media began to cash in on the hysteria. *Spring-Heeled Jack – the Terror of London* became an early Penny Dreadful. He even began to appear in the popular Punch and Judy puppet shows, taking the role in those gory morality plays usually reserved for the Devil. The first Spring-Heeled Jack stage play debuted in 1840. By 1885 his fame had crossed the Atlantic, with "Spring-Heel Jack; or The Masked Mystery of the Tower", appearing in *Beadle's New York Dime Library* #332.

Various theories competed in public opinion. For every one that proclaimed Jack a demon, spectre, or vampire there were those who thought him a lunatic butcher, a mad nobleman, or a cabal of rich men's sons reviving the antics of the infamous Hell-Fire Clubs.[72] Several copy-cats were caught; some were dealt with severely without recourse to the authorities.

The various traits of Jack's numerous claimed attacks were conflated: classic Spring-Heeled Jack had iron claws and burning eyes, belched fire and leaped great distances. He could change shape and melt into shadow. Weapons did not harm him. He dressed like a gentleman except when he was a bear or a ghost or wore tight-fitting oilskin beneath his flowing cloak.

The name of Jack was associated with woman-attacking monsters. The spring-heeled devil may well have inspired the soubriquet of his later murderous successor, Jack the Ripper.

So Jack entered folklore. His appearances diminished but his fame grew. He returned again in 1872 in Peckham and the next year in industrial Sheffield where a huge crowd turned out to see him jumping across the rooftops. But surely his most outrageous exploit was his haunting of Aldershot Army Base, then and now one of the UK's top-security military garrisons.[73]

In August 1877 a sentry there challenged a cloak-swathed figure that raced up and slapped him. Bullets appeared not to harm the assailant. The intruder disappeared into the night with uncanny bounds. A series of other appearances in and around the camp provoked news articles about "The Aldershot Ghost" and are mentioned in memoirs of officers serving at the time. Lord Earnest Hamilton's *Forty Years On* offers details but seems to fudge dates, and posits that the culprit was a prankster called Lieutenant Alfrey.

Jack sightings continued into the 20th century. His last "official" appearance after a couple of decades touring the country was in Liverpool in 1904. The most recent claim was of a family travelling home by car who encountered a "dark figure with no features" that climbed a fifteen foot wall in seconds "just like Spring-Heeled Jack" – in February 2012![74]

See what I mean about the pulpiness of Spring-Heeled Jack? From him proceeded Varney the Vampire, the Mad Gasser of Matoon, Pérák the Spring Man of Prague, Jason Voorhees, and a host of other characters claimed as real or creations of fiction. There is even a shadow of him in the Shadow's chilling laughter.

So a tip of the pulp hat to the scary old ghost – but don't look him in the eye lest he blind you with his fire!

---

72 For more Hell Fire Clubbery see Chapter 21.

73 This incident forms the background to I.A. Watson's short story "Spring-Heeled Jack" in *Sherlock Holmes: Consulting Detective* volume 7.

74 See *The Surrey Comet*, February 23rd, 2012, online at http://www.surreycomet.co.uk/news/epsom/9546587.Terrified_family_confronted_by__dark_figure__on_bypass/

Bibliography: Those who want to pursue Jack themselves are recommended to track down Mike Dash's excellent and definitive article published in *Fortean Studies* volume 3 (1993). Since that's very hard to find these days, a good alternative is Dash's website at http://www.mikedash.com/extras/forteana/shj-about that contains a version of his thesis along with complete reproductions of all the relevant source material.

***

14.
The Scooby-Doo Ending

YOU'VE ALL ENCOUNTERED the "Scooby-Doo" ending. At a story's conclusion apparently supernatural events are revealed as having some mundane explanation. Most often fraud is involved; smugglers were scaring folks away from the abandoned lighthouse, the strange lights beneath the loch were spies in a midget sub, or the murderer was covering his trail by making the deaths seem to be caused by witchcraft. Sometimes the ghost is literally unmasked, along with his sinister hidden motives.

Although popularised by the 60s cartoon adventures of Shaggy, Fred, Daphne, Velma and their dog and by the literary endeavours of the Hardy Boys, the not-supernatural-after-all story has its roots right back through the golden age of pulp and into those strange proto-pulp publications of the Victorian era.

A recent letter from anomalist Alisdair Moffatt, of Halifax, Yorkshire,[75] has focussed my attention on this. Most of what I'm discussing comes from his researches.

The rise of the Penny Dreadful – a cheaply printed disposable magazine-style story, with lurid line art and more lurid narrative – followed on from the pamphlets of "diverse wonders" that sprang up with the birth of printing. It wasn't a big step to jump from leaflets describing the horrors of supposed real-life cannibal Sawney Bean and his savage Highland family[76] to telling

75 *Fortean Times* #299, April 2013, pg 68-69

76 The lurid *Newgate Calendar* was the first publication to chronicle the supposedly historical tale of Alexander "Sawney" Bean and his 48-strong incestuous cannibal family. From a tidal cave at Bennane Head, Scotland, the Beans allegedly robbed, murdered, and devoured over a thousand travellers before being hunted down by King James VI (of Scotland; later also James I of England). Captured alive, the men of the clan had their hands, feet, and genitalia removed before they were hung drawn and quartered. The women and children were made to watch before being burned alive.

The complete text of the original *Newgate Calendar* article is available at various places online, including http://www.scotsites.co.uk/ebooks/sawneybeane.htm

Wes Craven adapted the story to contemporary America for his 1977 horror film *The Hills Have Eyes*.

fictionalised exploits of worse monsters still. Sensationalist periodicals like the infamous *Illustrated Police News* soon spawned similarly-formatted fiction from the same publishers.

By the late 1800s there was an avid market for material we would now characterise as pulp fiction. It usually saw print as short-form novellas, sometimes accompanied by additional unrelated short stories and articles. Often stories were serialised (as with *Treasure Island* and *A Tale of Two Cities*) or featured recurring characters (Sherlock Holmes is the best known). A significant section of the market was aimed at boys and young male adults of limited reading skill; amongst the weekly magazines targeted at that demographic in the UK were *Chums, Union Jack*, and *Aldine Half-Holiday Library*.

We often think of the late 19th century as being a time of superstition. It was an era when Spiritualism's popularity peaked, and many people believed in ghosts, fairies, and magic. But it was also the age in which Darwin's theories and scientific rationalism were taking effect. In Britain it was the time when all children first received school education. The reading public's tastes reflected that dichotomy. For every supernatural *Varney the Vampire* there was a *Ghost of Standgap Priory* (Union Jack Library, 1899), where a ghostly Cistercian friar turns out to be a jewel thief in luminescent robes.

The ghost explained was a popular trope. *The Legend of Ravenwood* (Union Jack Library, Christmas 1896) featured a 'mystic shadow' who was revealed as a man in a black suit with phosphorescent bones painted on it. *The Wrecker Witch of Death Island* (Aldine Half-Holiday Library, 1890) had a similar shtick. There are countless stories of thieves, smugglers, spies, escaped convicts and other wrongdoers counterfeiting the supernatural in the pulp literature of the time.

The appeal then was the same as now. For the majority of the story, the reader can thrill to the spooky events that the protagonists encounter. At the end, the world is affirmed as a rational, sensible place after all. It's the best of both worlds. This was especially important for serial stories where the supernatural could not be admitted. Sherlock Holmes encountered *The Hound of the Baskervilles* and *The Sussex Vampire*, but both were explained by the end of their tales.

But what inspired these fictional accounts of counterfeit spectres? Remarkably, the stories were modelled on real life incidents. The most famous man-dressed-as-ghost news report is probably the recurring 19th century accounts of Spring-Heeled Jack, but there were many others. In some, such as the Derby scare of 1885,[77] the perpetrator was caught and unmasked. Other would-be phantoms were chased by angry vigilante mobs.[78] Before the earliest pulp fiction accounts I can find of men dressing as ghosts for sinister or comical reasons there are reports of it happening in real life.

Such tales also undoubtedly inspired other actual attempts at such scares. The 19th January 1898 issue of *Chums* features the schoolboy protagonists dressing as ghosts to scare their fellows – only to encounter a strange and unexplained bat-like entity with glowing red eyes. How may actual japes and hoaxes did tales like that inspire?

But dressing as supernatural entities has a much older literary tradition. Shakespeare resorts to the device in *The Merry Wives of Windsor*, wherein Falstaff adopts the guise of the mythical Herne the Hunter, a green man or forest wose. The merry wives dress children as fairies to attack him. For that matter, various ancient Greek heroes impersonated divine beings, most often with intent to bed someone; since the gods impersonated kings when they felt randy regarding queens and princesses it seems only fair.[79]

The core of the pulp usage of seemingly-supernatural-then-explained events combines several themes. First, it allows for the spine-chilling narrative; reader and hero alike are unaware that truly diabolical events are not occurring. Secondly, it allows for a process of deduction, the thrill or revelation as the deceit is unmasked. Thirdly, it allows fantastic events to be grounded in 'real life', so that readers' suspension of disbelief is not as tested. This was perhaps an important get-out for some classic pulp readers who saw themselves as down-to-earth men of the world, who could get all the fun of a supernatural horror story yet still comfort themselves with it really only being a crime adventure.

In passing, it's perhaps worth noting the reverse strategy: the hero

---

77 This was first reported in *The Derby Daily Telegraph*, 1st October 1885. Frank Grey's evening walk beside the River Derwent with his sweetheart Isabella Scanlon was interrupted by "a ghostly figure". Grey challenged the intruder and struck him round the head twice, whereupon the phantom drew a revolver. Grey wrestled the gun from his assailant and the spectre fled. After the news became a national sensation, police identified the 'ghost' as one Christopher Burrows, who narrowly escaped imprisonment on firearms charges.

78 The best account is probably that of "The Dundee Ghost" who haunted that city in 1898, and who fled from pursuers despite tripping on his own winding sheet. The *Dundee Courier* of November 14th 1898 has the original story, but it is very adroitly summarised by Jacob Middleton in *Fortean Times* #297, February 2013, pg 36.

79 For example, the fair Alcmene, whom Hesiod says in *The Shield of Hercules* "honoured her husband like no woman before", was visited by Zeus (who was also her great-grandfather) in the guise of her beloved Amphytriton whilst he was away at war, and fathered Hercules upon her.

disguises himself as a supernatural being and the readers watch him scare the villains. "Criminals are a superstitious cowardly lot".[80]

These days some readers and writers deplore the "Scooby-Doo plot". Perhaps it has become cliché, or associated with childish 'comforting' endings. Perhaps technology and visual effects have made such perpetrations too easy to have much shock or novelty value. Even recent Scooby-Doo stories have encompassed the supernatural rather than supposedly-ghostly-explained endings.

I suggest, however, that there's still life in the old trope yet, with opportunities to baffle characters and readers alike by injecting a short dose of the impossible into even the materialistic of storylines.

If you don't believe me, look behind you...

✳✳✳

---

80 Bruce Wayne, *Detective Comics* #27, 1939, on deciding to become Batman.

15.
The First Whodunnit

LET'S SET SOME boundaries first. We're not talking about the first crime story. That might be Cain and Abel,[81] or one of the myths where gods do unpleasant things to each other. We're talking about a story where some unknown perpetrator commits an offence, is sought, and is discovered.

Other Biblical – or at least apocryphal - contenders are *Susanna* and *Bel and the Dragon*. These stories are from the extended *Septuagint* version of *The Book of Daniel*, which adds new chapters 13 and 14; the text appears in only one ancient source and these parts are omitted from most bibles (they were in the 1611 *King James Version* though).

In chapter 13, two lustful elders spy on the bathing Susanna. They threaten to accuse her of adultery unless she has sex with them. She refuses. They bring their allegations, and given the testimony of two prominent holy men the young wife is to be executed. Daniel intervenes to separately question the witnesses, and from their contradictory answers proves Susanna innocent. The accusers are executed instead.

Here we have all the trappings of the detective story, and one of the first reported interrogation scenes. I'd only discount it from my definition of "the first whodunnit story" because it forms one short incident in a much longer narrative, not the focus of the story as a whole. No doubt it is a proper detective mystery though.

By the way, one reason the ancient provenance of this story is questioned is that Daniel, in interrogating the witnesses (in Greek, the language of the *Septuagint*), uses outrageous puns that would not have existed in the original Hebrew. The key discrepancy of the testimonies is the kind of tree under which Susanna was supposed to have had sex with her young lover. One witness claims it was a short mastic tree, whose Greek name is similar to the

---

81 Okay, so at first Cain tried to lie about what he'd done, but since Genesis 4:8 tells us plainly what he did, before the story goes on to God asking what happened, I don't think this can really be called a whodunnit. Perhaps a divine procedural?

Greek verb for *to cut*, and Daniel asks if an angel was ready to cut the mastic down (σχίνον *vs.* σχίσει). The other witness describes an oak, whose Greek name is similar to the verb *to saw*, and Daniel asks if the angel was ready to saw that tree down (πρίνον *vs.* πρίσαι). Many scholars have gone into massive linguistic gymnastics to try and demonstrate how there might have been similar puns in an original Hebrew text. So this tale is also something of a literary whodunnit too.

In chapter 14, in a dispute with the king about the giant statue of the god Bel, the priests of Bel argue that their god miraculously consumes massive amounts of offerings laid out for him in his temple each night. A test is made, wherein the temple is sealed overnight and the food still vanishes.

However, detective Daniel has scattered flour on the temple floor, and from this demonstrates to the king the multitude of footprints that betray the priests' secret door, through which they and their families enter each night to consume the food. Bel is discredited, his statue shattered. So ends history's first locked room mystery. Technically it's more a howdunnit than a whodunnit, but it's definitely a contender.

But if we're dipping into biblical sources, why not dig back to Solomon's detection of who was the mother of the disputed baby?[82]

In my view, for the story to count as a detective whodunnit the mystery has to be the central feature of the story, not some incidental side-plot. There has to be an unexplained event, probably a crime, and a process of deduction. The mystery has to be explained by the end of the tale. Fair definition?

Assuming so, then which was the first whodunnit?

Historians mostly point to Wilkie Collins' *The Moonstone*, 1868. The story originally appeared in serial form in Charles Dickens' *All The Year Round* magazine, and it concerns the theft of the titular Indian jewel on the eighteenth birthday of the young Englishwoman who inherits it. Many of the familiar conventions of the modern detective story are set here, including the country house setting, red herrings, many suspects, a brilliant detective and bungling local policemen, a crime scene reconstruction, and the least likely suspect being guilty. There's even a locked room murder.[83]

---

82 1 Kings 3, 16-28; asked to judge between two claimants to the same baby, Solomon orders the child cut in half and given equally to each supposed mother. The lying claimant is satisfied with the judgement The real mother pleads that the child be spared and given to her rival. In this way the king discerns the true parent and bestows the child accordingly.

83 *The Moonstone* was hailed by crime fiction writer Dorothy L. Sayers as "probably the very finest detective story ever written". G.K. Chesterton likewise said it was, "probably the best detective tale in the world." T.S. Eliot described it as "the first, the longest, and the best of modern English detective novels in a genre invented by Collins and not by Poe."

Others make a case for Edgar Allen Poe's *The Murders in the Rue Morgue* and *The Purloined Letter*, appearing in 1841 and 1845, which predate Collins and include hallmarks of the genre.

I want to put forward "The Three Apples", from *The Arabian Nights*, which was written down at least as far back as the sixteenth century and probably much earlier.

Here's the plot. Judge for yourself.

A fisherman on the Tigris discovers a heavy sealed chest and gives it in tribute to Caliph Haroun al Rashid. The trunk is forced open and a dead woman's cut up body is found inside. The Caliph tasks his Vizier Jafar ibn Yahya to solve the case in three days or be executed in the murderer's stead.

The Vizier fails, but just as he is about to be executed two men appear and each confesses to the murder. The older man was father to the murdered woman, the younger was her husband. The husband proves he did it by describing the corpse's severed condition. His father-in-law's attempts to save him from punishment are thwarted.

That sets up the next mystery. *Why* did the murderer confess? Cue an *Arabian Nights* narrative flashback to back when the murdered woman was alive and well, wife and mother of three...

When the woman falls ill she can only be saved by certain rare apples from the Caliph's orchard in Basra. Her loving husband travels and acquires three of the fruits at great cost, but when he returns the wife claims to be too ill to eat them. Later that day he sees a slave carrying the same rare apple. When the slave is accused of theft he explains that he had the apple from his lover, who was given three special apples by her husband.

The husband confronts his wife, finds an apple missing, and in his rage he murders her. He cuts her body up, hides it in the trunk, and abandons it in the river.

But when the murderer returns home, his son confesses to stealing the missing apple, and having it stolen in turn by a slave to whom he had told the story of his father's quest to Basra. The husband has killed his innocent wife - hence his remorseful confession to the Caliph so that he can be executed.

Haroun al Rashid instead commands the husband to locate the slave whose lies caused tragedy, giving three days stay of execution for the task. This Caliph appears to have had experience of getting people to meet deadlines.

Again, the search fails. The husband bids his family goodbye before his execution. As he hugs his daughter he feels something in her pocket - the very stolen apple that the slave escaped with! She admits to buying the apple from the slave, whom she can name. And so the case is solved.

This being *The Arabian Nights*, the pardoned murderer then repays his Caliph's kindness by narrating another story.

I'd argue that this is an early detective story, albeit not a "play fair" type tale where the audience gets to race the investigator to a conclusion.

Or maybe that river box really contained nothing but red herrings.

16.
How Bad Guys Die

EVERYONE KNOWS that when the big baddie finally falls at the end of the story it's got to be gruesome, memorable, and satisfying. Some common ways of sending the archvillain to the reaper much beloved of adventure fiction are:

Desperate Last Struggle: The hero and villain slug it out one last time, for all the marbles. This often takes place in a significant location, such as the lip of a volcano or on a high girder over the city, or while a countdown clock ticks away to destruction. The hero seems outmatched – the villain cheats – but there's one final heroic push...

A Duel With His Opposite: "We're not so different, you and I." Hero and villain finally duel to discover who is superior with the weapon/technique/ skill of their choice in an honourable clash to the death. Turns out our hero was just that tiny bit better after all.

One Slim Chance: The villain is getting away or is about to launch his doomsday device or do something terrible to the heroine. "Nothing can stop me now!" Our hero has one long shot and he takes it. Mid-gloat, the villain's brains are splattered across the control console.

Delayed Retribution: The villain begs for his life. The hero spares him. Then as the hero turns away the villain pulls his hidden dagger. But the hero is ready for him, swings round, and shoots him dead. Hey, the villain had a last chance and he wasted it!

No Escape From Justice: Our hero is free. He lurks in the shadows, implacable, unstoppable. The villain loses his nerve, flees... but the henchmen he left behind to cover his trail are quickly taken down and terrible vengeance looms out of the darkness to bring the villain screaming to his final end.

Defeat at a Terrible Cost: To destroy the villain, the hero or someone close to him must also sacrifice his or her life! Common symptoms are lunging for the aircraft controls to force a power-dive, shooting into the reactor core, and grabbing the baddie then leaping into the lava pit.

Victim's Revenge: That girl he done wrong, that kid whose father he murdered, that dog whose puppies he slaughtered get their final, unexpected moment of triumph. The villain faces karmic reprisal. Natural justice is restored.

Villain's Own Hubris: He was warned not to open that casket, or to use that artefact, or to try and usurp the power of the gods. He didn't listen. Now nature/terrible monster/the gods have turned on him to accomplish his doom.

The Minion Snaps: Faced with one abuse too many, the villain's henchman finally turns on his master. The girl was the only one who was ever kind to him! And there the minion stands, right next to the lever that releases the mind-squids!

Killed By Irony: The villain's greatest weapon is turned against him. With the all-powerful death-cannon strapped to his arms he can't reach the 'cancel destruct' button in time. That useless peasant he killed in chapter three was the only one who knew where the antidote is hidden. It's a bad idea to discharge your taser disruptor into an enemy when you're both standing in the sewage.
Common variants of this include **The Briar Patch Trick** - goaded into some action which seems clever or evil, the villain in fact accomplishes his own doom, and **The Past Catches Up** – some early part of the villain's history, usually linked to his origin, comes back to haunt him and bring about his final downfall.

The Price of Failure: The villain allowed the hero to get away. His plans are ruined. Now his dark master/demon he sold his soul to/angry subordinates turn on the villain and punish him for his defeat.

An Unexpected Moment of Heroism: Hero and villain must team up to defeat an even greater menace. The villain makes a final noble act of atonement for his wickedness.

The Villain's Death Is Part of the Plan: Now nobody can input the lost launch codes and stop the end of the world. The villain dies to accomplish his goals and has one final laugh at his heroic enemy.

A variant of this is **Mutual Assured Destruction** – the villain triggers the explosion that destroys him and his adversary together.

Definitely Dead Till Next Time: And a special mention goes to all those "assumed" deaths where the body vanishes. Falls over cliffs or huge base-destroying explosions are best for this, but there are plenty of elaborate scenarios where the villain seems to be gone for good but isn't. They come in two flavours: 1. The villain planned it all along, and 2. The villain wouldn't have survived except for a lucky coincidence; in the second version he may also return horribly scarred.

"Defeat with honor is but victory delayed" – Victor von Doom, *Fantastic Four* #87

***

17.
On the Origin of Magic Swords, and their Makers

MAGIC WEAPONS are a staple of many fantasy stories because they're a staple from many myths and legends. They're ingrained into our storytelling DNA – with good reason.

Go back three and a half thousand years or more. In Britain and Northern Europe wandering hunter/gatherer tribes are transitioning to herder/farmers. Population has grown so there's competition for territory. Conflict is inevitable. There is a place for strong warriors. There is a place for powerful weapons.

The best weapon available is the bronze sword; this is the Bronze Age, after all. Bronze is the best technology. A dagger of bronze is more effective and keeps its edge better than a dagger of flint. New techniques are becoming available to increase the range of those bronze blades, combining the reach of a spear with the versatility of a knife. The first two foot long bronze swords appeared around 1600 B.C.. A man with such a weapon had a significant combat advantage. A man with such a weapon could be king.

Then came the discovery: fallen stars contain iron. Not the polluted, difficult-to-work stuff that could be grubbed from the ground, but pure, elemental material given by the gods. Meteor iron could be smelted just like bronze but it made blades that were stronger and lighter. And then the secret, passed down in guilds from smith father to smith son, making their line so important that today their descendants cover the Earth, making Smith the most common Western name;[84] add a pinch of carbon to the molten iron and it becomes steel!

A thousand years B.C., where the bronze blade was formerly the pinnacle of technology, iron was the magic metal. A steel sword could slice through even those amazing bronze weapons. A steel sword could pierce boiled leather

---

84 And by the time you add in the Schmitts, Smythes, Shmieders, Smeets, Fabrios, Fabers, Ferreros, Fabers, Haddads, Goughs, Kovacks, Sepps, Kajiyas, and Demercis that's a pretty wide number of people.

armour like it wasn't there. A steel sword could split shields and sever limbs. A steel sword made a good warrior great.

We know quite a bit about these swords. We've still got a lot of them, for a very odd reason.

In Northern Europe you can't throw an axe-head without hitting archaeology. So we've got plenty of evidence of the social and economic phases in the long millennia between the last ice age and the 'start of history'.[85] One of the more distinctive emphasises was ritual behaviour with rivers.

The oldest names in Britain are the names of the rivers, presumed to derive from the gods and goddesses to whom each watercourse was sacred. In England, the Don and the Sheaf, the Mersey and the Ouse, the Cam and the Thames all give us a glimpse back to a time when rivers were not only the safest highways but the most vital resource for a struggling population: food, transport, security, industry and status all began with a good river location.

It is perhaps not surprising then that there was ritual activity at these rivers. Again and again archaeologists discover deposits of valuable items tossed into the waters, buried in the mud. In some places hundreds of finds have been discovered, with post-holes where wooden walkway platforms were raised over the flood to reach the appropriate sacrifice spot.

Archaeologists love wetlands. For good scientific reasons we won't go into here, wooden and metal artefacts buried in the right kind of river mud don't oxidise or rot. We know what the weather was like in England in 3500 B.C. because we've got the tree-ring growth patterns from wood preserved from that era in wetland deposits.[86] And we've got hundreds of broken swords from those same deposits.

Hold on, though. *Broken* magic swords? How magic could they be if they broke in battle? But they didn't. Nearly all the river sacrifice items are broken; many show signs of deliberate destructions. The swords have been snapped in half. It's tempting to speculate that 'killing' these treasures was meant to send them to the afterlife, for the use of gods or ancestors; but our forebears left no instruction on their motives.

Hold on again! Iron weapons were *valuable*. The Iron Age is named after them but in Northern Europe they were rare right up to the coming of the Roman conquerors. Surely a warrior who broke a coveted near-impossible-to-find magic sword as a sacrifice was the most pious of men?

Well, yes and no. Yes, it showed a massive devotion to the gods. Yes, it

---

85 English history has traditionally 'begun' with the first invasion of Julius Caesar, 55 B.C.

86 The record is patchy, of course, but the longest dendrochronologies like those of the South German river oak and the Irish pine extend back more than 11,000 years.

showed his generosity and power off to the world. But there's probably a more pragmatic reason as well: *One man can only hold one sword.* If you fight an enemy and kill him and take his magic sword as well, then you have two. If you give your spare to an ally, even to a son, then two of you have miracle blades; you have a potential challenger. But if you break the weapon and send it to the gods then you have credit, fame, and a less itchy pair of shoulder-blades.

At least that's the way the archaeologists and historians like to spin it.

Dipping into myth for a moment, remember that King Arthur received Excalibur after the sword he'd drawn from the stone snapped in battle. Merlin brought him to a river and the Lady of the Lake caused a hand to rise from the water bearing the enchanted weapon. At the end of Arthur's life he had his oldest friend Bedevere hurl Excalibur back into a river, whereupon it was caught by that same hand, waved thrice, then taken under the waves again until it was required in a different age.[87]

But what of the men who forged the magic swords? Where did they come from? How did they learn their craft? What became of them after?

The most famous smith in Northern legend is Weyland, (proto-Germanic for "battle-brave"), called Volundr in the Norse, under which name he stars in the *Völundarkviða*, one of the poems of the Prose Edda. He also features in *Þiðrekssaga*, the saga of Theoderic the Great, and in the Old English sagas of Deor, Waldere and Beowulf. His legend is depicted on the Franks Casket[88] and on Ardre image stone VIII.[89] All of these sources are twelfth century A.D. or later, of course, but they seem to distil the surviving lore of smiths and smithies from an earlier time.

There are a couple of versions of how Weyland got started. In the most prevalent story he and his two brothers spy upon three bathing swan-maidens. It's well known that if you catch such a damsel and steal her clothes then she

87 *Le Morte D'Arthur*, Book I Chapter XXV and Book XXI Chapter V, by Sir Thomas Mallory
88 A small decorated Anglo-Saxon whalebone chest, probably originating in Northumbria. It is remarkable for its imagery, showing a variety of pagan and Christian themes, and for the writing carved on it in runes, Latin, and Old English script, some reversed. The majority of the box is kept at the British Museum except for the right panel which is displayed at the Bargello Museum, Florence. Weyland shares space on the box with the Adoration of the Magi, the Emperor Tiberius, Romulus and Remus, and other scenes tentatively suggested as Sigurd and Granu, Henga and Horgest, a wood god, the Penance of Rhiannon, and Satan and the Nativity.
89 Ten stones from the 8th to 11th centuries were recovered from the church at Ardre, Sweden, survivors of many image-stones that were reused as paving rubble or building materials. Preserved now at the Museum of National Antiquities, Sweden, Stockholm, the seventh stone depicts Norse mythology, including Weyland's story, Odin on his eight-legged horse Sleipnir, Thor fishing for the World Serpent, and the punishment of Loki. A woman bearing two swords also appears, but her legend may be lost.

has to stay with you as your wife, and that's what the three brothers did. Their valkyrie lovers taught them strange lore – including possibly what to do with the big iron stones that Odin cast down from the heavens on occasion.

After nine years the women returned to their own lands. Weyland's brothers went with their wives, but Weyland remained behind with his son. His departing lover, Hervör Alvitr (strange, all-wise creature) left him a ring to remember her by. Weyland forged himself a magic sword and became a renowned warrior and smith.

Weyland is credited with casting many magic blades. These include *Gram*, Sigmund's sword which Odin broke and was later reforged for Sigurd Sigmundson to slay the dragon Fafnir (*Völsunga* saga); Ogier the Dane's *Curtana* and Roland's *Durandil* (*Karlamagnus* Saga); *Mimung*, which Weyland forged to fight rival smith Amilias (*Thidrekssaga*); *Hatheloke*, the sword of Torrent of Portyngale (*Torrent of Portyngale*); and a good number of others. He also created a magic ring for Thorstein Vikingson in the saga of that name. His claim to forging Excalibur/Caliburn is of relatively recent origin.

Enter the villain: King Niðhad of Närke struck by night, capturing Weyland in his sleep. He had Weyland hamstrung so he could not escape then imprisoned him on the island of Sævarstöð where he would forge weapons that would make Niðhad unstoppable. Niðhad took Weyland's sword and wore it as his own. Hervör's ring was given to the king's daughter Bodvild.

As all story readers will know, it is a capital mistake for the bad guy to lock the main character up in a workshop, especially then that main character is the greatest smith of legend and a man with a grudge.

King Niðhad had two sons. Weyland worked on their enthusiasm and ambition, eventually winning their loyalty against their father. Then he murdered them in his workshop. He converted their skulls into goblets for their unsuspecting father to drink from and transformed their eyes into jewels and their teeth into a brooch for their unsuspecting mother to wear. He burned their other remains in his forge as he crafted wings to achieve his freedom.

Weyland had also befriended Princess Bodvild, who visited him often to see the wonders of his forge. Before he escaped he drugged her, raped her, and retrieved his wife's ring, leaving her pregnant with the child who would later become the hero Viðga.[90]

---

90 Modern readers will find Weyland's act abhorrent, but there is some possible mitigating cultural context here. To a Norse way of thinking, in choosing to wear Hervör's wedding ring Bodvild effectively made herself Weyland's property, his wife. His bedding of her as a wife was revenge for her usurpation

For the Scandinavians this was a pretty good ending to a revenge saga, and showed Niðhad that he'd messed with the wrong smith.

Of note in our present discussion, however, are the traits that Weyland was attributed in the legend. First off, he was lame. There's physical evidence – in the form of skeletons – that occasionally Iron Age folks had half their foot deliberately chopped off, including a few folks who, judging by what their bones can tell us about their diet and health, were otherwise of high status. This might simply be a way of non-lethally removing a competing family member from a leadership contest, but there are sufficient traditions about lame smiths (c.f. Hephaestus) for us to at least suspect it was a traditional means of ensuring that a valuable and dangerous resource could be controlled and contained.

Secondly we have the idea that smithlore was secret. Niðhad's sons were fascinated with it, lured in by hopes of learning the mystery through hidden initiation. It seems likely that there were craft secrets passed down by family or guild. After all, the ability to make magic weapons is a sure ticket to as good portion of the hunt-meat.

Thirdly, the smith's work was art as well as craft. Weyland made rings and jewellery as well as weapons of war. He made tools as well as killing devices. A man who can make a magic sword of star-metal can forge a cunning finger-band of fairy gold.

And fourthly, we learn that smiths were dark and dangerous men to cross.

The lore of swords and their makers have come down to us today via many generations of storytelling. Every magical tool, every SF miracle-weapon for that matter, comes from Weyland's workshop and from those ancient kings breaking their enemies' power over their knee before casting it to the gods. Every cunning scientist or technologist who solves the problem and overcomes the brutal adversary by using brains over brawn is a smith at heart.

Now go throw something in a river.

---

of a role she had not deserved. The legend is unclear as to the fate of Weyland's son by Hervör, but if he was murdered by Niðhad at the time of Weyland's capture then Norse listeners would have no difficulty with the revenge-slaughter of Niðhad's sons, nor with the 'justice' of Weyland fathering a new son on Niðhad's daughter. Or else those wacky Vikings just loved a good old rape-and-murder-your-enemy's-kinfolk revenge yarn.

18.
The Illusion of Change

STAN LEE, co-founder and architect of Marvel Comics,[91] argued that comics required series not to change but to have the illusion of change.

I agree that might be the case for those series which are intended to be ongoing forever. Titles like *Superman*, *Batman*, or *Spider-Man* have publishing histories older than most of their readers.[92] Many modern fans will not have read anything like the bulk of previous stories. Only the major milestones, like the death of Gwen Stacy,[93] have filtered through the years to significantly impact on the canon. For the rest, the same problems in different guises recur again and again - secret identity conflicts, returning villains, supporting cast problems - and when they're done right they can still be entertaining.

Plus ça change, plus c'est la même chose

LONG BEFORE the rise of the comic book, the weekly periodical story filled much the same niche. In the UK, magazines like *The Magnet* (1908-1940, 1,683 issues) featured ongoing series with many similarities to the

91 Begun as Timely Publications in 1939 then becoming Atlas Publications in 1951, the company became Marvel Publishing Inc. in 1961 and currently trades as Marvel Worldwide, Inc. It was acquired as part of the Walt Disney Company in 2009 for $4.24bn. Marvel Comics rise to success began in 1961 with the first issue of *Fantastic Four* and a quick succession of other popular titles including *The Hulk*, *Spider-Man*, *Thor*, *Iron Man*, *Doctor Strange*, *Daredevil*, *The Avengers*, and *X-Men* which remain the core published properties of the company to this day. In those early issues Stan Lee was generally credited as writer and editor but there was also significant creative input from the credited artists such as Jack Kirby and Steve Ditko.

92 Superman and Batman, from DC Comics, debuted in 1938 and 1939 respectively. Spider-Man first appeared in 1962.

93 Gwen Stacy, girlfriend of Peter Parker (Spider-Man), died during her rescue from the Green Goblin in *Amazing Spider-Man* #121 (1971 by Gerry Conway and Gil Kane). The story had a massive impact; up to that time no ongoing supporting cast member of such significance had ever died in a comic book (although Gwen's own father, Police Captain George Stacy, had died in *Amazing Spider-Man* #90). Some comics historians date the end of the Silver Age of Comics from this event.

comic book. *The Magnet* was notable for Frank Richards' Greyfriars School stories, adventure yarns featuring the original "famous five" schoolboys and their comedy relief Billy Bunter, "the fat owl of the Remove",[94] Frank Richards is listed in the Guinness Book of Records as the world's most prolific author. Richards produced about 100 million published words in his lifetime under a variety of pseudonyms (his actual name was Charles Hamilton). Amongst many other works, he turned out a 30,000 word Greyfriars novella a week for over thirty years, then continued his stories in novel form for twenty years more - and at the end of that time the schoolboys were *still* 14, *still* in the Remove, and still interacting in much the same way as they had before World War I. Harry Wharton and his chums make Franklin Richards (from the *Fantastic Four*,[95] no relation) look like a real fast grower.

Frank Richards knew that his audience was constantly turning over. His main readership was boys aged between eleven and sixteen, so every five years or so he had a virtually new audience for his tales. The details of the stories changed because they were always contemporary. When the Great War started, the schoolboys fought sinister agents of the Kaiser. During World War II they thwarted Hitler's spies. Compare this with Iron Man's various exploits,[96] from the much-revised war in which he was originally injured, once Viet Nam, now Afghanistan, and from his early commie-busting adventures to his contemporary anti-terrorist exploits. Comics have traditionally had a similar expectation of a limited-duration audience and a readership turnover.

But the same thing happened with Greyfriars as happened with superhero comics: some readers grew up but continued to read. Later in Richards' career his readership balance changed, with adult fans of the series supporting his novel releases. A fan club even produced facsimile editions of the original Magnet issues - 100 volumes in all, with even the original advertisement pages lovingly replicated. Again, compare to the hardcover deluxe collector's

94 That's the lower 4th form, Year 9s, 14 year olds for those not from British public schools. In the US they'd be 8th graders

95 Franklin Richards, son of Fantastic Four members Reed and Susan Richards (Mr Fantastic and the Invisible Woman), was born in *Fantastic Four Annual* #6, 1968. By 1987 he was five years old in the storyline; time progresses differently in ongoing comics. He remained five for many years but is now allowed to be twelve, dating the formation of the Fantastic Four and the start of the era of Marvel superheroes at a couple of years before that.

96 Iron Man debuted in Marvel Comics' *Tales of Suspense* #39 (1963), wherein playboy inventor Tony Stark was wounded in Viet Nam. As real-world time has passed and Stark has not aged within the flexible 'now' of comics, his origin was revised to shift the conflict in which he was injured to more contemporary events, such as the first Gulf War. His most recent version, in line with the highly successful movie franchise, places his injury in Afghanistan.

editions of classic comics that we see now with a high price tag. Greyfriars fans revelled in trivia discussions and obsessed over continuity (which, if the eternal 14-year-old-ness is overlooked, is remarkably good, given that a single writer steered the series over fifty years). Adult comics fans likewise obsess over reconciling discontinuities between older obscure events and new information; comics fans are often better informed about the characters than modern writers.

Event-driven comics

THE NEVER-CHANGING NATURE of ongoing comics means that changes which *were* meant to be permanent once had a major impact. At first these were "imaginary stories" - imagine if Superman married Lois Lane and they had a Superbaby! Later, memorable events were enshrined in 'continuity'; who can forget the paradigm-changing Wedding of Reed and Sue?[97] Still later, probably around the time of *Secret Wars* and *Crisis on Infinite Earths*,[98] publishers realised that 'big events' - and big meant future-comics-changing - sold. "This issue - someone dies!" became the key to reviving flagging market sales. Later still, 'going dark and gritty' - equated through some very shoddy logic with 'more realistic' - was considered an effective creative choice.

In fact change became a necessary sales tool. "Why read this issue? Nothing changes?" has become a common criticism of some comics, and especially of crossover events. The escalation of shock and trauma required to produce a sensation amongst an increasingly blasé and cynical readership has led to character deaths (and subsequent character resurrections), to infidelities, to new characters taking on the identities of older ones, to heroes turning evil, to rape, incest, and probably cannibalism. To be fair, the characters are only doing to each other what their publishers and hired creators are doing to them first!

Yet even in these event-driven traumatic days for comics, the illusion of change is there more than the reality of change. Captain America died and got real-world news coverage - but he's back now.[99] Same with Batman – but

---

97 *Fantastic Four Annual* #3 (1965) depicted the wedding of two of the series title characters.

98 *Marvel Super Heroes Secret Wars* #1-12 (1984/5) and *Crisis on Infinite Earths* #1-12 (1985) were early examples of "limited series" (i.e. deliberately short-run stories) and of comics-line-wide crossover events that have since become commonplace.

99 Captain America's assassination took place in *Captain America* volume 5 #25 (2007). The event was

he returned as a franchise.[100] Asgard was destroyed - but now its better.[101] Some heroes that did bad things were actually Skrulls,[102] or mind controlled, or did them on numbered alternate Earths that have now been erased or merged. Bucky Barnes and Jason Todd are alive, albeit changed and darkened to 'coolness'.[103] Reality gets altered by the Devil, or the Anti-Monitor, or John Byrne, or Mark Millar,[104] or whatever terrible menace to our heroes' wellbeing sells comics this month. And the change was illusory.

This cycle of apparent change, of life and death and reshuffling the pieces on the board, of the most-terrible-ever return of the Joker or Doctor Doom or Magneto, works pretty well for those new readers in their five-year reading span who haven't seen the previous most-terrible-ever return (remember the Doom who wore a flesh-mask of his true love Valeria?). But for that large

---

reported on AB.C. news, with analysis by Brian Robinson. Cap returned in *Captain America Reborn* #1-6 (2009). In the interim other characters wore Steve Rogers' costume and filled his role.

100 Bruce Wayne perished in the 7-issue limited series *Final Crisis* (2008/9) and was replaced by other heroes in the identity of Batman until his inevitable return in the 6-issue *Batman: The Return of Bruce Wayne* (2010).

101 Marvel Comics' version of Thor's legendary home was blown up in *Siege* #4 (2010). It was restored in time to be threatened again in the *Fear Itself* limited series (2011). Mind you, Asgard has faced Raganarok an average of once every sixteen months since Thor's comics exploits began in 1962.

102 The shape-shifting aliens who can look like anyone first debuted in *Fantastic Four* #2. They were adversaries in the 8-issue limited series *Secret Invasion* (2008) and its innumerable tie-in comics – during which time they too tried to destroy Asgard. Many poor creator choices leading to damaging character actions and plot developments can now be attributed to the hero being replaced by a Skrull at the time. In case of more poor writing, other methods of substitution and mind control are also available.

103 Bucky Barnes was Captain America's teenaged sidekick from his wartime comics. It was established at the time of Captain America's 1960s revival that Bucky had died in the combat that had placed Cap into suspended animation until the present day. In *Captain America* vol 5 #1 (2005) Bucky returned, having evidently been retrieved, experimented on, brainwashed, and cyborgised by the Soviets. He has since recovered from his ordeal and even filled in as Captain America during Steve Roger's leave of absence due to death, but remains a darker, more violent character than the one depicted in his 1940s appearances.

Jason Todd was the second boy to be taken by Bruce Wayne as his ward and trained to become his sidekick Robin. In *Batman* #429 he was killed by the Joker. He was revived to return in the "Hush" storyline, *Batman* #608-619 (2002/3), but was not confirmed to be the violent antihero Red Hood until the "Under the Hood" storyline commencing in *Batman* #635 (2005). Todd has also been somewhat rehabilitated in subsequent years.

104 In the "One Last Day" storyline in *Amazing Spider-Man* #544-545, *Friendly Neighborhood Spider-Man* #24, and *Sensational Spider-Man* vol. 2 #41 (2007/8), Peter Parker did a deal with the demon-lord Mephisto that reset much of his recent continuity, including his marriage and the public learning his identity.

The Anti-Monitor was the antagonist in *Crisis on Infinite Earths* limited series (1985) whose actions rewrote the continuity of the DC Universe, effectively 'rebooting' it from the start.

John Byrne and Mark Millar are comic writers with a penchant for ignoring the history established by creators who have come before them. Their inclusion in the article is a cheap shot.

segment of adult fans with longer memories there is definite trauma-event fatigue. The illusion of change is worn too thin. Eventually the magic is gone.

Kurt Busiek[105] reflected once that writers should only make permanent changes if what they put in place is at least as robust as what they destroy. You want to kill off Nick Fury? Come up with someone at least as compelling to do his job. Maria Hill and G.W. Bridge need not apply.[106] You want to marry off Peter Parker? You'd better have a damn good game plan for how that might work.[107]

Most stories have natural conclusions. Comics are a modern iteration of old legends, and in most of the greatest legends the heroes reach an end; either they get the girl, settle down, and live happily ever after or else they have an heroic passing - c.f. Hercules, King Arthur, Robin Hood. One reason that married superheroes struggle to find engaging ongoing storylines is that in our culture we view marriage as the ending of the 'adventure' period; what comes after is the reward, the settled time of enjoying love and children. So unless your series is about a family unit who face adventure (the *Fantastic Four* is the rare and best example) then your comic book is going to struggle once the hero and heroine have reached what we instinctively feel should be a rest point.

When comics allow events to progress in certain directions - marriage and death are two of them - then either they move towards a proper conclusion, or more likely they have to take extraordinary and usually incredible efforts to backtrack. The recent *Spider-Man* change and the rebooting of a now-single *Superman* are good examples.

Superhero Costume Changes

NO-ONE CAN DENY that superheroes have enjoyed a new lease of life after the blockbuster success of some recent movies, most notably the *Dark Knight* Batman films, the *Iron Man* trilogy, and *The Avengers*. Adaptation to the big screen has required, or been assumed to require, a number of changes

---

105 Award wining comic book writer of *Avengers*, *Superman* and others, creator of the highly-regarded comic series *Astro City*; in short, a man who really knows his comics.

106 Other characters who have served as head of Marvel's spy agency SHIELD.

107 Spider-Man Peter Parker married long-time girlfriend Mary Jane Watson in *Amazing Spider-Man Annual* #21 (1987), and various creators have tried to revoke, undo, or rewrite the marriage ever since. Even a potential pregnancy was 'retconned' out of the storyline. As of "One More Day", history has been rewritten by diabolic pact so that at last the marriage no longer happened. This has of course infuriated a number of long term fans who were supporters of the relationship and its development.

that have provoked much debate amongst fans. Amongst the most vociferous arguments has been the costume question: how much should a hero's 'iconic' appearance be modified for the big screen?

One side of the argument maintains that uniforms that were originally designed to look good in two-dimensional art in cheaply-printed four-colour comic books don't always work practically or aesthetically in live-action moving images. The other counters that it is those 'classic' looks which attracted the popular support that inspired the movie deals in the first place, and film creators should have faith in the properties that they are adapting.

This was never fiercer than in the "Winghead" debate, about the small white Mercury-wings that have adorned the sides of Captain America's mask since it was first designed by legendary comics artist Jack Kirby in 1941. In fact many of Cap's fellow Avengers jocularly refer to him as "Winghead" in the same way as Iron Man is nicknamed "Shellhead," the Hulk is "Greenskin" or "Jade Jaws", and Thor is "Goldilocks".

But for the latest movie version, these wings were eradicated as being unnecessary, likely to spoil suspension of disbelief for a wider audience. They appear as logo-style markings on the side of the some versions of the mask, but are otherwise conspicuous by the absence.

So let us consider superhero suits in general and Captain America's uniform in particular.

Back in the days when almost all the iconic costumes were created, comics had to be drawn with an economy of line and panel. Artists were expert at conveying story quickly – events that would take a six-issue mini-series now were packed into a 12-page feature then. The panels had to express movement, cause and effect, and yet still be quick to draw for by-the-page pay rates.

The male body is based around a downwards-pointing triangle with an upwards-tapering egg or triangle on top of it – plus arms and legs. The best superhero costumes accentuate that body triangle by design and colour. They place an emphasis on the chest then have lines that convey position and motion. Often a cape or cloak shaped like an upward-pointing triangle adds counterpoint and shows direction of travel. On the head, a mask with eyepieces emphasises the hero's determined eyes and his expression. This counterbalances the bold prominent square jawline that forms the head-triangle's base. Boots or gloves add weight to the ends of the limbs and help show movement.

The first superhero costume remains the best. Superman has almost all the elements of a successful comics page super-costume, lacking only the mask. First there's his chest, the muscled tapering torso accentuated by the shape of the prominent S-symbol. Spots of red at boots and trunks, along with pink hands and a red cape, balance out the other predominant primary colour of his costume. The cape can flare for flying and forward lunges, helping to depict action, showing force and direction.

Of course, Superman had gone commando in his latest movie, which sees his costume being adjusted to eliminate the red trunks. Unsurprisingly this means the eye is drawn away from the fussy reimagining of his S chest-symbol down towards the actor's, um, lower bulge; the very problem the 30s strongmen on whom his costume was modelled wore trunks to prevent in the first place.

Captain America is the other exemplar costume. Also in primary colours plus white, this Kirby creation uses all the same principles as Superman's outfit, sans cape but with added mask. There's the prominent chest star, which echoes the shape of the hero himself with arms and legs akimbo and serves as the same counterpoint triangle that Superman's cape accomplishes. Vertical red and white belly stripes guide the eyes upwards to the pectorals and that powerful patriotic logo. Horizontal lines at waist and trunks break the body up into sections to suggest a compact fighter; just use the horizontal lines alone and you've got a 1940s boxer. Red boots and gloves again emphasise pose and motion.

But there's more. Cap's original triangular shield continues with the torso-motif. The various lines, including the belly-stripes and chainmail indents, help to show Cap flexing and shifting. The mask emphasises his eyes and jaw by having a prominent A (another triangle) with the downward strokes pointing directly to those big blue eyes.

The change of the A-letter on Cap's forehead to a stylised-V eagle motif was one reason Rob Liefield's revision of the Cap costume didn't work, by the way.[108] Instead of enhancing Cap's eyes it emphasised the bridge of his nose, so his scowl became his most important facial feature and his eyes appeared smaller and beadier.

Which brings me to the visual images for movie-Cap. The costumes works, but it's the elements retained from the Kirby original that do that, in spite of changes that detract from the iconic version and suggest that the designer didn't really understand what he was messing with. Hence we have

---

108 *Captain America* vol. 2 #1, 1996. The 'reimagining' was cancelled after twelve issues and the 'original' Cap was returned.

a chest harness adding vertical lines that detract from the chest triangle, and shoulderpads with stars on them that emphasise yet more points of the body, points that don't particularly convey motion or emotion and drag attention from hands and face that do.

Most serious of all is the lack of Cap's mask wings. Now I admit that the wings seem goofy. They shouldn't work; but they shouldn't work as a costume accessory in the same way that "taking arms against a sea of troubles" shouldn't work as a literary phrase. Neither make sense by the usual rules but both are somehow right.

Cap's wings balance his mask to prevent him being some strange earless wonder. They trail backwards indicating forward motion. They help to depict head movement. They add the balancing splashes of white that prevent the white mask-A from appearing isolated and random. And they allow the other Avengers to call him "Winghead".

So for me, the movies' budget department could have saved designer costs and stayed with the costume that's worked for six decades and more now. Chainmail and canvas trumps plastic and spandex. Simple lines work better than harnesses and pouches. And head-wings work against all the odds; so if your costume team can't pull them off then get a new team.

On Continuity

I SUSPECT THAT what many fans value most about serial characters is their internal integrity.

Nobody's too bothered about whether Tony Stark took shrapnel in Viet Nam or Afghanistan. The key part of his origin is that a self-absorbed playboy got a hard lesson and literally remade himself as a hero by means of his technological genius. A story that portrays that well "gets it" and gets us. Conversely, when plotlines digress from that - for example if Stark becomes a techno-organic entity imbued with advanced nanotech wetware he didn't design that gives him a range of new super-powers[109] - then the essence of the hero and his situation is lost.

Many heroes' essential characters are established by their origins. That's why the further movies digress from those origins the weaker they become.

---

109 This version of Iron Man, popular at the time of Warren Ellis' six-part series *Iron Man* vol 4 #1-6 (2005/6), includes Stark receiving nanotechnology that allows him to "grow" armour from inside his body, to mentally control machines, and boosts his intelligence and thinking speed to superhuman levels. Some elements of the storyline were recycled into the third *Iron Man* movie.

I was very disappointed that the movie *Hulk* shied away from his nuclear bomb origin. The Hulk *is* that nuclear nightmare personified, an unstoppable uncontrollable destructive force that once released cannot be contained. He's Banner's curse for Banner's folly in designing the gamma bomb in the first place. He's Banner's tragedy because Bruce only took the gamma blast because of a last minute act of quixotic bravery. Substituting all that for Bruce zapping himself with rays in a lab dentist's chair because of scientific hubris reduces him and the Hulk to just another movie monster caused by arrogant scientific lab meddling; the paradigm is weakened.

Because comic books are episodic we come to know the characters rather well, to the point where we can predict how they 'should' react in most situations. Given a crashed alien spaceship with rampaging robots and escaping space-princess we can pretty much say how each of the Fantastic Four are going to react.

Good writers understand our understanding; they make the characters feel in character. The best writers can put the characters in situations where we're not too sure of their responses or can depict a response we didn't expect but then show us why its consistent with what we know of the hero anyhow. Think of Matt Murdock in Miller's *Daredevil* epic "Born Again".[110]

Much of the criticism of modern comics writing is that it "doesn't respect the characters" - that the heroes are bent to fit the plot. Stark is willing to imprison his closest friends in a governmental superhero-registration war.[111] Hawkeye is willing to cheat on his old friend and team-mate Hank by bedding Hank's ex-wife, the Wasp.[112] Gwen Stacy, Peter's first love, deceived him and secretly had Norman Osborn's bastards.[113]

It's hard to reconcile this behaviour with what we know of these characters from their longer publishing run. It destroys suspension of disbelief and pollutes what's come before because it colours what comes after. It's also bad business; a two-issue sales spike isn't worth losing 5% of your loyal readers

---

110 *Daredevil* #227-231 by Frank Miller and Dave Mazzucchelli featured a radical storyline in which the hero's whole life was destroyed by a villain who had discovered his secret identity. The powerful tale covers Matt Murdock losing everything dear to him then clawing his way back to a new kind of life and an inner peace. Recommended.

111 Marvel Comics' *Civil War* crossover, 2006-7

112 Avengers vol 3 #83, by Chuck Austen and Scott Kolins. Not recommended.

113 *Amazing Spider-Man* #509-514, 2004-5, written by J, Michael Straczinski, reveals that Peter Parker's former girlfriend Gwen Stacy, as previously footnoted a very significant character in Spider man's early comics and one of the first "major" characters to die in a comic book series, secretly bore twins to Spider-Man's archenemy the Green Goblin, which have been genetically accelerated to adulthood and now want to kill their father. It wasn't either Straczinski's or Spidey's finest hour storywise. Straczinski has since expressed a desire to "retcon" the characters and events from the series.

forever.

When it comes to movies there's another problem. The medium requires a full story, with a full character arc, to be told in under two hours. That's very different from the ongoing medium of comics. Our hero has to be introduced, given motivations and a modus operandi, meet the villain, save the day, win the girl etc before the end credits. There had to be a sense of completion.

The easiest way to do that is to tie the villain's origin to the heroes; see the *Fantastic Four* movie (2005). The mistake there was in assuming Dr Doom ever needed superpowers. Is he not... Doom? But these kinds of changes often mean the hero's origin has to alter, and that sometimes weakens the paradigm.

I suspect that what most people object to when they say that movie versions of superheroes "didn't get the continuity right" is that various changes that were made didn't respect the true character of the hero. If movie Peter Parker is a hot-headed smartass with an eye for the ladies then the game's over before it's started; I'm not suggesting he was, just giving a hypothetical example.

A more accurate criticism would be the *X-Men* movies' portrayal of an anal-retentive boring Cyclops who is far less attractive to Jean Grey than the kewl rough 'n' tumble Wolverine. Hollywood has a real problem depicting characters whose dedication and integrity require seriousness and application. To be fair, the last two decades of comics have done the same to Scott Summers; the heroic lynchpin of Xavier's dream vanished forever after *X-Men* #137.[114]

The essential character of the hero is expressed and portrayed in how he or she behaves, in how they relate to their supporting cast, in the detail of their lives and situations, and in how they respond to adversity. That's why changes from the comic book originals need to be carefully considered. Few variations have been for the better. Even minor alterations like changing Jane

---

114 This was the storyline in which the love of Cyclops' life, Jean Grey (Marvel Girl/Phoenix) died (for the first time; she's been back for several encores since). Its an excellent story from Claremont and Byrne, probably the peak of their very successful run on the series, and it sees the heartbroken Cyclops' retirement from the team that he'd been leader of since #1.

When he returned in later storylines his place had been taken by Claremont's favourite character Storm, who "defeated him in combat" for the right to lead the team. Cyclops was marginalised to an ineffective occasional character who suffered a series of unfortunate plotlines that saw him married to a Jean Grey lookalike, leave her, discover she was a clone of Jean, cope with her being possessed by a demon, leave her again when the "real" Jean Grey was resurrected... sorry, its just too long, complicated and depressing to even footnote.

Foster's profession from nurse to scientist in the *Thor* movie are ill considered; Jane the brave paramedic healer who runs into the combat zone to save lives seems to me far more likely to prove attractive to warrior Thor than Jane the theoretical particle physicist who can't drive; even Jane the gentle nurse from Thor's second Marvel Comics appearance in *Journey Into Mystery* #84 (1962) is a better fit.

The comics originals have mostly survived for a long time because of the basic strength of their early material. It's been refined by constant work. Things that didn't work have long gone - the umbrella on DD's billy club[115] and Ace the Bat-Hound,[116] for example - and what's left is golden. The strongest properties are the ones with distinctive themes that drive the character and dictate the kinds of stories they get - Superman, Batman, Captain America, and the Hulk are probably the most obvious. A good movie understands those themes, translates them to the screen with deft adaptation, substitutes only what is necessary to suit a different medium and a different story length. A poor movie allows a committee to 'improve' the product. Then we get *Avengers: United They Stand,* [117] or *Green Hornet.* [118]

Let's acknowledge that continuity is a great tool. Character is an essential element.

***

---

115 Blind Marvel superhero Daredevil uses a two-piece billy club as his primary weapon. These days it includes only a long shootable line for swinging between buildings or tethering foes. In its early days though it included a range of amazing gadgets, such as a boomerang (*Daredevil* #4), a curtain on a rod (ibid.), a smoke screen (*Daredevil* #7), a miniature tape recorder and a "snoop-scope" (*Daredevil* #8), nutritional tablets (*Daredevil Annual* #1), and subway tokens. Its greatest utility was probably in *Fantastic Four* #40, wherein it becomes a rifle and includes a "telescoping flexi-shield".

116 The crimefighting canine debuted in *Batman* #92, June 1955, by Bob Finger and Sheldon Moldoff, and appeared fairly regularly until 1964.

117 This short-lived 2009 Fox animated adaptation lasted a mere 13 episodes. It included a strange line-up of Avengers that did not include Thor at all outside the titles sequence and featured Captain America and Iron Man in one episode each. Perhaps its strangest feature was that the team all wore "battle armour" that obscured their traditional costumes and served no discernable purpose.

118 This refers to the disappointing 2011 film adaptation featuring Seth Rogen as the title character, which Roger Ebert gave one star, calling it "An almost unendurable demonstration of a movie with nothing to be about. Although it follows the rough storyline of previous versions of the title, it neglects the construction of a plot engine to pull us through."

19.
How Americans Come From Troy

THIS IS THE STORY of how modern Americans descended from the survivors of Troy.

According to Greek myth and later Roman glosses of it, Troy (or Ilium) was founded by Ilus, son of Troas – people liked naming cities after themselves back then. Illus was of divine lineage; he could trace his ancestry back to Zeus seducing the Pleiad Electra.[119] His family had a habit of marrying the daughters of river gods, and Illus did that too.

This line of kings carried on until King Laomedon annoyed Hercules by refusing to pay up for the monster-slaying that saved his daughter. Hercules wiped out the entire royal family except for one infant son, Priam, whom he placed on the throne before wandering off to his labours again. Priam grew up to become the powerful patriarch who ruled Troy at the time of the Trojan War. Paris, who stole Helen and triggered the conflict, was one of Priam's fifty sons.

The fall of Troy is best known from Virgil's *Aeneid*, which recounts the wooden horse gambit and describes the final destruction of the city that was thought to be impregnable. Nearly all the Trojans come to horrible ends, the heroes slaughtered and their women taken off into slavery; yet Aeneas, son of a Trojan prince albeit one who was only second cousin to the king, but whose mother was the goddess Aphrodite herself, managed a heroic escape. He saved Troy's household gods (their sacred statues, anyway) and probably the mysterious artefact known as the Palladium (but see below), then gathered together as many survivors as he could save and led them away to find a new

---

119 *Apollodorus* i.4 and others. 'Seduce' may be a soft word for Zeus' approach to the nymph. Electra and five of her sisters were eventually placed in the heavens as the constellation Pleiades. A seventh sister, Merope, the only one who married a mortal rather than caught the eye of a god (Zeus had three of them) was not so commemorated. Various pre-telescope cultures have counted the Pleiades stars differently, usually as six or seven, suggesting an astronomical event changed the magnitude of one of the objects.

land.

The Aenead, a politically-motivated and therefore very positive Roman account of Aeneas' journey, makes clear that he was instructed to do this in a dream by Hector, the greatest hero of Troy. Dead Hector directly handed the hero the sacred flame of Vesta, a literal passing of the torch from the guardian of 'Old Troy' to the guardian of the future of the Trojan people.

After a lot of adventures Aeneas found a new home for his people: Italy. On the way he romanced the Carthaginian queen Dido but he settled down in marriage with Livinia, daughter of King Latinus (from whom comes the name of the language and the people) and he founded a royal house.

Aeneas' alliance with Lavinia ensured peace between and culturally united the peoples that would be Roman. The dynasty continued through Aeneas' son Ascanius by his first wife Creusa. Ascanius was also called Iulus; the Julian-Claudio dynasty argued that Caesar was named after him due to direct descent. Aeneas misplaced Creusa while exiting Troy but she had been a daughter of King Priam, so while Aeneas himself was only peripherally royal his descendants came directly from the line of Ilus.

Generations later it was this lineage that produced the princess Rhea Silvia, whose usurping uncle forced her to become a vestal virgin so she could never marry and confer sovereignty on a king that might displace him. Despite this, the maiden was 'found' by the god Mars who fathered twins upon her. Since it really wasn't a good thing for a vestal to get pregnant, the children were exposed on a mountain to die. Instead of perishing they were suckled by a wolf and survived. Their names were Romulus and Remus, and they overthrew the wicked uncle and founded Rome.

So, according to Livy and others, descendants of the Trojan survivors founded Rome. Some of the Trojan sacred objects made their way to the city and were lodged there.

So to the account from 12th century chronicler Geoffrey of Monmouth, *The History of the Kings of England*. He claims that generations before Rhea Silvia, Aeneus' grandson Brutus was exiled from Italy for accidentally killing his own father with an arrow. Brutus could trace his ancestry not only back to the ancient kings of Troy and to Zeus but to either Ham or Japeth, sons of Noah.[120] Anyhow, Brutus went on his adventures, liberating Trojan slaves from the Greeks in Africa and leading them up through Gaul, founding cities as he went (Tours and Paris, for example).

Brutus received a vision of a distant isle at the ends of the world, a place

---

120 A story also promulgated by early British scholar Nennius.

populated by giants and monsters, and he led his people there to tame the land and settle it. The country was said to derive its name from him: Britain. He killed the fearsome giants Gog and Magog and founded a capital, New Troy (Trinovantium, the Roman name for London). So the descendents of Troy became the ancient Britons, the Celtic peoples.

This 'history' is now dismissed as fable by modern scholars, but it was taught as and believed as fact up to the seventeenth century. It was 'common knowledge'. To this day the annual Lord Mayor's parade in London includes carved images of Gog and Magog.[121]

Brutus' descendants were recorded as including old king Cole (a merry old soul) and King Lear. A female descendant of this house married a Roman governor of Britain, consolidating his "right" to rule the realm, converted her husband to Christianity, and gave him a son, Constantine, who rose to become the first Holy Roman Emperor.[122] Constantine's grandson was held to be Uther Pendragon. His great grandson was King Arthur.

Later waves of conquest mixed Celtic and Roman blood. Saxon invasion pushed many Celts to the lands they now occupy in Wales, Ireland, and Scotland; other Celtic princesses married into Saxon lines. Norman invasion took the land from the Saxons, but believing in the legends of Trojan kings the Normans were keen to intermarry with princesses of ancient lines – and

---

121 Mythological sources such as Geoffrey of Monmouth tell of giants who were defeated and enslaved by the survivors of Troy that tamed and settled in Britain.

By the reign of Henry V there were giant statues residing in Guildhall. By 1554 they appeared in the Lord Mayor's Show under the names of Gogmagog and Corineus. The earliest effigies were destroyed in the 1666 Great Fire of London and a second pair replaced in 1708. The current set was carved in 1953 modelled on the previous effigies that were destroyed in the London blitz.

Thomas Boreman's *Gigantick History* (1741) recounts that "Corineus and Gogmagog were two brave giants who richly valued their honour and exerted their whole strength and force in the defence of their liberty and country; so the City of London, by placing these, their representatives in their Guildhall, emblematically declare that they will, like mighty giants, defend the honour of their country and liberties of this their City which excels all others, as much as those huge giants exceed in stature the common bulk of mankind."

The Bible mentions "Gog and Magog" in Ezekiel 38.4 and Revelation 20.7-10.

122 This is Geoffrey of Monmouth's claim anyway. He maintains that Helena was a princess, daughter of the English King Cole, and that her son Constantine was therefore a rightful heir to the throne of Britain; so it was a Briton who went on to become the Roman Emperor who brought the empire to Christianity. Modern scholarship follows 6th Century historian Procopius who favours Helena being of humble Bythnian (Turkish) origin, possibly a concubine slave of Constantine's father Flavius Constantinus. As a saint, her feast day is either 21st May or 18th August depending on denomination.

Meanwhile, the historical Constantine's father rose to be Emperor as Marcus Flavius Valerius Constantius Herculius Augustus, co-ruling with Maximian then Galerius from AD 293-306.

For more on Constantine see Chapter 33 section 3.

did.

By the time of the recorded discovery of America, the English race as a whole had coalesced, and it was the English, Irish, Scots, and Welsh colonists that eventually established sufficient dominance in North America to ensure that language, law, and much of its culture derived from their own backgrounds. That's not to diminish the contribution of other European settlers or indigenous peoples, but for the sake of making this argument that's how Trojans came to be Americans and America became the New New Troy.

Q.E.D.[123]

If you're are European American then you're also descended from Zeus, Aphrodite, a bunch of river nymphs, and one of Noah's sons too. Congratulations.

The Palladium

ACCORDING TO Pseudo-Apollodorus' *Bibliotheca*, the goddess Athena was fostered with her uncle Poseidon and raised with his own daughter Pallas. One day Athena accidentally slew her best friend and confidante as they wrestled. Remorseful Athena forged the Palladium statue as Pallas' memorial. The sacred object was placed in the goddess' shrine, probably at Samothrace, where it became a mystery cult object.

Enter Elektra the Pleiad as previously described, pregnant by Zeus, distressed and outcast. Various sources recount that Elektra profaned the statue by touching it when not a virgin, or was granted the talisman to take with her as a blessing, or that it was gifted to her son Dardanus. In most versions the Palladium was cast into the territory of Ilium where it became part of Troy's founding myth. Ilus was said to have been blinded when he touched it to carry it from a burning temple.

The virtue of the Palladium was that while it remained in the city, Troy could not fall. During the Greek siege, Odysseus learned of the sacred object and he and Diomedes managed to steal it, thus opening the way for that gambit with that wooden horse statue later.

The Romans were very keen to establish that the Palladium had made its way to Rome. In some of their stories the stolen Palladium was a fake and the real deal was spirited away with Aeneas. Others claimed that it was stolen

123 At least if you're not an African American, Native American, Inuit, or from some family that didn't originate from Western Europe. That's a whole other essay.

again from Diomedes, or that he'd taken the object to Italy himself. In any case it ended up in the Temple of Vesta in the Roman Forum. Pliny the Elder recorded that Metellus was blinded like Ilus when he had to carry the statue to safety during the great fire of 241 B.C.

The Palladium was transferred again by the controversial and short-lived Emperor Elagabus into his temple to Deus Sol Invictus, the Elagabalium, around A.D. 220. It was said to have been moved by Constantine the Great away from Rome and buried under the Column of Constantine in Byzantium, thus finally transferring its protection to the new Roman centre. If true then the Palladium may still be there, since the Column still stands and is now a World Heritage Site.

Or of course the Palladium could have found its way to England and become the London-stone.

And In Other Pilfered Legends...

THERE'S A LONG TRADITION of the British trying to horn in on the big stories of history. One very ancient tradition, going back over eight hundred years in documents but allegedly much more than that in local lore, is that Joseph of Arimethea was a regular trade visitor to England, perhaps buying Cornish tin. After Christ's resurrection Joseph returned to England as a missionary, planted his staff at Glastonbury where it blossomed into a living thorn tree. He founded a wattle-and-daub chapel there, the first Christian church in England, and lived out his life preaching the gospel from it.

Other sources, following an early church tradition that Joseph of Arimethea was related to Jesus, perhaps his uncle, even go so far as to claim that some of Jesus' "missing years" before he began his ministry at around the age of thirty were spent travelling with Joseph. That tradition holds that the young Jesus also visited England. It's the source of William Blake's great poem and later the hymn *Jerusalem*, "And did Those feet in ancient times/ Walk upon England's mountains green?/ And was the holy Lamb of God/ In England's pleasant pastures seen?"

What is fact is that a flowering thorn tree still grows at Glastonbury today, an unusual mutant strain of winter-flowering - usually Christmas Day-flowering thorn. Tradition says it is a cutting from the original tree planted by Joseph of Arimethea. That first tree was chopped down by a soldier of Cromwell who was subsequently struck blind. New Age adherents of Glastonbury are convinced the tree was on a major sacred ley alignment.

The ancient tree in the ruins of Glastonbury Abbey died in 1991 and was felled in 1992. However, many cuttings had then been cultivated and some of them are old and mature trees themselves. Every Christmas Day a pupil from nearby St John's Infants School cuts a sprig of the flowering thorn (now from the tree in the churchyard of St John) to be sent to the British monarch; the custom dates back to around 1570, the reign of James I.

Another ancient thorn of the same stock on Wearyhall Hill outside Glastonbury was deliberately destroyed by vandals in 2010, and subsequent attempts to replant from rootstock have been sabotaged.

Medieval romancers maintained that Joseph not only retired to England but brought with him the two greatest sacred artefacts of Christ's life, the cup used for the last supper, which had also been used to catch Christ's blood as he bled on the cross, and the spear of the Centurion Longinus which had pierced Christ's side to prove his death; also known as the Holy Grail and the Holy Spear.[124] Joseph's descendants became the keepers of these mystic treasures, the Fisher Kings.

One such Fisher King, Pellam, was accidentally maimed with the Holy Spear, which Dolorous Stroke began the Enchantment of Britain at the time of King Arthur and eventually led to the quest for the recovery of the Holy Grail which could heal Pellam and the whole wounded land.[125]

Pellam's daughter Elaine slept with Sir Lancelot (he thought she was Guenevere at the time) and conceived Sir Galahad, the best knight in the world who would one day achieve the Grail.

It's remarkable to think that this kind of thing, along with other medieval "common knowledge" such as Prester John's kingdom, the Seven Sleepers of Ephesus, the Terrestrial Paradise, the Fortunate Isles, the siren Melusine, and the Mountain of Venus, was taught as fact for hundreds of years. It is the 'backstory' of much of our literary heritage.

As Miriam "Ma" Ferguson, the first woman governor of Texas (1924) is reputed to have declared to the head of the Joint National Commission of

---

124 This idea first crops up in the late 12th century *Joseph d'Arimathie* by Robert de Boron and was quickly adopted by the Grail legend literature industry that proliferated across the middle ages.

125 Pellam's unhealed wound was "in the thigh", a medieval euphemism like "between the legs". When he received the Dolorous Stroke his whole realm was reduced to wasteland and the usual laws of nature were shattered. Only the Fisher King being healed could heal the land.

This echoes back to ancient Celtic folklore about the realm's fertility being linked to that of its ruler. It's why old kings whose queens have died and who are therefore incapable of quickening the realm have beautiful princess daughters that require a hero who can make the land prosperous and whole again.

Languages, "If English was good enough for Jesus Christ, it's good enough for me!"

***

20.
A Pulpy New Year!

NEW YEAR is probably the most popular specific time of year for pulp fiction. That's when Honest Jack Action huddles in the corner of a smoky bar, lost in the booze and the past, almost oblivious of the classy dame shimmying towards him. It's exactly when Dr Destructo intends to set off his Mindworm Devices to conquer the Earth. It's when Vic Valiant has to chase the villain across the snowy rooftops while Big Ben tolls midnight and the fuses burn down around the Commissioner's daughter.

Christmas is a competitor, because it's fun to juxtapose those warm log fires and yellow-lit interiors with the bleak blizzard outside. Dark deeds seem that much darker against a cosy yuletide backdrop. But even Christmas can't match the pulpy power of the old year ending and a new one starting for good or ill.

Most stories set on Earth either ignore the season or generalise. Maybe the weather has to be bad for plot reasons, or the season is specific for pathetic fallacy; falling leaves are excellent for that, and so is frozen earth (especially around graves). But I'm hard pressed to think of *any* story that takes place on New Year's Eve or at Christmas by *accident*.

That's because fiction has to be more believable than real life, and because writers need to focus their readers on only those things relevant for the story they have to tell. In the same way that the hero doesn't bump into a neighbour who's on his way to the laundry and has a chat about his maiden aunt's lumbago unless it fiendishly turns out to be somehow plot-relevant in the end, so remarkable weather and notable times of year distract from the story and are thus omitted.

For example, how would *Farewell, My Lovely*[126] been improved by Christmas trees? In what way would "The Problem at Thor Bridge"[127] have

---

126   Raymond Chandler's 1940 Philip Marlowe novel.
127   From *The Casebook of Sherlock Holmes*, 1922, by Sir Arthur Conan Doyle

been bettered by occurring at New Year? Any stories *accidentally* happening at Easter, Hallowe'en, or any solstice or equinox are simply impossible.

That's because some holidays and some extreme weather forms are so distinctive that they have a narrative pull all of their own. New Year's Eve can never be a neutral backdrop. The characters simply *have* to react to it or else seem unrealistic. Unless the hero spends a moment with his old regrets or the villain is motivated by a burning resolution to wreak vengeance before the calendar turns, the time seems like a distraction, a nagging plot thread that doesn't fit. If it's New Year, or Christmas, or thunderstorming, or blizzarding, or a heatwave then it *has* to either be plot relevant or mood-setting. Literary convention insists on no less.

On the other hand, stories that do avail themselves of readers' expectations of an intimate family Christmas or of the countdown to the next millennium have a powerful tool. The problem is it's a much-used tool. If the writer wants to present a Christmas ghost story then the Ghost of Dickens Past peers over his shoulder. Any fictional teens who decide to spend a night making out in the old abandoned mansion on Hallowe'en must beware cliché as much as they shun the mad old groundskeeper. And archvillains about to launch the New World Order as the year turns had better book their place in the rota early, because there'll be a queue.

As each January 1st approaches, we ignore the fact that our calendar is somewhat arbitrary and take the opportunity to reflect upon joys, sorrows, and sins past, upon achievements and failures, upon lost friends and precious memories. We're also drawn to the future, to hopes or fears for the days ahead, to new resolutions, to changes that the coming days must mark. New Year is a birthday that the whole world shares, with similar celebrations and self-analysis. And so it is for our characters, with all the dramatic potential that offers. A writer's challenge is to use the setting as skilfully as any other pulp trope – the driving rain, the teeming railway platform, the unrelenting desert heat, the funeral of a friend etc – and make that countdown… count.

Let the world tremble. The hours comes!

Happy New Year. Whenever you are.

***

21.

How the Inventor of the Postal Service Was Responsible for the American War of Independence

NO, REALLY. He was!

Actually, there are over a dozen claimants for the honour of first inventing the postage stamp, starting with William Dockra's 1680 London Penny Post which hand-stamped paid letters. However, it's indisputable that the person who *formalised* the United Kingdom's postal service, setting mailcoach routes and delivery times and generally creating the format of the modern service as we know it now, was England's second Postmaster General, a disgraced senior politician titled Baron le Despencer.

He was better known as "the wickedest man in Britain", Sir Francis Dashwood, leader of notorious and decadent Hell Fire Club.

Dashwood was master of the revived "Knights of Hell-Fire" that had first flourished under the Duke of Wharton up to its suppression in 1721. Dashwood's incarnation of the gentleman's society began in the 1730s when he was in his twenties, but the Order of the Knights of St Francis was not properly instituted until 1746, by which time Dashwood was wealthy and powerful enough to command lavish parties with exotic and erotic entertainments.

His club enjoyed a high-class membership, including Cabinet members, Lords, and allegedly a Royal Personage. Amongst the key members were John Montagu, 4th Earl of Sandwich, for whom the well-known foodstuff was named, libertine Paul Whitehead, debauchee George Selwyn, George Bubb Doddington "the most corpulent man in England", and Thomas Potter, son of the Archbishop of Canterbury. William Hogarth was probably also a member; he certainly painted Dashwood in Hell Fire Club persona (in a parody of Renaissance images of Francis of Assisi).

Contacts like these, made closer by illicit debaucheries and secret "entertainments", made Dashwood both popular and connected in high society.[128]

In the 1750s an American traveller named Benjamin Franklin attended several events and was probably one of "the Monks of Medmenham" (so named for the Thames isle containing the ruined abbey where some of the Club's more private revels were held).

Dashwood and Franklin became friends and allies, and for a long time it seems to have been their dialogue which pushed forward attempts to reform Anglo-American trade, tax, and political representation issues.[129] At that time Dashwood, and probably Franklin, sought seats for elected American MPs in the British House of Parliament, in much the way that MPs were returned from the various parts of Scotland, Wales, and Ireland. This was the first meaning of the slogan "no taxation without representation".

Dashwood's political clout moderated much anti-American sentiment within his own party and held back the war-hawks who felt that America should be treated no differently than colonies held by Great Britain that were "not settled by Englishmen". There's at least a case for arguing that negative British response to American complaint was moderated for a decade in the quiet corners of Hell Fire Club revels.

In 1762 Dashwood was at the height of his political career. Tory Member of Parliament for his own estate of High Wickham, that year he was appointed Chancellor of the Exchequer (Americans would perhaps say Secretary of the Treasury), one of the three most important roles in government. Dashwood commented at his appointment that he was incapable of understanding "a bar bill of five figures", and went on to be one of the most unpopular and incompetent incumbents of that post - against some fierce competition for the honour. Less than a year later, after bungling a tax on cider and causing riots in the streets, he resigned in disgrace.

Everything began to crumble from 1763. The nation's tastes were changing, and the roaring boisterous years were ending. Prominent Hell Fire Club member John Wilkes was expelled and penned a damning expose for *The North Briton* news-sheet. Dashwood's "political cover" failed him for the first time when he had to resign his Cabinet post as Chancellor. The old boy network was shying from the spotlight of scandal. Dashwood suffered the fate of so many spectacularly failed British politicians – he was elevated to

---

128 Dashwood was an inspired prankster. While a guest of the Russian royal court at St Petersburg he created a stir by dressing as the King of Sweden, the Tsar's great enemy.

129 There's a variant view that Franklin was spying for America, looking for weak spots he could exploit for the colonies' benefit; but evidence is sparse and the possibility does not fit with our present thesis.

the House of Lords.

However, the Baron le Despencer was still in demand. In subsequent years he served as Master of the Great Wardrobe, a leftover medieval role which was one of the two greatest sinecure posts of the King's household.[130] He was appointed Postmaster General, at which he proved surprisingly effective. He even helped to write the Anglican *Common Book of Prayer*.

But worse was to come.

Wilkes was arrested for seditious libel against the King. His former closeness to Dashwood cast a shadow over the Baron le Despencer. Around the same time, a satirical novel by Charles Johnstone, *Chrystal, or the Adventures of a Guinea*, featured thinly veiled caricatures of the Monks of Medmenham, exposing them to mockery and moral outrage. The twin scandals broke Dashwood's influence over government and over Tory policy. He became a joke and a byword, and if he had good ideas or an advanced understanding about the American problem then nobody was listening. Not to him. Not to Franklin.

It's impossible to say whether Dashwood retaining his influence would have shifted British policy enough to offset revolution. Things had become so much more serious in Europe since those hedonistic days of young wastrels dressed as monks chasing prostitutes dressed as nuns through the pleasure gardens of Dashwood's High Wickham estate, or the satirical rites at scenically ruined Medmenham Abbey where the Earl of Sandwich had been terrified when he mistook an ape for the Devil.[131] There was revolution and terror in France, economic discontent at home. Perhaps those two unlikely Anglo-American partners might have held off their hotter-headed confederates. Perhaps not.

But once Dashwood's Hell Fire Club revels exposed him and his cronies, any chance for that was gone. Britain took a hard line. America dumped tea. Hence the Postmaster General's private life undermined international diplomacy and committed two nations to war that changed the world.

***

---

130 The other was Chamberlain.

131 It was rabble-rouser revolutionary Wilkes who once smuggled an ape with a horned head-dress and cloak into a Hell Fire Club ritual. At the height of the ceremony the creature was released to rampage amongst the "congregation", many of whom believed their mockery had raised the devil. It leapt onto Sandwich's back and clung there while the distraught and panicking Earl cried out and repented of his sins.

22.
The Dead Man Who Outsmarted Hitler

THE CORPSE of Major William Martin of the Royal Marines washed up on the beach at Punta Umbria, Spain, on 30th April 1943. A briefcase was handcuffed to his belt. A local pathologist decided that the courier had died when his plane had crashed into the ocean. Attempts by the British Consul to retrieve the documents on the body were thwarted by a German agent, and Martin's effects were spirited away to Berlin.

Amongst Martin's other property such as a photo of his sweetheart, a letter to her, and a receipt for an engagement ring was private correspondence from Lt. Gen. Sir Archibald 'Archie' Nye, Vice Chief of the Imperial General Staff to General Sir Harold Alexander, commander of 18th Army Group in Algeria and Tunisia, outlining the Allies' plans to invade Greece and Sardinia by feigning an attack on Sicily.

This intelligence breakthrough came at a critical time for the Nazis. The Axis war machine was being halted at terrible cost. Both sides knew that the next logical step for the Allies was to attempt mass landings in southern Europe, most likely Sicily but just possibly Greece. Now it became clear that Allied High Command hoped to pin vital German forces with a feint at the boot of Italy so as to divert attention – and hopefully divert Nazi tanks and planes – from a surprise assault through the Balkans.

Some German intelligence analysts were sceptical. Sicily was indeed the logical next target after Allied success in North Africa. Although the Axis powers had fortified the island so there'd be a terrible butchers bill if it was attacked, controlling the island would open the Mediterranean to Allied shipping. Even Churchill had privately admitted, "Everyone but a bloody fool would know that it's Sicily."

And that, of course, was why Major Martin's letter made some sense. If *everyone* knew Sicily was the target, then it would be easy to fool the German

High Command to concentrate resources there and leave Greece vulnerable.

Hitler congratulated his intelligence team, overruled Mussolini's doubts, and diverted divisions from Sicily to the Balkans and Greece. Rommel was sent to Greece to command the defence. Two weeks after the Allies invaded – Sicily.

The Nazis held back reinforcements because they expected the main attack elsewhere, because of Martin's information.

But the thing is, Major Martin never existed.

There was an MI5 group called the Twenty Committee. Twenty in Roman is XX, or a double-cross. This was the team that co-ordinated double agents, dirty tricks, and unorthodox war strategies. Part of their network was the Special Operations Executive, tasked with assisting overseas resistance and spreading disinformation. The SOE were based in Baker Street, London, and borrowed their nickname from the street-urchins who assisted Sherlock Holmes in his cases: the Baker Street Irregulars.

They were also sometimes called the Ministry of Ungentlemanly Warfare, and they prided themselves on tearing up the rulebook (preferably to use it to make an Axis fuel dump explode) so they often didn't wear uniforms or ID tags. This meant they were classified as spies if they were captured, and were therefore not covered by the humanitarian treatment supposedly guaranteed to military combatants.

The SOE core staff was about 13,000 strong. One third were women. They had an estimated one million "associate" operatives across the world.

Major Martin didn't exist – and he worked for them.

The Allies needed to take Sicily, but they needed the Axis to weaken their formidable grip on the island. Hitler must be convinced that the actual targets were Sardinia and Greece so he'd pull units out of Sicily to defend them. Department Twenty handed down the mission to the Irregulars.

The idea for how to do the job came from Ian Fleming – yes, *that* Ian Fleming.[132] It was his suggestion, developed by RAF Flight Lt. Charles Cholmondeley[133] and Royal Navy Lt. Cmdr. Ewen Montague, to create a fake officer to suffer a fake fatal accident and deliver fake vital information to real Nazi intelligencers.

Captain (Acting Major) William Martin, Royal Marines, assigned to Headquarters Combined Operations, was brought to life. His legend was mapped out in exquisite detail. He was born in 1907 in Cardiff, Wales. WAF

132 After the war Fleming became famous as the creator and author of James Bond. Much of Bond's character and exploits were rumoured to be autobiographical.
133 This surname is always pronounced 'Chumly'

officers were auditioned to be his fiancée "Pam"; clerk Jean Leslie got the part and posed for photos. Pam's love letters were probably penned by Victoire Evelyn Patricia 'Paddy' Bennett, later Lady Evelyn Ridsdale, who worked for Admiral John Henry Godfrey. Fleming would later model Moneypenny and M on the two of them.

Famed pathologist Sir Bernard Spilsbury found a suitable corpse. A tramp who had died by rat poison was "adjusted" to make it appear that he had drowned.

'Martin' was further equipped with a pompous letter from his father, one from the family solicitor, and a letter from Ernest Whitley Jones, joint general manager of Lloyds Bank, demanding payment of a £79 19s 2d overdraft, a used twopenny bus ticket, London theatre ticket stubs, a bill for four nights' lodging at the Naval and Military Club, and a receipt from Gieves haberdashers for a new shirt. All were on authentic stationary. So as to offset everything he carried being "just too perfect", Martin's HQ pass was deliberately forged to have expired a few days earlier, suggesting he had overlooked renewing it, and his ID card was marked as a replacement for one that had been lost.

The Gieves receipt was mistake, though. No gentleman would think of paying *cash* for his shirts at Gieves; but the Nazis didn't know that.

Martin's loss at sea was published in the Times' list of casualties and his body was conveyed by submarine to where it would wash on the beach. The whole action was designated "Operation Mincemeat".

When 'Martin' washed up on the shore with his vital documents in the briefcase secured to his belt, British ambassadors were instructed to demand the return of body and papers from the Spanish authorities. German agents and Fascist sympathisers colluded to get to the documents first and secretly copied them all; just as the Irregulars had hoped.

Hitler fell for it. Three Panzer divisions were diverted to Greece, two of them from the hard-fought Eastern Front. A group of R Boats were shifted from Sicily. When Operation Husky, the Allied invasion of Sicily, began, the Nazis delayed for three days before deciding that it was not a mere feint and sending in reinforcements. Sicily fell.

Moreover, the sting of being fooled by the Martin documents lasted for the remainder of the war. When later genuine Allied documents were discovered under similar circumstances their contents were dismissed by intelligencers determined not to be bamboozled again.

Major Martin was buried in the Nuestra Señora de la Soledad cemetery,

Huelva. The Commonwealth War Graves Commission amended the inscription on his tombstone in January 1998. It now reads, "Glyndwr Michael served as Major William Martin."

And that's how a dead man who never existed fooled the Fuhrer and changed the course of the war.

***

23.
The Wesley Poltergeist

THERE ARE AROUND 12 million Methodists in the world, over half of them in the USA. I wonder how many folks who follow the teachings of founder Reverend John Wesley know of the rather odd ghost story he was part of during his youth?

Wesley was brought up at Epworth, Lincolnshire in the early 1700s, in the parish rectory.

The place is very different now from how it was three hundred years ago. At that time the whole area was fenland, cold wet bog with lots of impenetrable tangled wetland woods stretching fifty miles or more to the sea. That part of England was notorious for its smuggling and poaching because the small inbred communities united to thwart revenue and customs men. It was near to 200 miles away from the civilising influences of Oxford and Cambridge or the authority of London – and probably about a century behind in social development.

To the village of Epworth in 1697 came new rector Samuel Wesley, the son of a vicar and a vicar's daughter, married to vicar's daughter Susanna on whom he fathered nineteen children, ten of whom lived to adulthood. High church, academic, fiercely Tory (Conservative), he was not a good match for the insular secretive people of the fens. Financial problems, including some time in prison for debt, did not help. His quarrels with the locals probably peaked in 1709 when some of them set his house on fire.

The most controversial of the things that Samuel preached from his pulpit was his support of government plans to drain the fens as the Dutch had in Holland, using a network of long dykes. This process actually happened over the 18th century and transformed the dense wild wilderness into the endless level pastureland that characterises much of Lincolnshire today. Suffice to say that the work was not done with wholehearted local support from any but landowners who would grow rich from the farming rights.

It was in this atmosphere of rural isolation and dislike that one of the best-recorded real-life ghost stories of all time played out. The source of the story: John Wesley's letters and his family's own diary accounts!

In December 1716, young John Wesley was thirteen years old. The significant events of his life as an Anglican vicar, his travels to America, the meeting at Aldersgate at which his "heart was strangely warmed", his expulsion from the Church of England, his role as the founder of Methodism and all the rest of his adventures physical and spiritual were all far ahead of him.

On December 2nd at 10pm, Samuel's manservant Robert Brown was sitting with a maid in the dining room when there was a knock at the door. No-one was there. He answered the knocking on four more occasions before retiring for the night; except that he found the hand-mill at the top of the stairs turning by itself! In bed he heard the sound of a turkey gobbling and then someone moving around his room.

The next morning, when Brown and the maid reported their fright the dairy maid mocked them, saying "What a couple of fools you are! I defy anything to fright me." That night as she stored away the butter she had churned she heard knocking from the shelf where the milk was kept. She searched with a candle but as the knocking became louder and louder she panicked and fled the room.

Mary 'Molly' Wesley, John's sister, then aged twenty, was in the dining room when she heard the door open and someone enter with a rustling of silk skirts. The sounds circled the room, passing round the table where Molly read, but she saw nothing. Reasoning that whatever it was would be able to run faster than she, Molly picked up her book and walked away normally.

She recounted the tale that night in the bedroom she shared with her 21-year-old sister Susanna (known as Sukey to distinguish from her mother), making light of the encounter. They were interrupted by a knocking from beneath the table, then a rattling of the iron casement. The frightened girls jumped into bed fully clothed and hid there until morning.

A few nights later, it was Mehitabel 'Hetty' Wesley's turn for an encounter. The 19 year old girl's rota chore was to wait outside her father's room until he was in bed then come when called to remove his candle. As she stood in the landing she heard footsteps descending the attic stair. Then, by her own account:

My sisters heard noises and told me of them, but I did not much believe them till one night just after the clock struck 10, I went downstairs to lock the doors, which I always do. Scarce had I got up the west stairs when I heard a noise like a person throwing down a vast coal in the middle of the kitchen. I was not much frightened but went to my sister Sukey and we together went over all the lower rooms, and there was nothing out of order. Our dog was fast asleep and our cat in the other end of the house. No sooner was I got upstairs and undressing for bed, but I heard a noise. This made me hasten to bed.

Eldest daughter Emilia's turn at removing her father's candlestick was likewise interrupted. Hearing a loud banging from the hall below, she too descended to investigate. When the sound moved to the kitchen she followed. When Emilia reached the kitchen the banging was from the outside kitchen door. When Emilia opened that door the noise stopped. When she closed it the drumming started again. When she opened the door a second time it was pushed back with enough force to pin the girl behind it. Emilia finally pressed the door closed and locked it. The hammering began again. She fled to bed. She reported her experience to her mother the following morning, from whose account this incident is known to us.

Events continued. Emilia summoned her mother to the nursery, where there was the sound of a violently rocking cradle though none had been kept there for years. Mrs Wesley attempted to banish the ghost by prayer. When that failed she told her husband what was going on; until then he had been unaware of the haunting!

That same day, family evening prayers were interrupted by another loud knocking – just as Reverend Wesley commenced his prayers for the King! Devotions on each night following were interrupted at the same point.

After this, Samuel Wesley began a journal of events. Susanna reported them by letter to her oldest son in London. John Wesley later drew on all of these when formulating his account.

By this time the household was speculating about what might be causing such disturbances. There was always the suspicion of locals playing pranks, given the animosity between the Reverend and some of his parishioners. Susanna (the mother) was concerned that the phenomena might be linked to the fate of her brother, who had vanished without trace in service of the British East India Company. Samuel considered it might simply be the work of the Devil. The children of the household nicknamed the ghost 'Old Jeffrey' after a man who had died in the house prior to the Wesley's occupation.

John Wesley's own later theory was that the trouble was a judgement from God on his father for breaking a sacred oath. In 1701, before John was even born, his mother and father had become estranged:

My father observed my mother did not say "Amen" to his prayers for the King. She said she would not, for she did not believe that William was more than Prince of Orange and no lawful King of England. My father vowed he would not cohabit with her until she did. He then took his horse and rode away, nor did she hear anything of him for a twelvemonth. He then came back and lived with her as before. But I fear his vow was not forgotten before God.

Samuel sent for help and advice from his friend and colleague, the Reverend Hoole, vicar of nearby Haxey. As with many modern-day poltergeist cases, the ghost fell silent with an outsider's arrival. Prayers that evening were uninterrupted. However, later that night, Brown warned that "Old Jeffery is coming," having recognised the signs. John Wesley wrote, "It was towards the top of the house, on the outside, at the northeast corner, resembling the loud creaking of a saw, or rather that of a windmill when the body of it is turned about in order to shift the sails into the wind."

When the knocking began, Samuel called out, "Come in, sir!" He and Haxey followed the sounds from room to room and thence to the nursery, where it frightened the three younger children therein: Martha ('Patty') 10, Charles, 9,[134] and Kesiah ('Kazzie'), 7. Kazzie was particularly scared, shaking with fear and sweating. Samuel pointed a pistol at her headboard and threatened to kill the ghost (!) if it did not quit. Haxey pulled the gun aside, warning, "Sir, you are so convinced this is something supernatural. Then you can not hurt it, but you give it power to hurt you!"

Samuel records his own answer: "Thou deaf and dumb devil! Why dost thou fright these children who cannot answer for themselves? Come to me in my study, that am a man!" The ghost responded with a knock like that the Reverend used to announce his own arrival at the gate, banging so hard that "the bedboard nearly broke" – then fell silent.

The following evening the ghost did as instructed. As Samuel attempted to open his study with the only key, the door was flung wide with such force that he was nearly knocked down. He followed knocking to his 14

---

134 If John Wesley was the father of Methodism then his brother Charles was the midwife. Charles wrote the lyrics of many of the most memorable Christian hymns, including "And Can It Be?", "Christ the Lord Is Risen Today", "Come, Thou Long Expected Jesus", "Hark! The Herald Angels Sing", "Love Divine, All Loves Excelling", and "Oh For a Thousand Tongues To Sing".

year old daughter Anne's ('Nancy's) bedroom and sent her away because, "Two Christians are an over match for the Devil. Go downstairs. It may be when I am alone he will have the courage to speak." When the knockings continued, Samuel asked if the spirit was his son Samuel (presumably one of the stillbirths, not his living eldest child, now an adult and away in London). The noises ceased, but from then Reverend Wesley was the centre of the disturbances.

John reported:

"My father was thrice pushed by an invisible power, once against the corner of his bed, then against the door of the matted chamber, a third time against his study door. His dog always gave warning by running whining towards him, though he no longer barked at it as he did the first time."

Susanna recorded:

"One night it made such a noise in the room over our heads as if several people were walking; then run up and down the stairs, and was so outrageous that we thought the children would be frightened, so your father and I rose and went down in the dark to light a candle. Just as we came to the bottom of the broad stairs, having hold of each other, on my side there seemed as if somebody had emptied a bag of money at my feet and on his as if all the bottles under the stairs (which were many) had been dashed into a thousand pieces. We passed through the hall into the kitchen and got a candle and went to see the children. The next night your father would get Mr. Hoole to lie at our house and we all sat together till one or two o'clock in the morning and heard the knocking as usual. Sometimes it would make a noise like the winding up of a jack; at other times, as that night Mr. Hoole was with us, like a carpenter planning deals; but mostly commonly it knocked three and stopped and then thrice again and so many hours together."

Next the family began to see things too. Susanna thought the spirit appeared as "a badger but without a head" when she saw it race under Emilia's skirts. A servant thought it a rabbit. The ghost passed through the house making turkey-gobbling noises and freezing one maid with fright by uttering "a death rattle". The poltergeist would answer raps with knocks of his own, but attempts to communicate with it were met only with animal noises. Latches lifted, doors moved, Nancy was lifted up, bed and all – the whole paraphernalia that we might associate with a modern-day poltergeist story. And as with many poltergeist cases, this one seemed to centre upon a young woman. Hetty was particularly disturbed by the ghost, so frightened that she sometimes had trouble breathing.

Word of the haunting spread. Reverend Wesley was counselled to escape the rectory. He responded, "No! let the devil run from me! I will never run from the devil!" He summoned his eldest son home to help face the situation, then wrote again to cancel the request; the disturbances had ceased!

All these remarkable occurrences took place in around two months. There were isolated later incidents, with Emilia still writing about Old Jeffery in 1750, but the first properly recorded poltergeist story in England ended as mysteriously as it began.

I stayed at Epworth Rectory in 1984, back before its conversion into a Bed and Breakfast, when it was still much the same layout as it had been when it was rebuilt after the 1709 fire. It's a rambling place with uneven floors and odd corners. It wasn't hard to imagine what it must have been like lit by nothing but guttering candles, in the shadow of the church and graveyard, surrounded by those oppressive fens and sullen fensmen. If ever there was a scene and a situation set for some explosion of repression or horror than that crucible must have been it.

Trickery, telepathy, delusion, spirits, devil, or God, take your pick. And yet from that strange soil rose two brothers who between them brought about a worldwide renewal of Christian evangelism.

***

PART THREE: BIOGRAPHIES
In which the author reveals illuminating
incidents from others lives and his own

24.
Monster Hunting For Beginners

"Let's split up. We can cover more ground that way."
– Famous last words

IT WAS 1985. I'd newly graduated from university and I'd got all summer before my first proper job contract started. Six friends and I set out in a battered minibus to see the world – which really meant we drove around the country visiting a bunch of people we knew at college who we'd only said goodbye to four weeks earlier.

Eventually we ended up on the bleak hills of North Yorkshire. Its all craggy steep cliffs and short turf used for sheep-grazing, blasted by a fierce wind off the North Sea. This was once Viking territory and all the place names end in –thorpe or –wick or -ton. The biggest town within fifty miles is Whitby, famous for its ancient abbey and for being the place where Dracula landed in England.

Being students – or very recently students – we were tight on cash. Fifteen miles out of Whitby's where we ran out of petrol. The engine stopped. But this is North Yorkshire, full of steep hills and unexpected ravines. I can tell you, having driven it, that it is possible to free-wheel a minibus fifteen miles down the valleys and coast into the garage just outside Whitby to buy another two gallons.

On the way back we took the scenic route, along one of the countless single-track roads that thread backwards and forwards over that ice age-forged landscape. The objective was to make it to Scarborough, where a girl we knew – let's call her Jane for legal reasons - was waiting to join the tour. I navigated by heading south-east by compass and choosing the forks accordingly.

We ended up down a particularly narrow, particularly windy "private road" that appeared to terminate in a stream. The water was about two feet deep. Closer investigation revealed that about a hundred yards along the watercourse was the other side of the road. It was clearly only used to drive cattle. Maybe a farm tractor used the track. Clearly we had to attempt to drive the minibus along the river bed and follow the route that perfectly led south-east on the opposite side.

It wasn't easy. I had the wheel. Everyone else was wading, directing me so I could drive on the higher stones so as not to plunge the bus into the deeper parts of the stream. On a couple of occasions the lads had to heave a rock out of the vehicle's way, or else push one over to fill a pit.

It took us about half an hour to move a hundred yards, but we made it – to the amazement of the farmer whose backyard we found ourselves driving through as we continued up the opposite hill.

Half a mile along that road we came to a village and decided to stop. The minibus' brakes were soaked and they weren't performing that well. Best to let the machine dry out in the July sun and take a look round the quaint old place we'd fetched up. How many horror films start out like this?

The village was called Egton. There were perhaps fifty houses and an old stone chapel. Having exhausted the possibilities of the local shop/post office – stamps or crisps were about as far as it went – we took a look around the church. It was built about the 1820s, which isn't at all old for England where we have plenty of mediaeval religious buildings and some that go back a thousand years. Still, the place had a pleasing gothic aspect to it, with some nice stained glass and some attractive interior woodwork. And it passed ten minutes.

There was a cheap home-stencilled guide book for sale for 5p (8 cents), with an honesty box. One of the lads, an amateur archaeologist (and years later, Secretary General of the British Pagan Association and a self-avowed witch), purchased the pamphlet and browsed through it. He immediately spotted the bit that explained that the present church in the village had been erected by public subscription "after the old church on the hill had to be abandoned because people were too frightened to use it."

That sent us back to the shop to ask what was so scary about the church on the hill.

The kindly lady behind the counter had clearly been asked this question before, presumably by other groups of young people who were about to be slaughtered by the local slasher. She explained that in the late 1700s the superstitious locals came to believe that the church and graveyard around it were haunted by a Barghest. So pervasive had this superstition become that the church had to be rebuilt at a less-haunted and more convenient spot that wasn't a long haul up a steep hill to the north of the village.

What's a Barghest? We were referred to "the Professor." No, really.

The Professor was an elderly Egton gentleman with an interest in local history. He had published a number of articles on the area in journals and magazines. He was remarkably happy to allow seven scruffy youngsters into his book-lined study and lecture us on local mythology.

A Barghest is the North Yorkshire name for a phantom black hound. It's also called Black Shuck, Padfoot, or Kirkgrim. It is traditionally the size of a horse, with glowing eyes a big as dinner plates. It was believed that the Barghest was a sign of coming death; anyone who encountered it, always by night, would die within a year.

Sometime around the late 1700s (the Professor had the exact dates but I no longer recall them) a series of items appeared in some of the gentleman's periodicals of the time regarding superstitious accounts of a black dog sighted in and around the church at Egton. The parish register, which records births, deaths, and marriages, evidenced an unusually high mortality amongst the villagers during that time. Shortly afterwards subscriptions were collected to move the church to a new location. The Barghest's culpability for the relocation is only inferred.

Barghests are sometimes said not to be able to cross running water.

The Professor had more to say on Kirkgrims (the word derives from the old dialect words for church and ghost). He pointed out that up to the 1700s the main industry of the area was sheep. Once a year farmers would drive their herds to market, travelling huge distances to get a good price for their stock. Many went as far as London, 270 miles away. Once there, these dour Northerners with money in their pockets would stay a week or two to indulge in the pleasures of the wicked city before returning to their sober livelihoods. These farmers drove their sheep with the aid of large, well-trained sheepdogs; not the collie or border shepherd breeds common later but big shaggy wolfhounds, able to protect the flock from large predators including wolves and bandits. When the farmers stayed in London they sent their dogs home, and remarkably the animals made the journey back unattended. The Professor's argument was that big dark-furred sheep-dogs travelling by night might easily give birth to superstitions about phantom hounds.

Black dog ghosts are a common motif in British folklore. The Ratchet Hound, Gabriel Hound, Wish Hound, Dandy Dog, Devil-Dog, Scratch, or whatever local terms is preferred, appears in almost every corner of the isle. They are often associated with night, curses, retribution, or death.[135] In Viking myth, Odin's twin wolves stalked to bring the vengeance of the gods. In Celtic legends, the Wild Hunt chased across the land, a pack of spectral hounds hunting sinners until dawn, and variously led by Herne, King Arthur, King Henry VIII, Sir Walter Raleigh, or the Devil. Sir Arthur Conan Doyle's account of the legendary Hound of the Baskervilles was not drawn wholly from his imagination. Bram Stoker's *Dracula* description of the spectral black dog leaping from the dead man's ship in Whitby was clearly inspired by local Barghest lore.

In any case, the Professor whetted our appetites for Barghests. We set out to ascend the hill to the graveyard where the old church had once stood.

It was an interesting place, atmospheric, overgrown, and so high that we could see for miles around, with a band of azure North Sea to our east. Where the church had once been now stood a locked and derelict chapel of rest.[136] Our archaeologist friend found some holes nearby that he wanted to open up. We restrained him, suggesting that they might actually be graves and that there are still laws about graverobbing.

Heading in a perfectly straight line from the graveyard was a long path of foot-square stones set across the fields. They were not continuous but laid down like stepping stones about three feet apart. We discovered later that this was a medieval lich path (lich coming from another old Viking word, *lik*, meaning corpse). It was the ceremonial route that a coffin was brought to interment when someone died in the neighbouring village that had no church of its own. Except there was no neighbouring village now; every single person there had died of the Black Death back in 1348.

All of this caught our imaginations. We speculated how the abandoned lich path to a dead village might be connected to an outbreak of phantom black dog sightings and deaths. We wondered whether that sinister avatar of death might still be hovering in the graveyard that had been its home. We discussed the matter as we set off in our minibus, and came to an inevitable conclusion.

We would have to come back at midnight and send someone to walk

---

135 Centuries apart Samuel Johnson of dictionary fame and Winston Churchill of prime minister fame used the expression "black dog on my shoulder" to refer to depression.

136 A chapel of rest is an area, though not necessarily part of a church these days, where a corpse is laid out in state for "viewing" before a funeral. These days it allows mourners time with the dead person to make farewells, and increasingly replaces the older custom of "laying out" the body at home. In medieval times, displaying the corpse in a chapel of rest was politically important as well as spiritually and socially - to prove that the deceased really was dead and inheritance could proceed.

through the graveyard alone and see if a Barghest appeared. We decided it would be traditional to acquire a virgin in a white nightdress for the occasion.

And then we went and picked up Jane in Scarborough and explained the plan to her. And in those days I was pretty good at the fast talk.

So, just before midnight we were back above Egton at the old church site. It was an ideal night, clear and full-mooned. It was windy, so Jane was probably pleased to have vetoed the nightgown idea. However, she was a game girl, so while the rest of us took cover behind a dry-stone wall with cameras to record any occult phenomena, Jane ventured into the graveyard to do a widdershins circuit.

It was a weird moment. We'd been joking about up till then, not really expecting anything to happen. It was a lark. Suddenly, as Jane moved off between the gravestones, we all went quiet. There was an atmosphere, a sense of the wild ancient land and the sleeping dead, of old superstitions and old secrets. For a moment we all imagined ourselves into a state where had a black dog with glowing eyes stalked out from the ruined chapel of ease[137] we might not have been surprised.

Jane passed out of sight behind the chapel of rest and did not reappear. I was nominated to go and die next. I hastened into the graveyard to check that Jane was okay.

Jane was okay. A side gate that hadn't been closed before was blocking her way and she was trying to figure out how to open it. She had not been torn to pieces by a monstrous hound. That meant we were fine to sneak behind the graveyard wall and circle round to come up behind the rest of the gang and scare the hell out of them.

We never did get to see the Barghest, which meant that all of us survived the year. The general view was that the no-show was Jane's fault, either for lack of appropriate attire or lack of appropriate virtue. Since I'd dated Jane the year before I was also held potentially partly responsible.

Anyway, Barghest-hunting's the sort of thing you do when you're twenty-one and just out of college, I suppose. It's a young man's game. I'm not sure I'd want to walk that lich-path now and approach that old graveyard by moonlight. I'm certain I wouldn't be luring a twenty year old almost-virgin with me. I don't think I'd want to risk the curse of the Kirkgrim.

---

137 A chapel of ease is a small additional sanctuary built within the geographical boundaries covered by a parish church, simply to make it easy for worshippers who live some distance from the main church to get to services. This was rather more important in days when attendance was compulsory. Chapels of ease were variously erected in rural outposts, as part of castle complexes, or on wayfarer routes. One such chapel formed a part of old London Bridge.

25.
The Most Powerful Woman In Europe
(And Other Monarchs)

ELEANOR OF AQUITAINE was the most powerful woman in the twelfth century, and a direct cause of Robin Hood! Here's why.

At 17, Eleanor was the most eligible heiress in Christendom. Her difficult father[138] had just died, leaving her Countess of Anjou and Aquitaine, then separate kingdoms, roughly 1/5 of modern day France. Not only was she rich she was also said to be the most beautiful woman in Europe.

Within three months of coming into her titles she was invited to visit the son of the King of France. Two weeks later she was his wife. Two years later he was King Louis VII and Eleanor was Queen of France.

But Eleanor wasn't content to stay home. When the French King went on the Second Crusade Eleanor went with him! In fact she organised what today we'd call the logistics, leaving her husband free to hit people in tin cans with heavy objects.

But things didn't work out well between Eleanor and the king. She bore him a daughter but found him an indifferent and unskilled lover - and a bit of a loser generally. Historians now suspect he may have been gay. She asked the Pope for a divorce on the grounds that she and the king were third cousins, and after the birth of a second daughter the marriage was annulled.

Three months later she married Henry, Duke of Normandy (whose father she may have bedded first). Two years after that her new husband became Henry II, King of England![139] Eleanor went from being Queen of France to Queen of England; the French weren't too happy.

---

138 The Count of Poitou carried off by force the wife of his subject the Viscount of Chatellerault and married her adulterously, despite the prohibitions of the church. Eleanor was the product of this scandalous marriage, and was sometimes considered accursed because of her blasphemous origins.
139 We return to Henry II see the section "Some Harrys and a Few Richards", and Chapter 32 section III, "Henry II and the Round Table."

What's worse from a French point of view, Eleanor and Henry between them ruled Normandy, Aquitaine, Anjou and more, the entire western side of France, roughly 2/3 of the modern day nation!

Eleanor fought with her new husband like cat and dog but they made an effective partnership, stabilising England after decades of civil war between the contending would-be rulers King Stephen (Henry's cousin) and Empress Maud (Henry's mother). Eleanor bore Henry eight children. The three girls all went on to become queens. The four boys who lived to adulthood all went on to attack their father, with their mother encouraging them.[140]

What's bizarre is that, as with a modern divorce, Eleanor and her French King ex had one of those strange ex-couple relationships. She married a guy who owned more of France than the French king did. Louis married again. Eleanor didn't get on with his new wife, but later brokered a match between her daughter by Henry and his son by wife #2. After Henry had found out about her backing his sons against him, she tried to go to the Louis VII to get military aid. Henry locked her in a nunnery, not because she was plotting against him, but because he didn't want her seeing her ex.

Stranger yet, Eleanor had Henry II interred at the same place where he'd had her confined, and arranged for herself to be buried beside him on her death. The carved sarcophagi are still there, Henry II and Eleanor side by side, their son Richard Lionheart buried at their feet. Eleanor got the last laugh, though. Her sarcophagus is a few inches taller than Henry's. Youngest son King John might have been buried there too, except by the time he died he'd lost Normandy and the church was in French hands.

What caused a final rift between Henry and Eleanor was the Fair Rosamunde, twenty-five years Eleanor's junior, the new most beautiful woman in Europe, and somebody who hadn't got any interest in scheming or power-struggles and seemed to genuinely care for Henry. Eleanor up with Henry's other mistresses, who were venal and corruptible and easily disposed of. Rosamunde was something out of a fairy tale and became the nation's

---

140 In *De Instructione Principis* (The Instruction of a Prince), Gerald of Wales records: "But it happened that there was a chamber at Winchester beautiful with various painted figures and colours, and a certain place in it which was left clear by the royal command, where a little time after the king [Henry II] ordered an eagle to be painted, and four young ones of the eagle sitting upon it, two upon the two wings, and a third upon the middle of the body, the fourth, not less than the others, sitting upon the neck, and more keenly watching the moment to peck out the eyes of its parent. But being asked by those who were on intimate terms with him what this picture might mean, he said, 'The four young ones of the eagle are my four sons, who will not cease to persecute me even unto death. The younger of them, whom I even now embrace with such tender affection, will sometime at the last insult me more grievously and more dangerously than all the others.'"

darling. In fact the greatest love ballads of the age were all about Henry and Rosamunde.

So Eleanor decided that Henry must go. She encouraged her sons to make it happen. The eldest, also Henry, known as "the Young King" because he was crowned co-ruler even though he never actually got to England's throne, was set on to his father because Henry senior had provoked the murder of Archbishop Thomas a Becket,[141] who had raised Young Henry since infancy. Junior nearly won, too, but died of dysentery. The third son Geoffrey also fought his father but died in a tourney.

That left two potential heirs: Richard, called by some Lionheart for his bravery in war, and John, called Lackland for his poverty (youngest son inherits least) and Soft-Sword for his less impressive battle skills and possibly bedroom deficiencies. Richard went to war with Henry II. John came in on Henry's side, then defected when he thought he might lose. Henry was broken-hearted, lost the will to fight, and died shortly thereafter.

When Richard became king he also went on crusade. During his ten year rulership of England he spent less than seven months in the country. Eleanor was left to keep an eye on things, including the two Justiciars Richard left to run the administration - and to keep John out. When John took over it was Eleanor who sent for her favourite son to come home. When Richard was captured and ransomed on his way back, it was Eleanor who terrified the barons and the church into finding triple the annual tax income of England to pay for his release. In fact Eleanor was formidable enough to force the church to part with a quarter of its wealth! John's attempts to pay for Richard to stay locked up were stomped flat by his mother.

Thereafter, Richard set off to reclaim Normandy, which the French had captured while he was imprisoned and John was being John. Eleanor came with him. Richard and his mum scared the hell out of the French - she knew exactly where their weak spots were. Richard spent the last seven years of his life campaigning in Europe. He died in his mother's arms.

And even then Eleanor wasn't done. She returned to England and "advised" John for the rest of her life. It was only after she was dead that the Barons rose against King John and forced the Magna Carta on him. I'm not

141 The Archbishop of Canterbury and the king had been at increasing odds for some time. Popular legend has it that Henry II angrily exclaimed "Will no one rid me of this turbulent priest?" Four knights interpreted this as a royal command, and on 29th December 1170 they hacked the Archbishop to pieces within Canterbury Cathedral. Within two years the Pope had sainted Becket. Henry humbled himself with public penance at Becket's tomb. The murderers were ordered to serve as knights in the Holy Land for fourteen years.

sure any of them would have dared try it while Eleanor was around to glare at them.

Arguably Eleanor put Henry II on the throne. She certainly but Richard I on the throne. She was responsible for at least a portion of the crippling taxes that are the backstory of many a Robin Hood tale. She was behind the Lionheart's return, which is the culmination of many a Robin Hood movie. There's even old stories of a queen summoning Robin Hood to seek his aid - Eleanor would be as good a candidate as any; she certainly had the charisma and intelligence to consider it (had Robin been real).[142]

In an age where noble women were often traded as commodities, Eleanor turned the system to her advantage and played major league politics with the top rank of European rulers - the Pope, the Holy Roman Emperor, the Kings of France and England... and Eleanor of Aquitaine.

When Disney Princesses Go Bad

NOT ONLY was there one woman who was successively queen of both France and England, there was almost another – and she'd have gone one better, because she'd *also* been Queen of Scotland!

Poor tragic Mary Stuart, Queen of Scots might well have been a pulp story heroine if only there'd been a hero to save her. Sadly there wasn't. Rarely has an innocent girl been so often and so badly betrayed.

Mary (who called and signed herself Marie all her life) became Queen of Scotland when she was six days old, when her royal father died from a surfeit of Englishmen. Her mother, yet another exported French princess, appealed to the French king for support against ambitious Scots nobles who were already clustering round the baby with wedding plans and offers to 'protect' her and her realm. The French king sent 2000 troops to bring Mary to the French court. They stayed to help the queen-mother rule Scotland.

Mary was five when she arrived in France, and she was already the most eligible girl in Europe. Not only was she the Queen of Scotland, whose husband would become King and gain all her lands and wealth thereby, but

---

142 I.A. Watson should know. He's the author of the award-nominated novel trilogy *Robin Hood: King of Sherwood* (2010), *Robin Hood: Arrow of Justice* (2011), and *Robin Hood: Freedom's Outlaw* (2013), and of the forthcoming *Robin Hood: Forbidden Legend*. He also wrote the Robin Hood comic strip "Lionheart's Gold" in *All-Star Pulp Comics* #2 (2013), which included the outlaw's meeting with Eleanor of Aquitaine. His website about Robin Hood, containing links to other features, is at http://www.chillwater.org.uk/writing/robinhome.htm

she was in line for England's throne too. She was a direct descendant of Henry VII. Number one heiress to England, Henry VIII's daughter Elizabeth, was a child of a marriage not recognised by the Pope, and therefore, to French thinking, illegitimate. Mary Stuart was next in line; her husband could claim England as well.

At age five Mary was betrothed to the French king's eldest son, Francis.

Mary had a Disney princess upbringing in France, probably complete with singing and dancing tableware. At fifteen she was tall (5'11), beautiful, witty, melodious, educated, cultured, and very French. She'd been mentored by Diane de Poitiers, the King's mistress (although not tutored in *those* arts), who was considered the most sophisticated woman in France. Catherine de Medici, the king's actual wife, apparently had holes drilled in her husband's bedroom ceiling so she could watch and learn when Diane visited him.

Anyway, Mary wed Francis. Her choice to be wed in white, previously a mourning colour of ill-omen, changed fashion forever.

So far so good. But Francis, a year her junior, was sickly and feeble, hardly a fairy tale handsome prince. His claims as King of Scotland were more or less ignored by the Scots.

A year later, King Henri II of France died in a jousting accident. His son was crowned King Francis II. At sixteen, Mary, Queen of Scots, was Queen of France. She immediately clashed with Catherine de Medici, the queen mother. Catherine, a true Disney wicked witch, did not like surrendering the royal jewels to a mere girl. Catherine's lifelong malice to Mary would doom the young queen.

A mere eighteen months later, sickly Francis II was dead too, of an ear infection. Catherine ordered Mary out of town, out of France. Mary's maternal family, who had been grooming her in hopes of sharing her fortunes, abandoned their support of her and hastily packed her off to England. England refused to let her land, so she made a perilous sea journey by French barque to Scotland; she recorded in her diary how distressed she was to have to order the sea-captain so often to stop flogging the oar-slaves.

Scotland was a foreign land to her. She wasn't really welcome there. She hardly spoke the language. But she was still very eligible; a dozen Scots plots immediately began, to beguile the young widow to marriage. Meanwhile, France continued to claim Scottish fealty based on papers they'd made Mary sign at 15.

Enter young, handsome, swashbuckling Lord Henry Darnley, Mary's cousin. Even at seventeen (three years younger than Mary) he was a heroic figure. "Falling ill" at Mary's castle, he allowed the young queen to nurse him back to health. At some point by his bedside she fell in love. Despite eighteen months of marriage, Mary was probably a virgin until she encountered dashing Darnley. She romantically married him and they set out to forge a new Scotland.

Except that Darnley was an idiot, a womaniser, and a bully. He squandered the popular goodwill Mary had begun to gain in her tours of the nation, swaggered over his political rivals, and sidelined his pregnant queen to run rough-shod over her subjects. When his enemies convinced him that Mary was having an affair with her Italian-French secretary, Darnley and his drunken friends hatched a plot that ended with them bursting into her rooms, stabbing the servant to death, and holding a knife to Mary's swollen belly. Only then did her pleas move the hearts of the assassins to spare her. Darnley 'forgave' her; Mary was broken-hearted that her hero was a swine.

Mary's son James was taken from her early on and became another political asset to be traded and fought over. The difference was that he grew up strong and ruthless and finally clawed his way to rule Scotland and England both and united them as a single realm.

Darnley? He was murdered while recovering from a bout of syphilis. The murderers tried to blow up his house. He heard them and jumped out of the window - on top of them. They cut his throat *then* blew up his house.

Mary was now back in play as an eligible king-making widow. Various Scottish and English lords promised her great things. Lots of Scottish armies gathered then let her down at the last minute. On the way back to Edinburgh, Mary was rescued by the Earl of Bothwell, who led her to the safe refuge of his castle - where he raped her until she agreed to marry him.

Mary's supporters rallied to save her - then faded away or joined Bothwell. A plea for help from France was intercepted and answered by Catherine of Medici. Rather than supporting Mary's claim for the return of her Scots-stolen jewellery, Catherine demanded a share of the loot. A letter begging Queen Elizabeth I of England for aid arrived the same day that the Virgin Queen bought some of Mary's pillaged jewel box from Bothwell.

Married to the villainous Bothwell, locked in a castle in the middle of a loch, Mary was the archetypal damsel in distress. Her plight moved the heart of one of her young jailors, who spirited her to freedom. Various Scots lords rallied to her aid, but when battle was imminent they all vanished again (young jailor included), leaving Mary alone. In fact there was hardly any significant Scottish lord who didn't let Mary down or betray her at some point in her life.

So Mary fled to England and threw herself on Elizabeth's mercy. Elizabeth didn't have any. Mary endured another nineteen years of confinement in various castles but never saw her cousin. Her son grew up and claimed the Scottish throne, but when England enquired if James VI would go to war should his mother be executed, he replied "No".

Sir Francis Walsingham, Queen Elizabeth's Nick Fury[143]-like secret service spymaster set a trap for Mary to incriminate herself through intercepted correspondence with another idiot would-be hero, Antony Babington; when Mary did not demur to Babington's suggestion that he assassinate Elizabeth they were both destined for the block.

Mary was beheaded at the Tower of London by two strokes of a butcher's knife. Her ghost is said to haunt the place; she has every reason to rest unquietly. So ended Mary, Queen of Scots and French, let down by both of them and destroyed by the English - surely one of history's most tragic heroines.

Some Harrys and a Few Richards

A QUICK GUIDE: England has had a series of King Henrys, eight so far, and a trio of King Richards:

• Before Henry II who wedded the redoubtable Elaine, there was Henry Beauclerc, William the Conqueror's fourth son (his older brothers ruled before him but died, one in a "hunting accident" with Henry).

• Richard I was the Lionheart, the crusader. He spent less than six months of his reign actually in England

• Henry III was the son of King John (the unpopular Prince John of Robin Hood fame). This Henry was nine when his father died, but he ruled for fifty-six years.

• Richard II was a son of Edward, the Black Prince, and suffered a troubled reign including the Peasant's Revolt He was eventually deposed by...

---

143 Marvel Comics' spymaster Nick Fury has recently become better known by his portrayal by Samuel L. Jackson in various superhero movies.

- Henry IV (Bolingbroke), the bloke who deposed Richard II. He was a tough warlord but his people never quite got over him seizing the crown, especially after Richard's mysterious demise in prison some months after he'd been replaced.

- Henry V, a.k.a. Bluff Prince Hal, was Henry IV's eldest son. He went on to win the battle of Agincourt and to be played by Sir John Geilgud and Sir Kenneth Branagh.

- Henry VI was Henry V's son and became king when he was nine months old. He never really had a chance; he was a pawn rather than a player in English politics all his life. The War of the Roses happened around him.

- Richard III came to the throne after his eldest brother died and his brother's juvenile sons vanished in the Tower of London. He may or may not have had a crooked shoulder or humpback, depending on who is shouting loudest at the history conference.

- Henry VII (Tudor) was the claimant who overthrew Richard and effectively ended the War of the Roses.

- Henry VIII was he of the six wives and substantial girth, although in his youth he was quite the sportsman and even took on the King of France – personally - in a massive tournament.

All clear? On we go then.

FOR THOSE WHO aren't intimate with English history, the Roses involved in the War of the Roses (1455-1485) were the white rose symbol of the House of York and the Red Rose symbol of the House of Lancaster, the two contending branches of the royal family and their extended network of followers. They don't really equate to the geographical counties of Yorkshire and Lancashire (although these two are ancient rivals, united only by their deep contempt of southern jessies); for example where I live in Barnsley, Yorkshire, was dyed-in-the-wool Lancastrian turf, cheering for Henry V and booing Richard III.

Although the textbooks put pretty clear dates on the civil war it was a long time coming. "The causes" as the history teachers like to call them, went back a long way to the beginnings of the Hundred Years War (England v France. Again)

So, the first thing to decide about the War of the Roses was when it really got started.

In either of the best two cases it was due to a weak king without popular support. Edward II was unpopular because he was a homosexual. He generally gave power, lands, and wealth to whichever lover he had at the moment, which annoyed his queen and his barons. His queen, by the way, was Isabelle, "the she-wolf of France", another in the line of French princesses imported to spice up English royal life over many centuries. Think a thirteen hundreds Joan Collins.

Eventually Edward was locked away in Pontefract Castle and his 15 year old son was crowned King Edward III (at least Isabelle *said* it was his son). Thereafter Edward II died "of a flux", or of starvation, or of having a horn shoved up his rectum and filled with molten metal, depending on whose propaganda you read.

Edward III promptly invaded France again and started the aforementioned Hundred Years War.

Or, it all started much later, near the official date for the War of the Roses (it was so signposted I'm surprised they didn't print invitations to be read to the nobles). Henry V died in his early 30s, leaving his nine month old Henry VI to rule instead. What started as political jostling to be the one to 'guide' the king became an all-out battle complete with poison and daggers, then sword and cannon, over who 'nurtured' the sickly and timid boy. Poor Henry VI got handed round like a present in a game of pass-the-parcel, each new Protector reversing the policies of the last and proclaiming all his personal enemies to be traitors.

In either case, the provocation for the Wars of the Roses can perhaps be casually summarised as a weak king following on from a strong one, perhaps with some trait which prejudiced people against him, with a powerful "showbiz" mother or wife (both were imported French princesses in the historical template), a series of factions with marginally different political goals (invade France vs. invade Holland, tax corn vs. tax wool; everyone was alright with kicking the Irish and Scots), and powerful enemies abroad requiring a strong domestic leadership in an age when there was no natural strong domestic leader.

The War ended romantically though, when the last surviving Lancastrian heir, Henry Tudor, returned from Europe to save the last surviving Yorkist heiress, Elizabeth of York, from a forced marriage to her uncle Richard III. Then Henry and Elizabeth united to found the House of Tudor! You just can't get more pulpy than that in an age before they'd invented railway tracks for her to be tied to.

Of course, the Richard-apologists' views of events may vary.

I once got damn near savaged by members of the Richard III Appreciation Society. I forget which ruined castle it was at, but it was one of the ones that still has towers you can climb, and I was on the battlements at the top of one when I happened to make comments to my wife about Richard that irked the Richardians. They were between me and the stairs. They vigorously defended their idol for around an hour and a quarter.

They had a few good points, though. Like all history, the chronicles of English kings are written by the winners. Most people make their judgements of Richard III based on Shakespeare's retelling of history, which, while artistic and exciting, tends to favour a good story over fact. Plus, Shakespeare was writing his history plays to perform before Queen Elizabeth I, a descendant of Henry V and of the young prince who defeated Richard III and 'saved' the last Yorkist princess.

So where do the Richards and the Henrys really rank in the royal league tables? At least the ones who crop up in or just before the War of the Roses; this is an essay, not a textbook.

Henry V: after a drunken youth he became something of a religious zealot. First he attempted to ethnically cleanse the Scots, and then he provoked an argument with the French to give him an excuse to invade them. He'd been building his navies for a year at the time of the 'trigger incident'.

The French assembled their best chivalry to stop him. He emptied England's jails of the worst cut-throats and football hooligans he could find. Then from the French point of view he cheated by shooting their knights with arrows while they wallowed in a muddy field unable to get to him. And then he stole their princess.

But it's hard to make a serious claim that Henry V was a bad egg. Other Henrys need not apply. Henry IV was a usurping brutal tyrant. Shakespeare glosses over his deeds by making him a guest-star in the plays named after him. Henry VI was a weak failure who lost everything his father Henry V had won. Henry VII did nothing memorable after getting rid of Richard III and was therefore, from the public's point of view, quite a good king. Henry VIII confiscated the lands of the entire church, set up his own denomination with him as boss, killed two wives, divorced two others, tortured and murdered a rebel leader who'd nearly overthrown him after vowing not to harm the man,[144] and left the nation bankrupt. Richard Crookback was a choirboy next to him!

And Richard? He was a patron of the arts and sciences, a supporter of courts over trial by combat, a founder of churches. It's not known whether he really did murder the husband of the woman he later married (she'd died before he went for the Last Yorkist, the Yorkists claimed by foul play) but its true he did convince her to get into bed with him even though she seemed to have believed he did it. That's either Bond-level charm or else its archvillainy.

Even if everything said about Richard was true, he was Dr Doom-evil not Red Skull-evil.[145] In Dungeons and Dragons he'd be lawful evil where Henry VIII was chaotic neutral.[146] All Richard's imputed crimes were either about becoming king instead of a series of less-than-stunning relatives who stood before him in succession or preventing internal civil strife by removing the problem before it got to the battlefield.

Britons tend to be tolerant of leaders who act like bastards as long as they're acting like bastards for England/Britain (c.f. Duke of Wellington, Winston Churchill). It helps if they're quotable too.

"We were, are now, and hopefully always shall be, detested by the French."
– The Duke of Wellington.

***

---

144   Robert Aske, a York lawyer, led the "Pilgrimage of Grace", a march from Yorkshire, Northumberland, Durham, Cumberland and Westmorland to protest the king's dissolution of the monasteries. His popular movement had a very real chance of overthrowing the monarchy, so he was invited to meet with the king in London under safe conduct. He received promises of redress from Henry VIII, along with safe passage home. Then, seizing on further unrest as an excuse, Henry had Aske waylaid on his journey, imprisoned in the Tower of London, then hanged to die in chains on Clifford's Tower in York.
145   A reference to the archvillains of Marvel Comics long-running *Fantastic Four* and *Captain America* comics.
146   Veteran roleplaying game *Dungeons and Dragons* classifies its characters' behaviour on two axis, from good to evil and from lawful to chaotic. Hence a lawful evil villain might keep his word while a chaotic good hero might bend the rules, or a lawful neutral adversary might offer honourable combat while a chaotic neutral one might cheat.

26.
Who's Afraid of Mary-Sue?

IN 1973, PAULA Smith published "A Trekkie's Tale", a parody of fan-written stories. In it, Mary-Sue, "the youngest lieutenant in Starfleet – only fifteen and a half", joins the crew of the USS Enterprise and proves to be essential to the survival of the ship, demonstrating a remarkable competence and claiming a place in the hearts of Kirk, McCoy, and even Spock. The wish-fulfilment character represents a series-enthusiast's fantasy of entering and interacting with the series they love.

Since that time, "Mary-Sue" has become a byword for non-satirical author-inserted characters who seem to be fulfilling the writer's own fantasies, often but not always in an ongoing series that did not originate with them. This character often speaks with the author's voice, correcting what the author feels are problems with the ongoing story, resolving long term situations, earning the gratitude of regular characters, and even displacing romantic leads to win the heart of a favourite cast member.

We see the phenomena in TV, books and comics. Rose Piper in *Doctor Who* is often cited. Of all the Doctor's many companions she alone wins his heart and proves essential to his wellbeing.[147] In Mantis' first appearance in *The Avengers*,[148] her creator Steve Englehart shows how great she is by having her easily beat Captain America and Thor in combat. Brian Bendis has faced

---

147 The author however has little problem with Rose and is a big fan of the series and of its Russell T. Davis era. Don't hurt him. Besides, similar criticisms have been levelled at Amy Pond and Clara Oswald.

148 *Avengers* #144, August 1973. Technically Mantis had appeared in the book before that in foreshadowing silhouettes, but this was her first meeting with the team. The author would also like to mention that he really likes Englehart's work on the series, with the scene being discussed as a rare exception. In fact Englehart even put the author *in* a story with Mantis (*Avengers: Celestial Quest #2*, December 2001) as a wry in-joke response to an article I.A. Watson wrote for *Assembled!*, an collection of essays on the Avengers series from White Rocket Books. The article was entitled "Why Mantis Had To Be a Whore," and the subsequent comic story included a brief scene where 'Ian' purchased the services of the aforementioned character. So at least he got sex with a superheroine – in continuity!.

"Mary-Sue" accusations for his use of his creation Jessica Jones,[149] retconned into Avengers history as a "dear old friend" who has now become an essential staple of the series and romances an established "cool" character.

Other authors write their own primary character as a "Mary-Sue" from the start. This criticism is sometimes aimed at Ian Fleming, for example. James Bond, whom "men want to be and women want", might be an idealised version of his own younger self.[150] There are many omni-competent and always-right characters in adventure and pulp fiction of whom a similar charge might be made.

However, just being generally right isn't enough to qualify a protagonist for Mary-Suedom. The Shadow, Batman, the Doctor, Sherlock Holmes and many other fictional heroes share those traits but cannot really be described as wish-fulfilment vehicles for the author; perhaps for the readers. There's a distinction to make between presenting a competent, dangerous, effective hero and a can-do-no-wrong paragon. Batman's obsessiveness is usually presented as a flaw, often with Robin or some other character poking fun at it. Superman's boy-scout attitude sometimes leaves him open to criticism too. Lots of nearly-perfect heroes are deliberately given some character flaw to humanise them. It's a good thing, because perfect heroes can get pretty boring since they have no story arc or possibility of character progression.

Likewise it's not enough for a new character to simply appear in a story and be helpful to the regular hero, or even to take a short-term spotlight and resolve that particular storyline. The "Mary-Sue" phenomenon precedes from an assumption that the series would be that much better and more fun with an authorial wish-fulfilment character.

Mary-Sues often tend to move the stories they intrude in towards a pat conclusion. They solve long-term problems for the hero with deceptive ease

149 Ex superheroine private eye Jessica Jones debuted in *Alias* #1, November 2001 (no relation to the TV series of the same name), created and written by Brian Michael Bendis. She was established to have been present at key Marvel universe events first depicted long before her character was conceived. For example, she was amongst the students present when Peter Parker was bitten by a radioactive spider. She was established to have fought the Avengers "and received a severe beating" that placed her into a coma. She received psychic therapy from X-Man Jean Grey, Phoenix. She had an affair with SHIELD agent Clay Quartermain. Jessica went on to become pregnant by Luke Cage, bore his child, and joined the Avengers as an old trusted friend of Ms Marvel. She played major roles in many of Marvel's twenty-first century Bendis-driven crossovers such as *Civil War*, *Secret Invasion*, and *Dark Reign*.
150 Fleming invests Bond with some dark edges, particularly in his violent treatment of women and his ruthlessness in achieving his missions. Whether those are meant to be seen as negative traits or whether Fleming was simply having Bond do what he'd like to - or did, according to some commentators - is up for question. For one of Fleming's real-life exploits, refer to Chapter 22, "The Dead Man Who Outsmarted Hitler".

and so earn his eternal gratitude. Romantic situations in particular come to whatever conclusion the writer feels is appropriate, driven by the dynamics of the wonderful new character in the mix.

Mary-Sues don't have to have perfect lives. In fact Mary-Sue's can suffer. Mary-Sues can be misunderstood and misjudged by the world, just like their authors. They can face terrible losses that leave us admiring their courage in the face of tragedy. They can 'turn dark' as long as it's a sympathetic kind of darkness caused by an indifferent and terrible world.

If fact one of the supposed hallmarks of a Mary-Sue character is a distinctive and traumatic background - the last surviving crystal elf princess who saw her whole family massacred and escaped her slavery due to her extraordinary abilities to take her place in our company of heroes, or similar

Consider Harry Potter. He's an untutored but naturally-talented lad whose skills impress all he meets and who regularly takes on the villain that makes all other wizards wet their pants so badly they won't even name him. Each book shows him becoming more powerful and more essential to the wellbeing of the world - and everyone says so. Or is he just an "author favourite" character rather than a character the author might want to be?[151]

It is perhaps also worth distinguishing between those "Mary Sues" put in place by a series originator and those added later by different authors, either by official writers who take over an existing property or by fan-fictioneers. Fans generally resent the intrusion of a later character from another creator more than a later character from the original creator, and a late addition from the original creator more than an original character being an "author vehicle".

Although "Mary-Sue" is often used to label and damn later cast additions to existing rosters by subsequent writers, the term is still regularly applied as criticism of an author's own original work. The *Twilight* series[152] is often condemned for it, for example. Others prefer to distinguish the original author's introduction of an avatar character as "Canon Sue"; I prefer not to get into the absurdity of the terms.

151 Don't think this is a slam on Potter or J.K. Rowling. The *Harry Potter* series offers some delightful tales with some excellent characters and it world-builds second to none. Harry himself stumbles occasionally, unlike the classic Mary-Sue who can do no wrong. In particular Harry's role in *The Order of the Phoenix* is to screw up. Overconfident from his former successes, Harry leads nearly everyone he loves into deadly danger and one of them dies because of it. For once, when Dumbledore told him what to do and not do, Harry should have listened, and he didn't. That's a very major twist that would never happen to a pure Mary-Sue.

152 Stephanie Mayer's popular fantasy romance series and the movies it has spawned centre around teenage girl Bella Swan and the supernatural suitors who adore her.

There are also characters which have been introduced into a series late and have come to dominate by their excellence, which aren't Mary-Sue's either. Popeye took over *Thimble Theater* and the Fonz altered *Happy Days* beyond recognition. Others have dominated by becoming an author's favourite without necessarily being a wish-fulfilment instrument. Wolverine, for example, was eventually written to be cooler, more experienced, and more competent than long-term X-Men leader Cyclops, even drawing Jean Grey's romantic interest, but I don't know that writer Chris Claremont thought himself to be Logan (or whatever name the character has in this week's origin version).[153]

And it must be admitted, all but the most disciplined authors (of which I am not one) allow a little Mary-Sueishness to bleed into their work. We're human.

Writers are often advised to "write what you know". What does a writer know better than him or herself? Don't we carve off and isolate fragments of our own character to form the traits of various of our fictional creations (including the villains, of course)? Aren't many of our characters drawn from some exaggerated aspect of ourselves, or of whom we would like to be? Who wouldn't like to believe that the best of our personal traits should win us success, love, or acclaim? Which of us doesn't have personal tragedies that we could mine for story material if only it did not hurt too much?

I'm conscious that I borrow from myself when I write male protagonists, but draw upon my preferences and idealised dreams of women for the female ones. I hope it doesn't make my heroes Mary-Sue (or Marty-Stus, or whatever someone has decided is the masculine form), only drawn from some observations of people's human natures, including my own.

So, while "Mary-Sue" characters are typically seen as juvenile, amateur, or series-spoiling, I wonder if there is a role for such personally-invested creations

---

153 Creators Len Wein and Dave Cockrum, and then Chris Claremont and John Byrne, relaunched Marvel's defunct *X-Men* comic in 1975, replacing almost all the original roster of mutants with a new line-up. Of these, one of only two that had previously appeared before was Wolverine who had debuted in *Incredible Hulk* #180 and 181 (he's only in the last panel of #180, but that still makes the issue very collectable). Wolverine's initial role in the X-Men storyline was to be the antagonistic short-fuse maverick. As his popularity grew his role was expanded. It has now been established that he is over a hundred years old, fought with Captain America in World War II (and gave him fighting tips), romanced a series of superheroines and supervillainesses, and is generally one of the most savvy and experienced heroes in the Marvel Universe.

Wolverine has been subjected to a series of origin stories, each proved to be false or incomplete by the next one. The current prevailing continuity comes from the mini-series *Origin* (2001-2), which revealed that his name was not Logan as had been thought for the last quarter-century of comics publishing but instead the suspiciously-apt James Howlett.

in their proper context. Can and should an author project themselves so fully into a character – and what happens then?

If you disagree, write some fan-fiction where your character goes in and tells mine where they're wrong.

"In every first novel the hero is the author as Christ or Faust." – Oscar Wilde

Mary-Sue Makes Good

ARE "MARY-SUES" always a bad thing? Dorothy L. Sayers tended to write versions of herself into her stories. Early Lord Peter Wimsey tales occasionally feature Marjorie Phelps, a young independent woman living a Bohemian life in Chelsea who sometimes assists the detective with his investigations. Sayers herself had lived a similar life. Strong-willed Oxford graduate Miss Meteyard from *Murder Must Advertise* works at an advertising agency just as Sayers herself did for a decade. Meteyard penetrates Wimsey's cover and solves the murder before him, but says nothing because "it's none of her business". *The Nine Tailors* fifteen year-old Hilary Thorpe wants to study at Oxford and become a writer. She is "striking looking rather than beautiful", whip-smart in helping solve the case, and by the end of the novel Lord Peter is her trustee.

Of course, all these reflections of the author pale into insignificance against Miss Harriet Vane, a detective novelist who graduated from Oxford and lived with a poet who claimed he did not believe in marriage, then left him when he offered her marriage anyway "like a good-conduct badge". Sayers herself graduated from Oxford, lived with a poet, and broke from him for the same reasons. Of course, Sayers' ex-lover was not found murdered in the same way as the victim of her latest book, but Mary-Sues must be allowed some wish fulfilment. Miss Vane's former inamoratas did perish in such a way, leaving her facing death by hanging unless rescued by Lord Peter Wimsey – who falls desperately in love with her.

Miss Vane appears in four of the Wimsey books.[154] Her debut in *Strong Poison* leaves a powerful impression, but her 'screen-time' is limited because she is behind bars. Her second appearance begins with her actually discovering

---

154 Plus a short story, and three subsequent volumes by Jill Paton Walsh authorised by the Sayers estate.

the body in the case. *Have His Carcase* is mostly told from her point of view. *Gaudy Night*, her third appearance, might properly be described as a Harriet Vane mystery with Lord Peter Wimsey appearances. The narrative follows her throughout, with the detective overseas on government work for two-thirds of the book. *Busman's Honeymoon* describes the discovery of a corpse on the morning after Wimsey marries Harriet, and was described by Sayers herself as "a romance story with detective interruptions".

From these summaries, a reader not familiar with the Wimsey corpus might conclude that the appearance of Miss Vane wrecked the series, robbing the central hero of the spotlight in favour of an idealised ego-trip character. But this is simply not true. The series is revitalised, moving away from mere puzzle-solving and plot analysis to a much richer, more emotional, more layered series of works – and fun stories; hence my citing it in such detail as an example of Why Mary-Sues Don't Necessarily Have To Be Bad.

So the Vane/Wimsey novels take on a fresh life. It's clear that Sayers was far more engaged with them than some others she wrote merely to fulfil a publisher's contract. Even Wimsey's absence helps the story. We get impressions of him from other cast and his eventual appearance comes with added impact. Harriet is fleshed out in all her tormented complexity, and if based on Sayers must have been painful to write. "What does pain matter if it makes a good story?" Wimsey asks Vane at one point. If there's wish-fulfilment in Harriet's eventual happy ending with Sayers' greatest literary creation, then it's paid for in the author's naked analysis of herself to tell a powerful narrative.

And then there's Captain America joining the *Avengers*.

The reason I picked on Cap as a possible proto-Mary-Sue is that when he appeared in *Avengers* #4 (1964) he was seen as "a big deal" by the others on the team and by the regular inhabitants of the Marvel universe. This was depicted as the case in the stories, but also had some truth in the real world. Captain America was one of the few characters that predated the great explosion of successful superheroes from Marvel Comics in the 1960s.

Cap had a publishing history extending back to 1941, and although his book had been cancelled and revived several times and he had not appeared for the best part of a decade, his reappearance was the equivalent of a big name star joining a regular show's cast.

Captain America gave the Avengers the credibility and cohesion they'd been lacking. This got ramped up more after the founding team left and Cap had his "kookie quartet";[155] for a year or two there, Cap was the seasoned pro who was always right and the others were rookies who could never do better than him. And yet the stories were classics. *Avengers* #23-24, where Cap tracks the kidnapped team to time-travelling warlord Kang the Conqueror's future and pulls them together - with Kang - to save Ravonna's kingdom from a worse menace yet, remains one of my favourite comics to this day.

But the point is, Stan Lee wrote Cap back then as unable to do any wrong, as the shining exemplar. In fact those issues set the template for pretty much how Cap's been treated ever since. So whether he was Stan-in-a-union-suit or just an author's favourite (Stan was a fan), those early Avengers Cap's might possibly be an example of the Mary-Sue-in-a-good-way I'm searching for.

Sometimes the audience might even miss a Mary-Sue! My son and I watched *Cabin in the Woods*, the clever but eventually bleak Joss Whedon horror/thriller movie. It's a smart story that plays on expectations and deliberately subverts slasher movie clichés, but, without getting into spoilers, the ending isn't happy for everyone. Afterwards my son said to me, "You know what would have made that movie better? If Buffy[156] had been in that cabin it would have been so much more interesting. Or Captain America."

In other words, he *wanted* a beloved character to come in and address issues that the movie deliberately chose to leave unresolved or that ended 'unfairly'. So maybe there's *some* demand for actually injecting competent, superior characters into certain stories?

***

---

155 From *Avengers* #16 the team's roster consisted of Captain America, Hawkeye, Quicksilver, and the Scarlet Witch. None of these characters had their own monthly series as founding Avengers Thor, Iron Man, the Hulk, and Ant-Man and the Wasp had.
156 *Buffy the Vampire Slayer* was Joss Whedon's most popular TV hit show, running for seven seasons, featuring Sarah Michelle Gellar as ' the Slayer' whose destiny was to fight the undead.

27.
The Finest Surgeon the British Army Never Had

WHILE LOOKING UP some background on London's oldest commercial cemetery, Kensal Green, I came across this odd story of one of its inhabitants:

Dr James Barry could be a figure from a 19th century adventure series. A British Army surgeon, he served at Waterloo, in India, in South Africa, in Mauritius, in Trinidad and Tobago, and at Malta, Corfu, the Crimea, Jamaica, and in Canada. In a career spanning 1813-1864 he relentlessly fought for better conditions for medical patients, even lepers, although this brought him into regular conflict with 'the authorities', who felt him to be a dangerous maverick.

So who was he and, despite having a grave at Kensal Green, why did he never exist?

The records show that in 1809 young James Barry arrived to study literature and medicine at the University of Edinburgh's School of Medicine. His fees were probably paid by friends of the family, since his father, Jeremiah Bulkley, was in prison for debt. The student elected to register under his mother's maiden name; his uncle was Royal Academy painter James Barry. Another sponsor may have been Francisco de Miranda, the Venezuelan revolutionary, who was a family friend.

Barry was an apt student. A medical doctor by 1812, he went to London for courses at Guy's and St Thomas' hospitals before passing his exam for the Royal College of Surgeons and qualifying as a "regimental assistant" – a military physician.

By 1815 he was promoted Assistant Staff Surgeon – and that was Waterloo year. Barry probably got his first taste of action in that historic clash between the might of England and France, the decisive battle that broke Napoleon's grip on Europe and shattered his ambitions to invade the United Kingdom.

From there he was posted to India and South Africa. Such was the life of an army medical man. Within two weeks of arriving in Capetown he was appointed Medical Inspector for the colony. He overhauled the town's water system but soon clashed with the medical authorities who disliked his criticism of their methods. Somewhere before 1821 Barry performed the first successful Caesarean section in the British Empire,[157] delivering James Barry Munnik hale and healthy.

Barry was 'got rid of' by his enemies, posted to Mauritius, Trinidad and Tobago. He was arrested and deported for "politicking" on St Helena. He scandalised the clergy of Malta when he sat in a pew reserved only for bishops. He quarrelled with Florence Nightingale at Balaclava. He fought at least two duels when people insulted his appearance or professionalism.

His military record included many punishments for insubordination and discourteous behaviour, but as many citations for medical innovation and brilliance. A vegetarian teetotaller, he introduced the pear to the diet of the common British soldier.

In most of his latter adventures he was accompanied by his faithful Negro manservant John and his dog Psyche.

After a career that spanned the globe, Barry retired back to England – unwillingly – in 1864. He lasted less than a year before he was taken by dysentery.

And that's where things get strange.

It was only after his death that Barry's secret was revealed. When he was laid out for burial it was discovered that Dr Barry was actually... a woman! That makes him the first female Briton to be qualified as a medical doctor.

The matter came to the attention of George Graham of the General Register Office, who wrote a letter of enquiry to the physician that had issued the death certificate.

The reply has survived:

"I had been intimately acquainted with the doctor for [a] good many years, both in London and the West Indies and I never had any suspicion that Dr Barry was a woman. I attended him during his last illness, (previously

---

157 A caesarean was performed by Dr Jesse Bennett of Mason County, Virginia, in 1794, upon his wife Elizabeth.

An article by R.W. Felkin, "Notes on Labour In Central Africa", 1879, recorded witnessing a native caesarean being performed in Uganda. Felkin concluded from the well-developed technique that such operations had been done in that culture for a long time. *Source:* "Caesarean Section, a Brief History", U.S. national Library of Medicine, http://www.nlm.nih.gov/exhibition/cesarean/part2.html

for bronchitis, and the affection for diarrhoea). On one occasion after Dr Barry's death at the office of Sir Charles McGregor, there was the woman who performed the last offices for Dr Barry was waiting to speak to me. She wished to obtain some prerequisites of her employment, which the Lady who kept the lodging house in which Dr Barry died had refused to give her. Amongst other things she said that Dr Barry was a female and that I was a pretty doctor not to know this and she would not like to be attended by me. I informed her that it was none of my business whether Dr Barry was a male or a female, and that I thought that he might be neither, viz. an imperfectly developed man. She then said that she had examined the body, and was a perfect female and farther that there were marks of her having had a child when very young. I then enquired how have you formed that conclusion. The woman, pointing to the lower part of her stomach, said 'from marks here. I am a maried (sic) woman and the mother of nine children and I ought to know.'

The woman seems to think that she had become acquainted with a great secret and wished to be paid for keeping it. I informed her that all Dr Barry's relatives were dead, and that it was no secret of mine, and that my own impression was that Dr Barry was a Hermaphrodite. But whether Dr Barry was a male, female, or hermaphrodite I do not know, nor had I any purpose in making the discovery as I could positively swear to the identity of the body as being that of a person whom I had been acquainted with as Inspector-General of Hospitals for a period of years.

D.R. McKinnon"

This revelation troubled the British Army. It sealed Barry's records from his death in 1865 for a hundred years. But Inspector-General Dr James Barry was buried under that name – not Margaret Anne Bulkley as she had been born – and her grave remains today for those who wish to seek it at Kendal Green. She remains one of the most swashbuckling soldier-adventurers of the Victorian age.

***

28.
On Swearing

HOW WELL I REMEMBER our school House Master's annual lecture on the subject of Swearing. The entirety of Thoresby House would be gathered in the junior common room; for fourth years and younger these meetings were the only times they were admitted to that hallowed space now that fagging was abolished. Prefects and wardens were obliged to wear their gowns. Mr Farrell would stand up before the crowd, clutch his lapels, gather the room's attention with a steely eye, and begin:

"There is a place for swearing. It expresses shock, dismay, pain, and anger. As such it must not be part of our everyday common language. Rather reserve it for when you need to vent your spleen, or for rare and extraordinary emphasis in making your point. If you season your regular conversation with profanities and foul words you will have no reservoir to dip into when more significant need occurs.

"There are those who believe that swearing is a sign of masculinity, of adulthood, or of toughness. When you are grown you will understand that there is no need of bad language to be a man. The toughest and greatest of men need not prove themselves with crude words, but demonstrate it in their character and deeds. Beware those who seek to project an image of themselves though coarseness. They are invariably of inferior breeding and usually insecure in their manhood.

"Do not swear in the presence of ladies, or women of any class. Even if ladies are aware of or use such vulgarity - which most will do in private circumstances - always conduct yourself as a gentleman, as you would wish others to speak to your wife or mother. Do not use harsh language with domestics and lackeys who cannot answer you back. That is the attitude of a coward and a bully.

"If you are accosted with foul language from a peer of your own age, do not respond in kind. I do not say resort to combat at first provocation, but do what honour demands and circumstances warrant. As an adult, defend others from the course behaviour of inferior characters. This is the role of any man, and especially of an Englishman.

"It goes without saying that any boy heard swearing will receive three of the best, an afternoon in quod, and ten pages of Livy.[158] That is all."

Or words to that effect.

If that sounds remarkable for the 1970s, you should have heard his sixth form lecture on the proper etiquette of mistresses and other paid companionship.

***

---

158 That is three strokes of the cane on the backside, detention after class, and additional homework translating ten pages of Latin into English.

29.
Churchill Shot First -
Scruffy Nerf Herder vs. Imperial Sun King

TRUE OR FALSE? Churchill probably slept with at least one English queen. In the seventeenth century.

True. Except it wasn't Sir Winston Churchill, it was his son John. And it wasn't *that* Sir Winston Churchill, it was a distant ancestor. John Churchill is a character that deserves a pulp novel – except that it would only be a biography!

The *first* Sir Winston Churchill was around from 1650 to 1722. He was one of those romantic Cavaliers supporting the king's cause in the English Civil War. He wooed and won the equally romantic and beautiful Elizabeth Drake, who would fit anyone's definition of a dime-store romance story heroine. But fines for being on the wrong side of the civil war nearly ruined the Churchills, so their romantic son John Churchill had to make his own way in life and carve out his own romantic fortune.

When the monarchy was restored, young handsome, charismatic John was appointed as page boy to King Charles II's brother James (later King James II). His looks, wit, bravery, and all round main-characterness won him lots of attention, including from James' young wife, whose biographer delicately notes "[she] indicated more kindness and favour to the young aspirant than her husband thought prudent." Suspecting that John and the future Queen of England were aspiring like rabbits, James arranged for the 17 year old to get his life's ambition as a commissioned soldier – far away in the most dangerous posting possible.

John joined the Guards in defending Morocco from the Arabs, where he proved to have a good eye for tactics and to be excellent with the sword (insert crude bedroom comment re King James' wife here). Instead of getting horribly killed, John got horribly covered in glory and came home with a shining record to a hero's welcome.

But John didn't go back to aspiring with the princess. This time he romanced society beauty Barbara Villiers, one of the massively romantic and powerful Buckingham family, and shared her bed and her massive fortune. Unfortunately, Barbara was King Charles II's favourite mistress, and the money she gave to John was what Charles had given to her. In fact she gave John about the equivalent in Charles' money of what Sir Winston had been fined all those years before. Imagine how happy King Charles II was.

This all culminated in that classic cliché of the King bursting into Barbara's boudoir and catching John and the lady in the act. Well, technically he found John hiding in Barbara's bedroom closet. Charles pulled John out, laughed, and forgave him, saying "You only do it to get your bread." The King then found a foreign military situation more dangerous than Morocco and sent John there.

John Churchill was attached to the 6000 men under the command of the Duke of Monmouth sent to join the French in an invasion of Holland in 1672. This pairing was either a bad mistake or brilliance on the king's part. Monmouth was Charles' bastard, only a couple of years older than John; it was like introducing Butch Cassidy to the Sundance Kid. The two of them took a dodgy losing situation and turned it into a string of impossible victories. When the French suffered a major setback at Nimenguen and lost the town, the French Marshall de Turenne wagered a supper and a dozen claret that "my handsome Englishman will capture the town with half the men it took to lose it." Churchill did.

By the time of the critical siege of Maastricht, John had become a legend to the soldiers he commanded, somewhere between James Bond and Captain America. When he volunteered for "the forlorn hope" – the first squad of soldiers who charged the fortifications, usually taking up to 100% losses so the main army could get close during the distraction – dozens of his men vied to go with him. John was first onto the ramparts and planted his army's (French) flag there. As well as ensuring victory he found time to squeeze in saving Monmouth's life. King Louis XIV, France's shining Sun King, was so impressed that he promoted Churchill to lieutenant general and gave him joint command with de Turenne of the rest of the war.

In 1701, during "the Glorious Revolution" where English King Charles II and then James II were deposed by Parliament in favour of William of Orange, John was smart enough to pick the winning team. He'd got very disillusioned with the old monarchy while on a series of 'diplomatic' overseas missions for them. He backed the new King William and was rewarded with the title of Earl of Marlborough. And yes, he made money from the tobacco trade.

Old King Louis XIV was a sneaky one, though. When he thought he could get away with it, he broke the treaty he'd made with England and recognised James II's son as James III, the new if exiled King of England. He began equipping young Jim to go get his throne back off that Dutch pretender. William of Orange replied by falling off his horse and dying shortly after, which didn't help. Allegedly his dying words were advice to his daughter, who would be Queen Anne upon his passing: "Send for Marlborough."

So the young Queen, beset with imperial forces threatening to invade her land and oppress her people, met the young Jedi who... oh wait.[159] Well, actually, that's not too far off what happened. Churchill undertook a series of dazzling diplomatic and 'diplomatic' missions for Anne and somehow managed to pull together a rag-tag rebel alliance of all the countries France had annoyed or annexed. King Louis XIV was not happy when his unstoppable soldiers were beaten in the field by the military equivalent of a bunch of Ewoks.[160]

Queen Anne was satisfied though – some suspect well satisfied – and she upgraded Marlborough from Earl to Duke.

The other important character in the story is Lady Sarah Jennings. She was Queen Anne's best friend and bedmate (although that didn't necessarily imply any sexual relationship in those times). She was the Queen's most influential unofficial advisor. She was the most courted and eligible woman in England after the Queen herself.

Lady Sarah was a tender fifteen when she first met the young Churchill - and distinguished herself in his mind by refusing to become his mistress. Of course she then had a fiery romance with him, became his most loyal supporter, covering his back from politics at home while he was overseas campaigning - and was secretly his wife.

Later on her pregnancy somewhat gave the game away. Contemporary accounts remarked how close a relationship the Duke and Duchess of

159 These *Star Wars* references may confuse the casual reader. The author suggests that various traits of one of the principal characters of the original movie trilogy, swashbuckling outlaw space-pirate Han Solo, described by the princess he eventually wins as a "scruffy-looking nerf-herder", had many characteristics in common with John Churchill. Of course, Han was not a Jedi knight, so its perhaps best not to push comparisons too far.
160 *Star Wars: Return of the Jedi* includes a battle between the oppressive cloned Imperial troopers and an indigenous race of cute fluffy teddy bears known as the Ewoks. Assisted by the heroes including Han Solo and Princess Leia, these unlikely creatures overcome a powerful and superior invading army.

Marlborough enjoyed and what a formidable team they made. At various times Lady Sarah stood up to Queen Anne, to King George II, to Prime Minister Walpole and others. By the time she died she was one of the richest women in Europe.

So we come to the bit that still gets taught in military colleges. Louis XIV correctly deduced that Marlborough was the dangerous one. He sent forces to pin Marlborough in the north so the French and their Bavarian clone armies could take Austria without interference.

In return, Marlborough vanished with his whole army into the German Rhine valleys and didn't even tell his allies where he was going. Somehow he convinced his army to a supposedly-impossible forced march, covering 125 miles in five days, popping up in the Danube in time to cause trouble after all.

Normally a forced march like that would wreck a column, leaving them in no fit state to fight. Churchill however used what the modern war-teachers call "logistics". He had food and water stations en route, men setting up camp ahead of the main column and tidying up after them, and vast supply lines. In fact one of his staff wrote, "the soldiers had nothing to do but pitch their tents, boil their kettles and lie down to rest."

He also changed route several times, so that every time the French thought they had anticipated and blockaded him he turned out to be going somewhere else. All requests for modifications to the French battle plan had to go back to King Louis in Versailles for approval, which didn't make for a very mobile engagement doctrine. Dispatches to the French Sun King could only be read to him at certain times of the day so as not to interfere with his court routine. The lesson, the military historians intone at this point, is about proper delegation of tactical authority within strategic guidelines and rapid lines of communication. Or maybe it's don't take on a mad Englishman who can infect a whole army with his romantic swashbuckling notions.

All this led to the Battle of Blenheim, 1704, where the Austrians were reinforced by Marlborough's sudden army so that 52,000 soldiers turned up to oppose the 56,000 French and Bavarians. The French commander had fortified his troops in the village of Blindheim (Blenheim is the English name), protected by big guns, marsh, and woodland. He sent King Louis word that "the enemy would never dare to attack" - just before Marlborough marched over the horizon.

Churchill won by being flexible in his attack plans. When the French centred too many men in the village he drew back his ground forces and concentrated artillery on the overcrowded streets. When the French commanders argued over strategy, leaving a thinly defended spot in the perimeter defences, Marlborough hammered all his infantry through it. 30,000 French died, 10,000 surrendered. 3,000 elite cavalry drowned trying to escape across the river. As French defeats go, this one was up there with Crecy, Agincourt, Trafalgar, and Waterloo.

Nobody wanted to actually tell Louis XIV. In the end his mistress Madame de Maintenon was sent in to explain to him, "You are no longer invincible." Meanwhile, Churchill featured in the catchy popular song *Marlbrouch s'en va-t-en guerre* (Marlborough goes to war). It wasn't that popular at Versailles.

Marlborough went on to do a victory lap of Europe, kicking the French each time Louis broke his peace treaties. You can hear the poor Sun King chewing the carpet even this far down the corridor of history. Eventually Louis had to sign the Treaty of Utrecht, acknowledging the new line of English kings, promising never to unite the thrones of France and Spain to conquer the world, and ceding vast tracts of Canada to the English. He then died.

The English did what they always do to their greatest heroes. They turned on Marlborough, accused him of corruption and self-aggrandisement, then sacked him. To be fair, the nation did pay for Marlborough's retirement home, the glorious Blenheim Palace; to this day the Marlboroughs annually present the monarch of Great Britain with a replica French banner to commemorate all the ones Churchill sent to Queen Anne.

All of which goes to show that a daring young man with a swash in his buckle can go a long way.

***

30.
The First Defenestration of Prague

HOW HAS HISTORY come to overlook an event so gloriously named as the First Defenestration of Prague? Come on! It's an event that set a good part of Europe ablaze. As the title implies it involved people in the capital of Bohemia being thrown out of a window. And, as the name also suggests, this was only the *first* time it happened in Prague.

Charles University is probably the oldest university in mainland Europe. Founded by the Holy Roman Emperor Charles IV at the height of his power, the Prague-based Universitas Carolina Pragensis was a seat of liberal learning and pioneering scholarship in the fourteenth century. But in 1402 it got a new rector, the fiery young reformer Jan Hus, a priest who admired the English radical Wycliff and read his works from the pulpit – and a scholar who argued for a doctrine of impanation.[161]

This was important and controversial stuff at the time. Hus' teachings later inspired Luthor, Calvin, and Zwingli and played a major role in the Protestant movement. Hus was reprimanded by Pope Gregory XII, but since Gregory was currently one of two warring Popes (the other being Benedict XIII), Hus did the only logical thing and threw his support and that of his institution behind a third candidate, Alexander V, whom the Catholic church now considers an Antipope. No, honestly.

However, Antipope Alexander turned against Wycliff, ordering all his works destroyed, threatening terrible retribution on those who followed his "heretical teachings" (such as translating the Bible into anything other than Latin). Hus fell out with the new Pope in fine style, ignored the Papal Bull, was excommunicated, and carried on regardless. He crusaded against the giving of indulgences – pre-paid forgivenesses for sins yet to be committed.

---

161 The theological belief that the bread and wine of Christian sacrament are not physically mystically transmuted to the flesh and blood of Christ as Roman Catholic doctrine holds but rather undergo a symbolic and spiritual metamorphosis.

The Pope interdicted Prague, meaning Christians there were no longer allowed to participate in the rites of the church. They did anyway, because Hus said so.

Alexander responded by dying. The new Antipope was John XIII, who called for a crusade against the anti-indulgenists. There was civil unrest in Prague. Three common men who denied the efficacy or authority of indulgences were beheaded. Hus preached a seminal sermon arguing that, "man obtains true forgiveness of sins by repentance, not by money". His followers began to argue that Hus, not the Pope, should be the authority of Christian doctrine.

The Council of Constance convened in November 1414 to try and heal the schisms that were tearing church and states apart. Hus was offered safe passage there to state his case, but once he arrived he was arrested and imprisoned. He was chained in a dungeon, starved, and isolated while he faced a series of trials at which he was not allowed to offer evidence in his defence. Refusing to recant, he was burned at the stake in 1415. His ashes were scattered in the Rhine. It was over.

Except that now, instead of being a living annoyance, Hus was a dead martyr. Does nobody learn from history? Strike him down and he became more powerful than you could ever imagine.[162] Within months, what would become known as the Hussite Wars had begun.

There are lessons to be learned from the aftermath of Hus' execution, such as:

1. If you are Sigismund, Holy Roman Emperor, do *not* send follow-up letters to Bohemia, Hus' homeland, warning that you will "shortly drown all Wycliffites and Hussites".

2. Do *not* persecute the Hussites so they spread all across Europe taking their message with them to whip up flash mobs into a spontaneous army.

3. Do *not* throw stones at Hussite parades from the windows of the Prague New Town Hall. It can lead to serious defenestration.

Yes. We're at the first defenestration at last. On 30th July 1419, Hussites protested Prague town council's refusal to exchange their Hussite prisoners. Someone hurled a stone from the Town Hall window at the priest leading the procession. An enraged mob stormed the building and threw the judge, the burgomaster, and thirteen councilmen out of that same window. Those who survived the fall were beaten to death by the crowd. King Wenceslas (not the

---

162 Yet another *Star Wars* reference, in this case paraphrasing some of the final words of Jedi master Obi Wan Kenobi before he died and became "one with the Force".

good one, his descendant) of Bohemia was so shocked by the news that he fell sick and died.

And then there was war. The Hussites formed militia, very effective "cart units" with unusual tactics that proved very successful against medieval military methods. Rings of upended wagons formed makeshift defences to protect against cavalry charges, while combinations of crossbowmen, hand-gunners, and flailmen targeted horses first. It was the first time knightly charges proved ineffective against infantry.

Catholics were hounded from Bohemia. Pope Martin V proclaimed a crusade "for the destruction of Wycliffites, Hussites, and all other heretics in Bohemia". A vast crusading army, including huge numbers of fortune-hunting adventurers, descended on Prague and captured it; but as soon as the army had dispersed, the citizen of Prague themselves besieged the fortress and recaptured it. King Sigismund, who claimed the Bohemian crown, tried to break the siege in the winter of 1420 and was decisively defeated by the Hussites' carts.

The year after, a second crusade attacked, this time with German troops. Sigismund, whom I picture as a medieval Dick Dastardly[163] for some reason, managed to capture a town before being chased off again by the Hussite peasant army. Drat and double drat!

Between then and the third anti-Hussite crusade (of five), the Hussites amused themselves by schisming. The moderate Utraqists wanted religious tolerance and the extremist Taborites held that there were only two sacraments, baptism and holy communion. Their weapon of choice was the *Böhmischer Ohrlöffel* or *Knebelspiess*, a triple-spiked polearm whose name translates into English as the Bohemian earspoon. No civil war fought with Bohemian earspoons can possibly be dull.

The consequences of defenstration rippled on, though. The Pope proclaimed his third crusade to interrupt the internal earspooning. Nobody came. Well, the Danish got part way but went home when nobody else turned up. The Hussites got bored waiting to be attacked and invaded Moravia instead. For the next couple of years they amused themselves by intermittently conquering Germany.

The amazing thing is, though, that this rag-tag force consistently defeated organised military resistance and managed to terrorise the crowned heads of

---

163 The Hanna Barbera cartoon villain debuted in 1969 and has appeared in a variety of cartoons since. He is very much the archetypal villain, based on actor Terry Thomas' typical roles and on Jack Lemmon's "Professor Fate" character from *The Great Race*, 1965. He is perhaps best remembered for his catch-phrase, "Drat, drat, and double-drat!"

Europe and the Catholic church. They were like that shabby new neighbour who tosses his garbage into your yard then asks what you're going to do about it. They brought down the property values but nobody was able to object. And they continued to kill each other on the issue of how many sacraments God had authorised. Whole cities proclaimed themselves as Utraquist or Taborite; Tabor, for example, was Taborite.

The Hussites were so powerful now that they were offering various crowned heads of Europe the monarcy of Bohemia – they had serious problems recruiting to the post. Their chavauchées ('beautiful rides') saw them raiding through Silesia, Saxony, Hungary, Lusitania, Meissen, pretty much everywhere that had ever supported the crusaders earlier on. Their adversaries included the marvelously-named Monastic State of the Teutonic Knights (incorporating the Livonian Brotherhood of the Sword – I'm not making this up). They eventually conquered as far as the Baltic Sea near Danzig and boasted that only an ocean could stop the march of the Hussites.

By 1431 the only chance of peace was the Council of Basel, at which the Catholic church reluctantly admitted the Hussite heretics but drew the line at Greek Orthodox clerics being present. But the Papacy decided that before the conference it was best to prepare things by throwing one last really good crusade at Bohemia. The Elector of Brandenburg lead an invading force to siege the city of Domazlice. When the Hussites arrived singing their battle hymn – of *course* they had a battle hymn – the Papal forces ran away again.

Basel didn't solve anything. In the end, the Hussites were defeated by their worst enemy, the Hussites. The factions warred, then split, then warred with the sub-factions. Earspoons flew. On 30th May 1434 the leaders of the Taborite Hussites fell in battle against the Utraquists at Lipany. The storm unleashed by Jan Hus' burning and a badly-judged rock from a town hall window finally passed into drizzle and bluster. Bohemia was a scorched wasteland. The remaining Hussites began to call themselves Protestants.

A peace settlement guaranteed religious tolerance in Bohemia and Moravia, which lasted right until 1618 and the *second* Defenstration of Prague that triggered the Thirty Years War. But that's another story, and besides on that occasion the defenstrated clergymen fell into a pile of manure and were miraculously saved.

***

31.
The Lone Ranger Rides To The Box Office

"A FIERY HORSE with the speed of light, a cloud of dust and a hearty Hi-Yo Silver! The Lone Ranger! ... With his faithful Indian companion Tonto, the daring and resourceful masked rider of the plains led the fight for law and order in the early western United States! Nowhere in the pages of history can one find a greater champion of justice! Return with us now to those thrilling days of yesteryear! From out of the past come the thundering hoofbeats of the great horse Silver! The Lone Ranger rides again!"

There are heroes that can be treated ironically. The Lone Ranger should not be one of them.

The Lone Ranger exemplifies two places and times. He is probably the best known Western hero of series adventure, epitomising many of the finest values of that era: self-reliance, grit, honour, intrepidness, and ingenuity. But he is also very much a product of 40s and 50s American popular culture, exemplifying positive characteristics that were in many ways the defining ones of a modern USA: justice, fair-play, responsibility beyond self interest, and decency.

When the original show's writer, Fran Striker, established the character, he also established a written code for the Lone Ranger. It starts:

"I believe...
- that to have a friend, a man must be one.
- that all men are created equal and that everyone has within himself the power to make this a better world.
- that God put the firewood there, but that every man must gather and light it himself.
- in being prepared physically, mentally, and morally to fight when necessary for that which is right."

In other words, the Lone Ranger was portrayed as an unambiguous hero, a role model that others should strive to emulate. This is at the very core of the character. Any version that doesn't understand that this masked man is meant to personify the greatest characteristics of a nation - and is often pitted against the worst characteristics of it - has completely missed the point.

That's not to say that the Ranger has to be two-dimensional or boring. There are other aspects to him which make him distinctive and special.

First off is his origin. Six rangers led by Captain Daniel Reid are treacherously ambushed and gunned down by Butch Cavendish. The villain assumes they are all dead, but Reid's brother survives. In most versions of the origin the last - lone - ranger is found and nursed to health by Tonto. Six graves are prepared to fool Cavendish that his hunters are all silenced. One survivor dons a mask made from his brother's tunic to bring anonymous justice to the evildoer. As origins go, that's mythic; but more, it provides an underpinning for the Lone Ranger's quest - after he should have died, a hero continues without a name but with an unshakable code.

The mask stays, too. This is a hero who does not remain to receive rewards or adulation. There is always a new horizon with a new challenge. There is no finer example of 'the hero who comes to town' that this one. "Who was that masked man anyway?"

Then there are silver bullets. The Lone Ranger uses them because they are expensive; they remind him that every life is precious and that gunplay should never be casual or without supreme reason. In real life it's not usually feasible to shoot to disarm, but the Lone Ranger uses trick-shots whenever possible because life has value to him.

And there are his companions. Tonto elects to accompany the Lone Ranger on his quest because he believes in him. But the wild stallion Silver willingly gives up his independence to carry the Ranger too (and in one episode brings Scout along for Tonto). And there are other, temporary partners and companions who also get caught up in, and transformed into something nobler by, adventuring with the Ranger. The masked stranger may come, address the trouble, and vanish, but he leaves more than a silver bullet. He changes everywhere he goes, not only causing the downfall of the bad guys but leaving good people stronger and better.

Finally, like many characters with early radio history, the Lone Ranger has many catchphrases associated with him. "Hi-ho, Silver!" and "Get 'em up, Scout!" might serve to tell radio listeners that our heroes are now riding, but there are very few series with such a comprehensive sound palette. And of course, *The March of the Swiss Soldiers* has become an iconic superhero theme tune. The visuals were also quite distinctive; in modern terms both the Ranger and Tonto have unique 'silhouettes' and command any scene in which they appear. Attempts to change or modernise the phraseology or appearance of the characters much will always fail because the franchise has been so closely associated with these sounds and sights.

So what does need updating for a contemporary version of the Lone Ranger? It might not be politically correct to call Tonto an Indian now, but that's certainly what Native Americans of the Potawotomi tribe were called in the era the stories are set. The relationship between the Ranger and Tonto was very much ahead of its time anyway (see item 2 of the Ranger's creed above). I think the challenge is actually in depicting a genuine honest good-guy hero in a world where that is rare (then and now).

For the rest. If it's not broke...

The Lone Ranger Revived

THIS PIECE ISN'T schadenfreude for the 2013 Disney version of *The Lone Ranger* featuring Johnny Depp and Armie Hammer that took just $29.4m in its opening weekend, a fraction of the $250m it cost to make and market, and that received domestic takings of just $89.3m.[164] However, its clear that this version, like other *Lone Ranger* revivals before it, failed to capture the popularity of the original. Rotten Tomatoes, the website that aggregates critic and public response to movies, recorded 66 "fresh" vs 151 "rotten" professional reviews, a miserable 30% score on their "tomatometer".[165]

Some commentators assume this is because "the Western is dead". Others point to creative conflict and budget overruns in the production process. One blames the washed-out colour palette of the trailer. There are certainly plenty of pundits ready to nominate scapegoats. However, assuming there isn't a simple blame game to play, what does go wrong when classic 'properties' are revived or revised for the big screen?

All historical fiction reflects our current age. The sensibilities of the 1950s coloured the presentation of the 1880s in the original *Lone Ranger* stories. The sensibilities of the 2000s coloured the way a similar time was portrayed

---

164 Sources: *The Hollywood Reporter* http://www.hollywoodreporter.com/news/disneys-lone-ranger-could-lead-581503
Box Office Mojo http://www.boxofficemojo.com/movies/?id=loneranger.htm
165 http://www.rottentomatoes.com/m/the_lone_ranger/

in HBO's *Deadwood*.

Modern movie and TV audiences these days are educated - or perhaps conditioned - to expect certain things from a story that older audiences were not. The main change is that viewers are constantly provoked to ask "what's the angle on this guy?"; everyone has a hidden fault or failure, everyone has feet of clay. Our protagonist is an alcoholic/ex-conman/wifebeating/sociopathic/ emotionally scarred/womanising/wiseass piece of damaged goods. Otherwise he's not 'realistic'. Plotlines are overtly sexualised and more violent than in many older pieces. Examine the screen combat:non-combat ratio between even a major cowboy movie like *The Good the Bad and the Ugly* and any modern CGI-flick to prove the point.

So a 21st Century update for the Lone Ranger isn't questioning the time period. It's questioning how that period and its characters are portrayed.

Let's look at how a studio might internally debate the Lone Ranger property. I think they'd start with two problems:

1. There's a Native American secondary hero, and that's going to raise race issues.

2. The main character wears a mask and has a 'golden age' legacy that can sometimes seem camp and goofy

Now you and I might think the way to address that would be to tackle it head on. That's the property; deal with it. But studios nervous of focus groups might choose to try and differ the concept to address the concerns they fear their audience would have.

Problem #3 is that the original Lone Ranger shoots to disarm. That will raise questions for a modern audience used to Bruce Willis and Clint Eastwood tearing though hordes of thugs with guns blazing. It certainly makes large-scale action sequences against multiple opponents very difficult. The *A-Team* movie addresses the same problem by throwing out the non-lethal, but that was never an implicit part of the characters' personalities, only a studio censorship directive. The Ranger's respect for life is a major driver.

So the first choices a studio probably (and reasonably) makes are:

1. The Lone Ranger shoots to kill (but hopefully not unnecessarily).

2. Tonto needs to be majorly kick-ass and hold his own (not that he didn't anyway) and be as "authentic" as possible.

3. The Ranger doesn't spend all his time in the mask.

Now comes the tough part. Modern audiences expect their quota of grime and squalor in Westerns. There are less school-ma'ams and more bar whores. Authority is likely corrupt. Life out West is cheap, brutal, and venal. And audiences also expect 'the big plan', a high-stakes (often unrealistic) plot to do something unspeakable. A mere bank heist won't do it anymore.

So that means that the Ranger's brother and comrades were probably *betrayed* into Cavendish's ambush, as part of a bigger plan to do something massive like overthrow the President. In a good interpretation the Ranger plays as the last honest man in a corrupt world (c.f. Judge Dredd[166]), holding to values nobody else believes in and somehow making them work. In a less-good version he's an outdated fool clinging to unrealistic morals, a sad figure or a comedy one; and his heroine/romance interest is either going to be a prostitute or a rape victim or both.

I'm trying to illustrate the range of adaptation choices, good and bad, before a studio. To truly capture the spirit of the Ranger he has to be an absolute, an unstoppable force of justice who won't even let a grave get in the way of his duty. Tonto sees the good in him and matches it with his own, in a true and equal friendship. After that, the baddies can be as nasty as you like, as long as they get the silver bullets at the end. In fact putting the Ranger in *Deadwood* would work; they came quite close with Bullock at times.[167]

The producers and financiers of Hollywood productions are often just following the marketing primer. To sell a product - pretty much any product - requires a hook, something that grabs the potential purchaser and reels them in. Traditionally these hooks have been one or more of:

- Brand recognition (either a known product or a known originator of that product)
- Gimmick (either innovative marketing or secondary tie-in)
- Concept (a new idea or a clever twist/combination/repackaging of old ones)
- Price (something significantly different to competing products in the marketplace - both lower and higher actually work)

For a marketing-led product (i.e. a luxury or leisure item rather than staples like bread or milk) the doctrine is that the specific nature of the product is determined by the choices made about its marketing and distribution. A micro-beer for enthusiasts is handled very differently from a celebration champagne vintage, which is again done differently from a twenty-year-

---

166 The ultimate cop in futuristic Mega City One debuted in the UK weekly comic *2000AD* #2 (1977).
167 The sheriff of Deadwood in history and in HBO's award-winning TV series

matured Scotch. And if the production company feels it needs to get more into, say, the 25-40 male demographic, then even the actual choice of selling an alcohol option in the first place as the way to grab that market might determine what the eventual product is.

Hollywood is an extreme example of investor-led single-product market competition. Every investor expects their movie to give them a significant return in a high-risk potentially-high-yield marketplace. That means the money behind the productions will mostly back what look like sure-fire winners, with the occasional wild toss of the roulette ball to pad out the portfolio.

But the traditional hooks still hold good. The only change is that price remains pretty fixed (3D and Blu-Ray are the latest attempts to vary it) although cost is a key factor. Otherwise, *brand recognition* means a known character (Batman, James Bond, Bridget Jones), a sequel, a known actor (Brad Pitt, Johnny Depp, Bruce Willis), or perhaps a known director (there are maybe six out there with the pull required). *Gimmick* could be a viral internet marketing campaign, 3D (in 2009), controversy, TV-series tie-in. *Concept* is what the movie's about - Star Wars meets Jaws, undead serial killer in girls school, teenager knocks up girlfriend's sister, whatever.

But its important to know what the main hook is. If your main hook is "adaptation of *Lord of the Rings*" then it can't also be "Christopher Lee" or "Peter Jackson" or "video game tie-in". Those can all be secondary hooks, but marketing is a simple beast. Get the main hook right and the rest follows.

But if your property is, say, the Lone Ranger, then there has to be a sober balancing of which is going to draw in more purchasers; is the hook a beloved 50s TV series, or is it Johnny Depp? There's a case for either, but if the hard truth is that if Depp sells more tickets than the Lone Ranger then it'll be a Depp movie first and a Ranger movie second. After all, while movies can be somebody's labour of love, they're also a studio's expectation of a 160% return over layout.

Once that hook is decided on, the rest has to bend to facilitate it. An authentic Lone Ranger tale becomes secondary to servicing the reason most viewers paid for their ticket: to see Depp.

The problem comes when that hook is around a concept which doesn't quite match the original franchise. When the action-adventure hero Green Hornet becomes the feelgood-comedy-of-the-summer *Green Hornet*, it's an uncomfortable fit. And mostly it doesn't work, because the first creative decision - what's the hook? - was fundamentally wrong. No budget can save it after that.

I submit that some movies that many 'core fans' have hated have been commercially successful because the finance boys were cynical and picked the right hook. Many more movies have tanked because the right hook was not understood and followed through, or somebody tried to change horses half-way through the race.

Consider the recent *John Carter* debacle. The hook there really had to be Carter himself, an archetypal SF/fantasy character from a classic and known pulp writer, the inspiration for *Star Wars*, *Flash Gordon*, and half the sci-fi movies ever made. Arguably the hook might have been the concept, "Earthman goes to fantasy version of Mars and fights for freedom". But somewhere along the way Disney moved away from both those hooks to "This has great CGI", "This has explosions and hitting things", "Wouldn't you like to find out who John Carter is?" and latterly "Please, please, come and look at what we made!" And potential viewers were off the hook.

In summary, while we might feel a frustration with 'Hollywood hacks' messing with classic properties, sometimes its down to wider economic and business practices rather than mere creative incompetence. Give most studios the choice between a loss-making classic movie and a piece of rubbish that makes them a billion and see which they pick.

Studios might want to be more astute with creative properties in considering the relative merits of various hooks. If they're handling a beloved character with sixty or a hundred years of successful publishing history behind him then clearly someone somewhere got the hook right before. Perhaps they even had a better hook than Johnny Depp? Perhaps if the studio chose their hook with conviction and backed it with faith and passion they might get the extraordinary return they are dreaming of?

When big money and complicated production processes meet creative genius and fan expectations there are going to be some casualties. Better consideration of 'the core hook' of any creative property might make sure they're the right casualties.

***

32.
The Man Who Wrote More Than Lester Dent

MOST PULP AFICIONADOS will know of *Doc Savage* writer Lester Dent's prodigious 30s and 40s output, 159 novels in 16 years.

But between 1958 and 1965, an English schoolteacher wrote part-time after classes. In that time, R.L. Fanthorpe, a.k.a. John E. Muller, a.k.a. Karl Zeigfried, a.k.a. Bron Fane, Pel Torro, Leo Brett, etc, produced at least 170 novels for Badger Books. That's twenty-one books per year![168]

Nowadays this author is better known as the Reverend Lionel Fanthorpe, ordained Anglican vicar, broadcaster, non-fiction writer of religious volumes and of studies on Knights Templar and Rennes-le-Chateau. He's got a filmography on IMDB.[169] He's even had his own TV series, investigating "real-life mysteries and strange phenomenon" in his leather jacket on his vintage motorbike.

Badger Books were as pulpy as they get. Their paperbacks had distinctive yellow spines and covered all the usual genres: crime, westerns, war stories, supernatural, SF, and titillating romance. The covers typically had a strapline that explained the plot. For example:

Space No Barrier by 'Pel Torro' – They discovered the secret to a mystery older than time itself!

The X-Machine by 'John E. Muller' – The Ultimate Weapon had been unleashed, humanity could only wait.

The Negative Ones by 'John E. Muller' – There was terror in the ominous cloud above the doomed city, the day the *bomb* had arrived.

Black Infinity by 'Leo Brett' – If this was only a dream – why couldn't she wake?

Negative Minus by R.L. Fanthorpe – The thing swooped out of the darkness like an animated cloud!

---

168 For another prodigious author output see Frank Richards from Chapter 18 section two.
169 International Movie Database, an online site that does what it says in its name.

Badger Books were not prestigious. The publishers provided no editor and paid 15 shillings (40 cents) per thousand words. Badger authors were fast and cheap. *Radar Alert* by 'Karl Zeigfried' was produced in just 11 hours on 2nd November 1963, dictated to tape with typists working in parallel to transcribe it. For those who are wondering, the tale describes an invasion of Earth by an electronic lifeform subverting military radar systems.

The paperbacks had very strict word counts. More than once Fanthorpe would be warned by his typists that "he had three pages to go before the end", so he would have to introduce some *deus et machina* to conclude his narrative quickly. On other occasions where the word count was short, filler was required. *Dark Continuum* includes a one and a half page account of the heroine brushing her teeth.

Some paragraphs in the published works are garbled where secretaries misheard or misunderstood sentences. And the urgency of day-by-day submission of part-finished material means that occasionally dead characters reappear later in the text since the author has forgotten they have died!

Another Badger quirk was that the covers were commissioned before the text. Writers would receive a copy of the image then be expected to provide a title and cover blurb. Thereafter a story was commissioned.

Fanthorpe's output is not always well regarded by SF enthusiasts. The aforementioned *Negative Minus* is effectively a retelling of Homer's Odyssey, featuring Captain Suessydo from the planet Ahcati encountering the one-eyed alien Sumehpylop and the beguiling Ecric. Read the names backward to work out Fanthorpe's cunning code.

On the other hand, much of Fanthorpe's output reflected his eclectic and erudite obsession with weird phenomena and arcane studies. His work references J.B. Rhine's ESP experiments, Abdul Alhazred's *Necronomicon*[170], Paul Kammerer and the midwife toad hoax (Google it), and *The Rubaiyat* of Omar Khayyam; and that's all in just one short novel, *Unknown Destiny* by 'Bron Fane'. *The Last Valkyrie*, which is actually a story about Daedelus, Icarus, and King Minos, was clearly running short and so includes a full chapter retelling the entirety of Norse myth.

Fanthorpe's novels are liberally populated by a variety of adventuring vicars, tough two-fisted spiritual warriors with holy water and handguns, always ready to battle lycanthropes, nosferatu, cultists and demons. One might suspect a certain authorial identification with these characters. Woe

---

170 The fictional volume mentioned in the writings of H.P. Lovecraft has now been published in a variety of 'discovered' editions.

betide the Satanist who tries to raise something nasty in Reverend Fanthorpe's parish today!

The point is, Fanthorpe is one of the 'forgotten' many of pulp writers who produced some forgettable work, some execrable output under mitigating circumstances, some variable tales with moments of genius, and a few hidden gems. As a writer I'd probably be happy with that record. Time to offer him a little corner of the Pulp Hall of Fame; somewhere where his works' bright yellow spines can ward off evil and serve as a memorial to a forgotten age of frantic budget paperback publishing.

Further Reading: The author owes a debt of thanks for source material to Andrew May's excellent article in *Fortean Times* #297. There's a relatively full list of Fanthorpe's publications at http://www.isfdb.org/cgi-bin/ea.cgi?R._L._Fanthorpe but I possess at least one volume not included there. A cover gallery of many of his works is found at http://www.peltorro.com/gallery.htm

***

33.
The Once and Future King

KING ARTHUR PENDRAGON hunts mysterious Inglewood Forest for a white hart – ever a symbol of sovereignty. After capturing the beast the monarch is confronted by the mystical knight Sir Gromer Somer Joure. This warrior has a grudge against the Pendragon's cousin, Sir Gawaine, whom he claims has stolen his lands. Arthur is unarmed for the hunt and so is at the mercy of armed and armoured Sir Gromer.

A bargain is struck. Arthur must return in a year's time and yield his life unless he has discovered the answer to Sir Gromer's riddle: "What is it that women most desire?"

Arthur returns to his court, where Gawaine learns of his king's pact. The pair of them quest for the answer. Eventually Arthur ventures again into Inglewood.

A disfigured crone, Lady Ragnelle – the Loathly Lady – claims to know how to respond to Sir Gromer's question. She will reveal the solution to Arthur, but only on condition that handsome, swashbuckling Sir Gawaine will marry her!

Gawaine, prince of Orkney, one of the greatest of the Round Table knights, is renowned for his good looks and success with women. Marriage to the hag will make his an object of scorn and pity; court life can be cruel. Still, Gawaine accepts the bargain to save the king. Ragnelle tells him what women want more than anything: "Their own way."

And since Ragnelle turns out to be Sir Gromer's sister it's the right answer. The mystic knight is thwarted.

Sir Gawaine has given his word. His marriage to the Loathly Lady goes forward with great ceremony, and with derision from his peers. The crone is crude and disgusting at her wedding feast. The knight adheres to his promise.

In their nuptial chamber on their bridal night, Ragnelle disrobes – and becomes a most beautiful damsel. She reveals that she is under a curse, and gives her husband a choice. Will he have her appear as a beauty during the day in public but a withered smelly hag in bed, or have her desirable to him alone in their private bower but an ugly monster outside?

And Gawaine replies, "Whichever you choose." Women, after all, want more than anything to have their own way.

This breaks the curse of Inglewood. Ragnelle is cured and remains beautiful day and night, and many knights who had scorned Gawaine envy his great fortune at acquiring such a lady.[171]

Violence, revenge, intrigue, mockery, and sex. The Matter of Britain makes excellent pulp fodder.

I'm talking about that thick corpus of medieval French, Latin, Welsh and Old English fiction, poems and ballads around King Arthur and his knights, of which *La Morte D'Arthur* by Sir Thomas Mallory is the best known version.

I'm far from the only one to recognise the Pendragon's story potential. There are dozens if not hundreds of modern Arthurian stories out there that are well written, well researched historical novels, elegiac modern romances, intellectually layered metaphors, the lot. But go back to the first Arthur stories, the ones the bards told, the ones finally written down in the *Mabinogion*,[172] in the *History of the Kings of Britain*, in the Vulgate tales, and in Mallory's *Morte D'Arthur* and really you've got the medieval equivalent of pulp. It's stirring mass-market bestseller fare that peddles a complex continuity of interlocking stories published in serial form.

So Arthur adapts easily to the contemporary pulp format, right? After all, his literature forms some of the genre's deep roots.

The problem is that the things that were important to a medieval audience aren't always as important to us and vice versa. Mallory is fascinated by recording who won every single joust at a tourney, right down to whose surcingle[173] snapped and whose cruppers[174] brake, but he names virtually none

---

171 This is a summary of the 15th century poem *The Wedding of Sir Gawain and Dame Ragnelle*. Other versions appear in *The Marriage of Sir Gawaine*, Child ballad 31, and *The Wife of Bath's Tale* by Geoffrey Chaucer. Earlier Loathly Ladies who become beautiful when embraced include the Celtic one in *The Adventures of the Sons of Eochaid Mugmedon* who encounters Niall of the Nine Hostages, and the monster who shared a bed with Helgi, Hróarr's brother in the Old Norse *Hrólfr Kraki's Saga*.
172 Probably the oldest extant Arthur source, this collection of old Welsh legends features Arthur in the tale of *Culhwch and Olwen*. It's amazing how many of the later elements of Arthur's stories appear in it - his brother Kay, his best knights Bedevere and Gawain, his dog Cavall; even his wife Guenevere gets name-checked, with his sword Caliburn and his ship Pridwyn. It illustrates how at that early time Kay, Bedevere, and Gawain were the main characters in the stories.
173 That's the leather band that goes around a horse's girth (under his chest).
174 A loop and strap used to stop the saddle from slipping forward.

of the many damsels who feature prominently in the stories. For example, the quest maiden who leads Galahad on his Grail hunt, who braves temptation and danger with him for love's sake, and who finally dies to break a terrible curse on the also unnamed Leprous Lady (no relation to the Loathly Lady above), is only ever known as "King Pellinore's daughter". 50% of all other Arthurian ladies are called Elaine (see below for a guide to Elaines).

And medieval literature hadn't quite developed dialogue in the way that modern readers expect it. The Matter of Britain offers detailed action sequences, quite well described battles, reported debates and wooings and disputes, but relatively little quoted speech. The kind of interaction banter we'd usually expect of a group of heroes on a mission, or old comrades taking their ease, or young lovers embarking on their romance is wholly absent.

Perhaps most difficult for the modern reader is that Mallory and his compeers tell us *what* happened but don't always explain *why*. The motivations are sometimes opaque. Sometimes we can fathom it for ourselves; for example there's an incident in the Grail quest where Sir Bors, a less-than-perfect knight trying to make good, has to choose between saving his naked captive brother from being scourged with thorns by the wicked Sir Bruce sans Pitie or rescuing a damsel who is about to be ravished by brigands. He chooses the maiden but we're not told why. Only a close reading and some additional comments when Bors' brother turns up furious "for his betrayal" help us realise that Bors chose to save the maiden because that was the chivalrous and Christian thing to do. He believed his brother to be so noble as to choose to suffer rather than allow the maiden's dishonour.

Bors next test is whether to defend himself when his brother tries to kill him.

Other occasions simply don't offer enough context to fathom the reasons for events. For example, the treacherous Sir Meliagrance, maddened by lust for Guenevere, cuts down her unarmed companions and carries her to his castle to rape her. Once there however he changes his mind and instead locks her in a tower to tend her wounded knights, leaving time for Lancelot to ride to the rescue (in a cart, which is a great shame for a knight). Meliagrance yields and begs for mercy.

It is right after this rescue that Lancelot and Guenevere finally act upon their long-suppressed passion and become adulterous lovers. Seeing sheets bloodied by du Lac's reopened wounds, Meliagrance accuses them of the deed and is again challenged by Lancelot. But like all good villains, Meliagrance has a trick up his sleeve and manages to trap the hero in a dungeon. The best knight in the world escapes (with the help of a damsel) and still turns up just in time for his scheduled duel. Sir Meliagrance refuses to face the hero. In the end he agrees to duel if Lancelot is unarmoured with one hand literally tied behind his back. Lancelot kills him.[175]

It's all rousing stuff but the Mallory text gives little insight into why each of the principles of the story act quite as they do.

Modern versions such as T.H. White's excellent *The Ill Made Knight*[176] offer plausible reasons for Meliagrance's change of heart and why Arthur's queen and his best friend betray him, but the gloss comes from new material not the original stories.

Then there's the aforementioned Leprous Lady whose castle lay beyond the waste forest near Cartelois, who could only be cured by a dish of warm blood from a virgin princess (a specific one, at that, and no-one knew who), another example of the "what but not why" stuff. Everything in the Grail Quest tends to have deeper significance,[177] but why the lady was cursed with leprosy, why other maidens were not suitable to cure her except Galahad's true love, and why God's wrath then toppled her castle and destroyed her after her cure (which seems somewhat to render the Grail Maiden's selfless sacrifice pointless) remain open to many interpretations.

Another problem is that much material is missing; it's like having only half the books in a series, or half the comics in a long run. Some stories assume familiarity with others.

To illustrate: many later tales that start with a new hero beating up Sir Kay, Arthur's half-brother and seneschal. He gets pounded so often he seems like a real wussy. Actually the story is trying to say "That's how hard this new guy is - he can take even Kay!" It's like somebody introducing a new character

---

175 *La Morte D'Arthur* recounts the incident in Book XIX, Chapters I.- IX.

176 The third volume of T.H. White's seminal retelling of King Arthur's story, collectively titled *The Once and Future King* (1938-58).

177 For another version of the Grail, there's also the Celtic idea of the Four Treasures (as described in the Four Branches tales from the *Mabinogion*). The kingly sword, deadly spear, cauldron/cup of regeneration and stone of kingship can be argued to reappear in the Matter of Britain as Excalibur, the Holy Spear that gives the Fisher King his dolorous wound, the Grail, and the Round Table. So there might be independent sources for the Grail content before the French romancers got involved.

On a side note, the Irish claimed that the Stone of Kingship resided at Tara, the crowning place of kings, and would emit a great shout when a true monarch sat on it. The Scots claim that this stone ended up as the Stone of Scone (pronounced scoon) beneath the Scots king's throne. This stone was taken to London when James VI of Scotland also became James I of England and the two nations thereafter shared a common monarch. It was placed in the Palace of Westminster (Houses of Parliament) under the seat used by the monarch when he presided there. The Stone of Scone was only returned to its former place in Scotland around a decade ago.

to DC Comics and having him beat up Superman to show how tough he is. Sadly, the original stories that show Kay being the main hero are pretty much lost.[178]

All of this means that a pulp treatment of the Matter of Britain is fertile loam to grow stories in but requires the dots joining to punch home the stories to a modern readership.

A Brief Guide to Arthurian Elaines

Elaine of Tintagil was one of "the three lovely Cornwall sisters", daughters of Duke Gorlois of Cornwall and his lady Igraine who was accounted the most beautiful woman of her generation. Her elder sister was Margawse, who married King Lot and bore him four sons, Gawaine, Agravaine, Gaheris, and Gareth, and on whom Arthur fathered the bastard Mordred. Her younger sister was Morgana le Fey. When her father was slain, her mother was wed by force to King Uther Pendragon; the offspring of that liaison was Arthur, Elaine's half-brother. Elaine was married off by Uther to King Nentres of Garloth and little is heard of her thereafter except that she is the mother of Sir Galescin.

Elaine of Benwick was the wife of King Ban of Benwick (a bit of France). Her husband was murdered by major Arthurian villain King Claudas, who conquered the kingdom. Her young son Galahad was saved when he was spirited away by the Lady of the Lake. Thereafter this boy took the name Lancelot du Lac; his son by Elaine of Carbonek was named after him and is the more famous Sir Galahad. Widowed Elaine of Benwick founded the religious house known as the Royal Minster on the site of her husband's murder and became its saintly prioress.

Elaine of Carbonek is the daughter of Pellam, the Grail King, keeper of the sacred chalice.[179] She was rescued by Lancelot from a curse that confined

---

178   The exception is a Mallory account (Book IV, Chapter III) of the Battle of the Humber, a desperate war with Saxon invaders where Arthur, Bedevere, Gawain and Kay (always the king's companions of choice in the earliest stories) had to ford and swim the River Humber to escape capture. Guenevere, accompanying Arthur on campaign, is offered the choice of risking death with them or yielding to the Saxons; she elects to go with Arthur. Soaked and exhausted on the other side of the wide estuary, Arthur and the others stumble upon the Saxons' headquarters tent – and attack. Kay is the hero of the battle, defeating the Saxon king and breaking the invasion.

179   See Chapter 20, Part Two, "And In Other Pilfered Legends".

her to a scalding bath,[180] and he also killed a dragon for her. With her old nurse's connivance she slipped into Lance's room by night. He slept with her, believing he was finally bedding Guenevere. This actually worked twice on different occasions. After Lancelot and Guenevere's affair finally shattered the Round Table, Lance retired with Elaine to Joyous Garde where they lived content for a time until the knight was persuaded back into action. The bastard child born from their first union was Galahad, "the best knight in the world" and the one who finally achieved the Grail Quest.

Elaine, the Lily Maid of Astolat, was also deliriously in love with Lancelot. She is the only lady whose token he consented to carry at tourney and she nursed his battle wounds, but he refused to make her his mistress because his love was reserved only for Guenevere. Elaine "died of her love for him."

Elaine, daughter of King Pellinore by the Lady of the Rule, loved a young knight called Sir Miles. Her knight was treacherously slain by villainous Loraine le Savage. Her father Pellinore rode past, urgently pursuing the kidnapped Lady Nimue and neither recognised Elaine nor stopped when she called him for aid. When he eventually returned she had slain herself with her lover's sword. Fortunately, the lions that were devouring her had left her head till last so that her father was finally able to identify her.

And so on.

We have a plethora, possibly a surfeit, of Elaines.

Questing for the Round Table

KING EDWARD III (1312-1377) was a massive King Arthur fan. Seriously. He had a special court built at massive expense at Windsor Castle (its remains are now under the Queen's ceremonial lawn), complete with a round table, and he "re-formed" an order of knights of that name. In 1344 he held a huge feast and tournament in his new Camelot that was heard of all across Europe.[181]

---

180 According to T.H. White and others. Phyllis Ann Karr in her excellent and definitive Pendragon A-Z, *The Arthurian Companion: The Legendary World of Camelot and the Round Table*, (ISBN: 1568820968 - invaluable and recommended) argues against conflating this Elaine with the troubled bather, and her opinion should never be discounted.

181 Edward wasn't the only English king keen to identify himself with King Arthur. At Winchester

Polydore Vergil, "the father of English history", records in his *Anglica Historia* (1534) how young Joan of Kent, Countess of Salisbury, accidentally dropped her garter at a ball at Calais, to her embarrassment and the delight of the mocking crowd. Gallant King Edward responded to the ridicule by tying the garter around his own knee with the words, "honi soit qui mal y pense" - evil be to he who evil thinks.

And then he formed The Most Noble Order of the Garter with that motto, modelled after Arthur's chivalrous knights, turning the lady's shame to a singular honour. It remains the most prestigious rank of British knighthood to this day. Current and recent members include Margaret Thatcher, John Major, and Tony Blair.

Henry II was another fan. Remember him from earlier? Eleanor of Aquitaine, the Fair Rosamund, Richard the Lionheart's dad? Henry was very keen to find an Arthurian link in England. After all, at his time both Wales and France were claiming King Arthur too, so it was only right that God should reveal Arthur's essential Englishness.

Luckily, "an ancient British bard" revealed to him exactly where King Arthur's tomb happened to be – in the cemetery at Glastonbury Abbey. A little excavation revealed a grave with "giant's bones", clearly the skeleton of a mighty king, along with those of a female presumed to be Guenevere. To further the miracle, the carving on the presumably 6th century coffin was in high medieval (10th century) Latin.[182] Anyhow, in an age of pilgrimages and the income they brought to religious houses, having the relics of Arthur was a great draw. The bones went missing about the time Thomas Cromwell destroyed many Catholic foundations during Henry VIII's dissolution of the monasteries.[183]

The other theory about the discovery of Arthur's bones was that even then the "once and future king" story was commonplace. There's a rich

---

Castle, which many early sources identify as the original Camelot, there is a massive Round Table dating back to the 13th century. It may have been created for King Edward I's earlier version of a Round Table tournament. The table was elaborately repainted for the Holy Roman Emperor Charles V's state visit to Henry VIII in 1522. The artwork depicts Arthur in his high seat – an Arthur who looks suspiciously like Henry VIII himself!

182 Giraldus Cambrensis in his *De Principis Instructione* (1193, two years after the discovery), records the inscription as "Hic jacet sepultus inclitus rex Arthurus in insula Avalonia" ("Here lies interred the famous King Arthur on the Isle of Avalon).

183 Glastonbury Abbey was sacked in September 1539 on the orders of Thomas Cromwell, then Henry VIII's chief minister. Abbot Richard Whiting, previously a major supporter of the king, resisted and was hanged, drawn and quartered as a traitor on Glastonbury Tor. His head was put on show over the gate of his abbey and his severed limbs were displayed to the public at Ilchester, Bridgwater, Bath, and Wells.

stream of folklore around a sleeping hero returning; it's also claimed of Barbarossa and Charlemagne, for example, and possibly of Elvis. Perhaps the current monarchy was feeling threatened by the peasantry comparing the current rulership with how good things would be when the "true king" returned. Having Arthur's dead body show up would be helpful in quashing their hopes.

Glastonbury is a fascinating place and should be on any visitor to the UK's tour itinerary. Stonehenge is near enough to do in the same day. The archaeological evidence suggests that Glastonbury was pretty much a dry island in a dense marsh until the 9th century or so, making it an ideal sacred place to Christian and pre-Christian traditions alike. It has long enjoyed being associated with the legendary Isle of Avalon. As a place where Arthur might be carried across water in a barge sailed by nine mystical queens it's a fair candidate.

Arthur still had the power to inspire a nation in 1834, when a disastrous fire destroyed the Houses of Parliament, requiring the entire Palace of Westminster to be rebuilt. The monarch's House of Lords robing room was decorated with scenes from *La Morte D'Arthur*. Perhaps as a reminder of how kings should behave? Or die?

Other legends about where Arthur went are rife in European folklore. A prevalent legend, sited all over the place, is of a farmer, hunter, or artisan who gets lost in the woods. He finds an ancient door in a hillside and somehow through strength or trickery manages to get into the cave beyond. There he finds a hall of sleeping knights and a bellrope. When he pulls the rope the bell sounds and the sleepers begin to wake. "Is it time?" they ask. "No," he tells them. Sometimes an old man with a white beard is present as their keeper. Perhaps he is Merlin. In any case, the protagonist escapes and can never find the place again.

Then there are the Wild Hunt stories. Similar to the distinctive English Black Shuck, that huge phantom dog with glowing saucer-sized eyes (of the Egton variety; see chapter 24) are the Wish Pack, Gabriel Ratchets or Devil's Chase. On stormy nights, horsemen and hounds ride or even fly cross the countryside, hunting down sinners to drag them to hell. Sometimes those who witness them feel compelled to join in the chase and are never seen again.[184] The chief huntsman is variously named

184 In *Memoranda*, 1664, the Reverend Oliver Heywood of Coley Hall in the Calder Valley noted, "There is also a strange noise in the air heard of many in these parts this winter, called Gabriel-Ratches (sic) by this country-people, the noise is as if a great number of whelps were barking and howling, and 'tis observed that if any see them the persons that see them die shortly after, they are never heard but

as Henry V, Henry VIII, Sir Francis Drake (of Spanish Armada fame), Herne the Hunter, some local hero, Lucifer himself - or King Arthur. Finally there's what we can perhaps term "the reincarnation theory", the idea that Arthur is reborn and 'returns' in the person of some contemporary hero. Henry II and Edward III were especially keen on that one. Some claimed it of the Duke of Wellington who defeated Napoleon. Even today there is a new-age eco-warrior who has legally changed his name to King Arthur and who turns up at protests with a sword he calls Excalibur.

The Imagined Or Historical King

WE'D BETTER get back to this. I promised it at the start of the book and now we're nearing the end.

There's a mini-industry out there writing books about "the real Arthur", finding evidence placing him all around Great Britain and sometimes elsewhere in Northern Europe. For example, Dr Norma Goodrich (1917-2006) was a formidable linguistic scholar who argued in her many books on the subject that Arthur was actually a Scottish chieftain (hence the MacArthur clan). She based her case on a belief that key works had been mistranslated.

For every expert there's an equal and opposite expert. There's similar scholarship making cases for Arthur in Wales, Ireland, Cornwall and France. The main counterargument to the Scottish location is the very early adversarial association between Arthur and the Saxons. Arthur at the Battle of Baden (wherever Baden was) is probably the oldest reference to him. Scotland did not suffer the Saxon depredations that England did so any theory has to explain who Arthur opposed with his united nation. Nor was Scotland ever colonised by the Romans, so a Scottish Arthur loses his mythical associations with post-Roman national rulership (his lineage from Aurelius Ambrosius and Constantine the Great, for example). But I wouldn't want to overstate the opposite case; Goodrich did her homework.

Generally I'm not convinced by any of the 'discover the historic Arthur' research. Some of it's robust, some wildly imaginative, but the problem is that Arthur's reign is usually dated smack in the middle of the Dark Ages, a period when there was no Christian church in Britain chronicling history, few

---

before a great death or dearth."

"Though Narrow Be That Old Man's Cares", an 1807 Wordsworth sonnet concludes "For overhead are sweeping GABRIEL'S HOUNDS/ Doomed, with their impious Lord, the flying Hart/ To chase for ever, on aerial grounds!"

non-wooden buildings to leave archaeological traces, and no authenticated overseas evidence to help work out what happened. We know the country was a seething turmoil of tiny and ever-shifting kingdoms, suffering waves of invasion, colonisation, or migration (depending on which historian you favour). All the rest depends on later Christian ecclesiastical sources which are obviously secondary.

Another complication which might speak for or against the theories is the rather strange migration of the indigenous Highlands people to Ireland and the old Irish migration to Scotland. Myths from the one tended to travel to the other.

And let us not forget that St Patrick, patron saint of Ireland, was a Welshman.

Ethnically, the Welsh and Scots are the remnant race of Celts who once occupied all of Britain before being displaced by the Saxons. If they have Arthurian legends those stories could have retreated with them to the marginal territories of Wales and the Highlands.[185]

If there *was* a historical figure who was the basis for Arthur then the two most likely candidates are either a survivor or descendant of the Roman administration or else a tribal warlord leading resistance to Saxon incursion. If he was the former then he might well have been Christian, especially given the emphasis Princess Helena (assuming she was a princess) and her son Constantine the Great had on the English ruling class. If Arthur was the latter then a pagan background becomes more likely, although its not clear what the prevalent pagan faith might have been at that time.

Going back to original sources, Geoffrey of Monmouth's description of the history or England, including Arthur's extensive role in it, were part of a mythographying for the new Norman overlords. As such it assumed a Christian gloss on the events it described, even those taking place before Christ. Most ecclesiastical historians did the same thing, probably without intentional bias. Many of the hagiographies and histories did not distinguish between statements of fact or of surmise and of faith; these differences were just not important to the original audience.

As mentioned earlier,[186] Mallory went a step further, setting his accounts firmly in a world that was technologically and culturally not much different

---

185 I'm told – but can no longer find the source - that "Welsh" was actually a Saxon term of insult meaning "bloody foreigner", which the displaced Celts claimed in much the same way that some black people have embraced the word "nigger". Proper scholarly theories such as the word being adapted from the Celtic Volcae tribe need not apply.

186 Chapter Ten, "Writing Historicals".

from the one his contemporary readers knew. Knights, castles, chivalric codes, laws, taxes, feudal arrangements, and social customs were all assumed to have been the same in the sixth century as the twelfth. Of course the assumption was extended to the church having the same role and authority as it did in Mallory's day.

Let the historians and archaeologists have their entertainment. Fortunately I'm more interested in the legendary Arthur. His themes of unity against invasion, of might being harnessed for right, of divine kingship and so on underscore some of the national characteristics of Britain and other European countries over many centuries. In fact the rationale for the British Empire – "the white man's burden" (read: an Englishman's burden) to civilise and protect the rest of the world - is implicit in Arthur's Round Table mission.

I worry that fiction which cuts out the 'unrealistic' parts of Arthurian anachronism also cuts out some of the heart of the story. These tales were anachronistic at the time they were first told, as realistic as 1950s TV series doing westerns; nobody cared. The search for the 'real' Arthur doesn't start with a map or a trowel but by digging into ancient folklore and the hearts of a nation.

***

34.
The Remarkable Adventures of the Earl of Uxbridge's Leg

UXBRIDGE'S RIGHT LEG may be the most famous limb of the Napoleonic era. Indeed, few limbs have had poems written about them, provoked so many memorable quotes from so many illustrious people (Lord Uxbridge included), nor inspired a new industry.

Henry William Paget, later Lord Paget, later the Earl of Uxbridge, had a remarkable career as soldier and statesman and was a scandal of the early 19th Century. His military service included the Flanders campaign during the French Revolution, distinguished command of the cavalry during the Corunna campaign, and similar feats at Sahagun and Benevente during the Peninsula War. He led the heavy cavalry charge at Waterloo. Amongst the posts he held during his long career were Master-General of the Ordinance, responsible for all British army artillery, and Lord Lieutenant of Ireland, responsible for ruling the country in the name of the Crown.

In 1809 though, his affair with Lady Charlotte Wellesley left him sidelined and reviled. Lady Charlotte was the wife of Henry Wellesley (later Lord Cowley) who was in turn brother to the Duke of Wellington, then commander in chief of the war against Napoleon and later Prime Minister. In 1810 Uxbridge divorced the wife on whom he had fathered eight children and married the similarly divorced Lady Charlotte. The broadsheets had a field day.

Despite the difficulties between Uxbridge and the Wellesleys, Uxbridge's ability meant that he could not be completely excluded from the fight against Napoleon. He was appointed cavalry commander in Belgium, a charge that Wellington later very fairly extended to include the whole allied artillery and cavalry. Hence Uxbridge was a senior officer at the battle of Waterloo, where on 18th June 1815 he led the spectacular charge that stopped d'Erlon's threatening advance dead. During the battle he had eight or nine horses shot out from under him.

And so to the leg. One of the very last cannon shots of the battle hit Uxbridge. He reportedly remarked to Wellington, "By God, sir, I've just lost my leg!", to which the great general replied, "By God, sir, so you have!"

Uxbridge was evacuated to the village of Waterloo, where surgeons prepared to amputate his ruined limb above the knee. His aide-de-camp reported him as saying, "I have had a pretty long run. I have been a beau these forty-seven years, and it would not be fair to cut the young men out any longer." To the surgeons who operated upon him without anaesthetic or antiseptic he remarked, "Those knives appear somewhat blunt."

After the operation he was visited by his friend Sir Hussey Vivian. Asked how he was, Uxbridge replied, "Ah, Vivian! I want you to do me a favour. Some of my friends here seem to think I might have kept that leg on. Just go and cast your eye upon it, and tell me what you think." The knight viewed the severed limb and reported back, in his own words: "I went, accordingly and, taking up the lacerated limb, carefully examined it, and so far as I could tell, it was completely spoiled for work. A rusty grape-shot had gone through and shattered the bones all to pieces. I therefore returned to the Marquis and told him he could set his mind quite at rest, as his leg, in my opinion, was better off than on." When told of the defeat of Napoleon, Uxbridge commented, "Who would not lose a leg for such a victory?"

All of this was widely reported in the newspapers back in England. Jubilant at the final defeat of the French bogeyman Bonaparte, the broadsheets went wild with tales of brave soldiers, and Uxbridge had lost just the right amount of body parts at just the right time to be lionised for his bravery and sacrifice.

Prompted by an enthusiastic public, the government offered Uxbridge a pension of £1200 a year (around $400,000 in modern money), but Uxbridge turned it down. The saw that severed his leg is still held by the National Army Museum.

As for the leg itself, it was placed in a reliquary shine in the garden of the house where the surgery had taken place, 214, Chaussée de Bruxelles, Waterloo. This became a place of pilgrimage. Visitors first visited the bloody chair where the operation had been performed, then progressed to the garden monument that was inscribed: "Here lies the Leg of the illustrious and valiant Earl Uxbridge, Lieutenant-General of His Britannic Majesty, Commander in Chief of the English, Belgian and Dutch cavalry, wounded on the 18 June 1815 at the memorable battle of Waterloo, who, by his heroism, assisted in the triumph of the cause of mankind, gloriously decided by the resounding victory of the said day."

However, a graffito on the tombstone suggested: "Here lies the Marquis of Anglesey's limb; The Devil will have the remainder of him."

The newspapers published a poem by Thomas Gaspey:

Here rests, and let no saucy knave
Presume to sneer and laugh,
To learn that mouldering in the grave
Is laid a British calf.

For he who writes these lines is sure
That those who read the whole
Will find such laugh were premature,
For here, too, lies a sole.

And here five little ones repose,
Twin-born with other five;
Unheeded by their brother toes,
Who now are all alive.

A leg and foot to speak more plain
Lie here, of one commanding;
Who, though his wits he might retain,
Lost half his understanding.

And when the guns, with thunder fraught,
Pour'd bullets thick as hail,
Could only in this way be taught
To give his foe leg-bail.

And now in England, just as gay -
As in the battle brave -
Goes to the rout, review, or play,
With one foot in the grave.

Fortune in vain here showed her spite,
For he will still be found,
Should England's sons engage in fight,

Resolved to stand his ground.

But fortune's pardon I must beg,
She meant not to disarm;
And when she lopped the hero's leg
By no means sought his h-arm,

And but indulged a harmless whim,
Since he could walk with one,
She saw two legs were lost on him
Who never meant to run.

Ouch!

The Pagets appear to have been generally careless with their limbs. Uxbridge's brother, Major-General Sir Edward Paget, lost his right arm in the Second Battle of Porto, 1809. His daughter lost a hand in Spain tending her husband on the battlefield.

The Waterloo monument became a nice little earner for the family Paris who owned the garden. Visitors such as the King of Prussia and the Prince of Orange were amongst many 'top-drawer' pilgrims who paid tribute to Lord Uxbridge's leg. But trouble loomed; a visit from Uxbridge's son in 1878 found the bones exhumed for display. A diplomatic incident followed, with Britain demanding the repatriation of the leg of an English peer. The Paris family refused, demanding money for the bones, to the outrage of the British public. The Belgian Minister of Justice was forced to intervene before – honestly – military action was contemplated. He ordered that the bones be reinterred.

But they were not. The Paris family hid them away. The widow of the last Paris found the bones in her husband's Brussels study in 1934 along with provenance documents. She burned everything in her heating boiler "to avoid more scandal".

Even that's not the last legacy (no pun intended) of the Uxbridge limb. The rest of Lord Uxbridge returned to England to receive a Knight Grand Cross of the Order of the Bath and to be dubbed Marquis of Anglesey. On the actual island of Anglesey, a 27 yard high (bipedal) statue of him was erected. He went on to become Lord High Steward of England and a member of the Privy Council.

But these duties required a mobile man. Hence James Potts designed an artificial prosthetic, one of the first modern appliances of its kind, articulated at knee, ankle, and toes. The design became known as the Anglesey Leg and is a milestone in disability equipment. A whole new industry burgeoned creating jointed false limbs for veterans. One of Uxbridge's actual false legs is preserved at Plas Newydd, Anglesey, along with the Hussar trousers that the hero wore at Waterloo!

Lord Uxbridge's leg marches on!

***

35.
The End

AND THEY ALL LIVED happily ever after. Or until the end of their days. Or until the sequel.

A story's ending is as important as its beginning. The start hooks the reader. The ending sends him or her away satisfied. It's no accident that old-style publishers used to require of their applicant authors a story outline and the first and last chapters of the book. Getting the ending right is a critical writing skill.

There are all kinds of choices the author can make, depending on the effect they want to leave with their audience. Medieval playwrights and performers mostly wanted to ask that the audience clap now and possibly give them money: "Give me your hands if we be friends, and Robin shall restore amends."[187] Children's storytellers often wanted to get the moral across, "And that is why we never talk to strangers in the woods." Hagiographers wanted to draw out the spiritual meaning. Victorian authors assured their readers with philosophical musings on the events of the narrative.

I like the old Russian ending to every tale of a lost princess or a peasant-boy-made-good. "I was there, and I danced at their wedding." There's the more pointed variant too, "My tale is done, and thirsty work it was," - presumably illustrated with the proffering of an emptied beer-mug in need of remedy.

A story's ending can be like coffee at the end of dinner, a final grace-note that completes the feast and announces its conclusion. It can be like the crescendo of a musical piece, weaving together each of the themes that has come before it. It can be the moment of sexual climax that pays off all the mounting excitement; or the pre-smoking-ban post-coital cigarette.

The kind of ending the author chooses depends on the effect the story is

---

187 Puck's closing speech in *A Midsummer Night's Dream*, by some Elizabethan playwright or other.

meant to have on the audience. If the main purpose is to entertain, then a last laugh, thrill or chill might be in order. If the book is to have a sequel, then something that intrigues or teases for another volume might be the thing. If the story is meant to provoke us to action – to outrage us at trafficking, or to warn us about materialism or religion or love, or to enthuse us to join the army for our nation's defence – then the ending is the last shot to get the point across.

Here are just a few of the many endings popular for bringing a text to a close:

The Set-Piece: This is the showdown. Everything else leads up to this. It might be a duel to the death between hero and villain in a sword-fight. It might be the cast in the library for the detective to reveal the murderer. It might be the family manor burning. In any case, it's the big finale with all the stops pulled out, leaving the reader stunned and breathless when the physical or emotional pyrotechnics are done.

After the Set-Piece: Where its not enough to go out with a bang, some authors then have the quiet "down-time" scene after. This can serve to offer explanations and justifications for what has gone before, or we can see the cast coping with the consequences of what occurred.

What Happened To Them In The End: Where we've been invested in a cast, sometimes the writer steps out to offer an authorial summary to tell us how things turned out: "William never returned to the hall. He set up shop in a small seaside town and never again opened the yellow casket..."

Shocking and Sudden: A last minute event comes out of left field, or some final revelation changes everything that has gone before. "Wait a moment – she was his *mother?*" Really clever writers can have set up the Chekov's gun hundreds of pages before so as to play fair.

Musing On the Point Of It All: Popular in bygone days and still sometimes used now, this technique involves the author summing up his themes and drawing conclusions from what has happened. "Marcia couldn't understood why Tom had left. Some aspects of the human heart are unfathomable. Sometimes things left unsaid are more hurtful than those screamed aloud..."

Resetting to Default: Useful for a series where the illusion of change requires the cast restored and ready for another adventure next time, this ending shows how the hero has recovered from his gunshot wound and is heading back to his cluttered desk to pick up the next case file.

The Joke: Related to Resetting to Default, this ending depends upon a moment of humour to tell us that things are all right now. In 1960s stories and earlier this almost always comes from the comedy sidekick/talking animal/funny alien/cute robot/hilarious foreigner etc.

The Romantic Bit: The hero and heroine have found each other at last. They kiss and head off into the sunset together. It's a traditional ending, offering a sense of completion for characters whose relationship we've invested in. Nor is this ending really confined to lovers. Any ending where we see the characters receiving the rewards of their labours and leaving content fits this trope.

Bleak Hopelessness: Much beloved of Russian realists and teenage Goth writers, this ends things on a note of existential despair, where all crumbles to nothing. A variant of this is "Everybody Dies", often seen at the end of horror stories and Greek tragedies.

I Promise It's True: Those Victorians loved to preface their tales with accounts of how they heard this story from a gentleman they once met or got it from an ancient manuscript account or whatever. The more fabulous the tale the more important to ascribe it. They liked to finish with a nod to their tale's hard-to-credit parts. "It seems strange to me now, thinking back over the years to those curious events at the vicarage…"

The Sermon: When the story has a point, sometimes the writer just comes right out and says it, either via one of the story's cast or directly in the authorial voice. "Just like Mandy, one in twenty people in sub-Saharan Africa has AIDS, two-thirds of the total number of infected people in the world. The West spends less money combating it than it does on buying Viagra."

Full Circle: Especially favoured in epilogue endings, the last scene goes back to link up with the first scene. It might even be the bookend framing sequence. In any case, it echoes or amends what that opening was all about, bring us neatly back to where we started, to find out what's the same and what has changed.

Goodbye to the Cast: A favourite of mine, the closing scene or scenes revisit all the people we've met in the story and gives them each a last character moment.

Let's do that one now, shall we? Um, Churchill? Could you put Rhodopis down for a moment? I'm pretty sure that's *not* where she's hiding her slipper. And King Arthur, your majesty, please stop hitting William the Conqueror with the Earl of Uxbridge's leg. You're getting the Henrys and the Elaines overexcited. Medea, step away from Dr Barry's medicine cabinet. Spring-Heeled Jack, you *really* don't want to stalk Eleanor of Aquitaine. Especially not when she's chatting to that masked man, whoever he was anyway. Beside the London-stone.

Most importantly when approaching the ending, you need to find the perfect place to stop before your word-count runs out and your editor simply cuts you off in mid-

***

About the Author

I.A. Watson was at a Buckingham Palace garden party. The gardens there are really huge, big enough to have a whole lake. The lake has ducks. The garden party had little elegant triangular sandwiches. I.A. Watson decided to introduce the sandwiches to the ducks.

This was a tactical blunder. Royal ducks are not used to being fed by the Very Important Personages who usually turn up at these garden parties. Now, granted license by this common oik from Yorkshire in the barbarian North, these privileged birds discovered a ferocious lust for Her Majesty's sandwiches and swarmed in their hundreds across the lawn, eager to locate more of the delicacies.

Ladies in expensive designer summer frocks squealed and screamed. Gentlemen in perfect formal daywear shooed the invading poultry aside with their top hats. Foreign visitors, many of them in their traditional national costume, watched with bemusement, wondering if this was some obscure British custom, the Saluting of the Ducks.

I.A. Watson reflected that it was half a century since anyone was actually been locked away in the Tower of London and that another incarceration was probably about due. He sidled away casually and dodged into the drinks tent. He found an Important Personage there and struck up a conversation to make it look like he'd been here for hours and had certainly not been organising pond-dwelling aviforms to a plebeian rebellion.

The conversation covered some interesting topics and ended up with literature. I.A. Watson owned that his hobby was writing fiction, but that he was reluctant to seek publication, afraid that his refuge from work would then become another job. The Personage argued that there was no harm in showing something to a publisher. He'd heard that some of them were quite good eggs.

Meanwhile, in a mythical fantasy land called America, a publisher – whose relationship with eggs will not be examined – found he was short a story for an anthology that was pending and asked another of his authors to suggest someone who was a fast writer and could come up with 15,000 words ASAP. I.A. Watson's name was mooted and he was invited to submit a tale.

Basic politeness required a story be provided. Basic politeness has required quite a lot of stories since. There's a full list at **http://www.chillwater.org.uk/ writing/iawatsonhome.htm** but here's the short version as of April 2014:

Novels:
Robin Hood: King of Sherwood (2010)
Robin Hood: Arrow of Justice (2011)
Robin Hood: Freedom's Outlaw (2013)
Blackthorn, Dynasty of Mars (2012)

Short Stories in:
Sherlock Holmes, Consulting Detective, volumes 1-6 (2010-14)
Gideon Cain: Demon Hunter (2011)
Blackthorn: Thunder on Mars (2011)
The New Adventures of Richard Knight (2012)
Blood-Price of the Missionary's Gold, the New Adventures of Armless O'Neil (2012)
Sinbad: The New Voyages (2012)
Monster Earth (2013)
Grand Central Noir (2013)
The Spider: Extreme Prejudice (2013)
The Many Worlds of Ulysses King (2014)
Pride of the Mohicans (2014)
Sentinels: Alternate Visions (2009), a *very* short story!

Magazines and Comic Books:
Planetary Stories #18 (2011) – "Loss Adjustment"
Pulp Spirit Magazine #14 (2012) - "Robin Hood and the Slavers of Whitby"
Wonderlust Magazine #8 (2012) – "Rostherne" and "The Tulpa"
All-Star Pulp Comics #2 (2013) "Robin Hood: Lionheart's Gold"
Pro Se Presents Winter/Spring 2014 "Robin Hood and the Maiden of the Tower"

Non-Fiction:
Assembled! – Five Decades of Earth's Mightiest
Assembled 2!

Some of the stories got nominated for pulp industry awards and things. Some of them won. But when people starting publishing I.A. Watson's fiction, he really needed a new hobby to relax from his old hobby. He started writing little articles that he e-mailed to unsuspecting correspondents. Odd histories, opinions, reflections, correlations. Sometimes they helped him prepare for things he was writing, others were just things that had caught his attention.

And then there was an e-mail from Pro Se Press, and they wanted to collect those essays and maybe some more and put them in a book also. Bastards.

And here we are.

I.A. Watson is considering taking up fishing.

www.ingramcontent.com/pod-product-compliance
Lightning Source LLC
Chambersburg PA
CBHW070108290526
45789CB00005B/1965